Griffiths' stated intentions are to analyse the relationship between cultural and political change by looking at Scandinavian artists and their works, and to provide an 'outsider's' view of the history of the area without the all too common parochialism and regional bias of local historians. He has succeeded remarkably well on both counts. There is an astonishing amount of information in *Scandinavia*'s 200-odd pages, yet the lively style makes page after page read like a good story.

Marjatta Forward, *Australian Book Review*

An heroically compressed history of the politics and diplomacy by which the four nations have won and held their independence, and a witty and affectionate account of their leading writers, artists and businessmen.

Hugh Stretton, *Adelaide Review*

Griffiths gives an account of the cultural history in a general historical survey. I wish that similar surveys in Scandinavian languages also had this ambition.

Sune Jungar, *Scandinavian Journal of History*

He blends together, in a fascinating way, history, politics and culture, and draws illuminating pen pictures of the archetypal nordic heroes.

Ulf-Erik Slotte, *Hufvudstadsbladet*

The reader may set off for Scandinavia safe in the knowledge that whether conversation turns to Moomin Trolls or Gro Harlem Brundtland, she will not be in the dark.

Anglo-Norse Review

Scandinavia

Tony Griffiths has taught Australian
and Scandinavian history in Australia,
Japan and Europe. He lives in Adelaide,
but revised this book while a Visiting
Fellow at the Robert Schuman Centre
for Advanced Studies at the European
University Institute in San Domenico
di Fiesole.

Scandinavia

Tony Griffiths

948
Griffiths
v 2004

First published in Australia in 1991 by
Wakefield Press.

First North American edition published in 2004 by
PALGRAVE MACMILLAN™
175 Fifth Avenue, New York, N.Y. 10010
Companies and representatives throughout the world.

PALGRAVE MACMILLAN is the global academic
imprint of the Palgrave Macmillan division of
St. Martin's Press, LLC and of Macmillan Ltd.
Macmillan® is a registered trademark in the
United States, United Kingdom and other countries.
Palgrave is a registered trademark in the European
Union and other countries.

ISBN 1-4039-6776-8 hardback
ISBN 1-4039-6753-9 paperback

Library of Congress Cataloging-in-Publication Data is
available from the Library of Congress.

This edition published in association with
Wakefield Press, Kent Town, South Australia

A Cataloguing-In-Publication data record for this book
is available from the British Library

First North American edition: September 2004
10 9 8 7 6 5 4 3 2 1

Printed in China

CONTENTS

Understanding the living, said Marc Bloch in *The Historian's Craft*, is the master quality of the historian. Bloch recounted his visit with Henri Pirenne 'to Stockholm; we had scarcely arrived, when he said to me: "What shall we go to see first? It seems that there is a new city hall here. Let's start there." Then, as if to ward off my surprise, he added: "If I were an antiquarian, I would have eyes only for old stuff, but I am a historian. Therefore, I love life."' The basis for historical research remains the documents in archives and libraries, the indexes, the bibliographies, the records, the conflicting testimonials, but it must be remembered that with ink anyone can write anything. The written sources must be tested, and to do this I have followed Bloch's advice to get out of the archives and into the field as much as possible. There are interesting places to understand the living in Scandinavia, and to future historians I would suggest the Sogne Fiord in the west of Norway, a Finnish sauna on the Silja Line, the smörgåsbord in Stockholm's Opera Källaren Restaurant, and Copenhagen's Nyhavn and Tivoli Gardens.

This short history of Scandinavia from the Napoleonic era to the present differs from other accounts in two ways. It analyses the relationship between cultural and political change in Scandinavia by looking at the works of imaginative artists as touchstones of their societies. This theme has hitherto remained largely unexplored, although exchanges between Scandinavian artists and their politicians have produced many of the western world's archetypal political and cultural motifs and symbols. Scandinavian intellectuals, artists and theorists have often been studied as individuals, but rarely in their cultural context. These men and women provide ready access to the unique qualities and internationalism, and the successes and failures, of Scandinavian societies. Henrik Ibsen's observation, for instance, that to live is to war with trolls, provides a good starting point for outsiders wishing to understand Scandinavia's modern history.

Scandinavia also departs from convention because it relates the Scandinavian countries to each other, and does so without regional bias. Some of the relatively few books written on Scandinavia and published in English have been translations of original works on specific countries by national scholars. Finnish, Norwegian, Swedish and Danish-born historians have naturally concentrated on areas that illuminate their national preoccupations and have not tried to connect separate countries to each other except to illustrate victory, conquest or regional superiority. To a large degree this parochial approach has been brought about by the competing interests of neighbours and the need to express national identity in order to survive in difficult circumstances. Similarly, whenever an historian from an English-speaking background has become interested in Scandinavia it has usually been for a personal reason that has coloured the scholar's view of the subject. In this way, the idiosyncratic approach of nationalist historians has been reinforced rather than modified by writing originating outside their borders. For example , a British historian married to a Finn writes history as 'Finnish' in its focus as any Finn would, and a British historian who helped the Norwegian resistance during World War II has a Norwegian perspective that would do credit to the most patriotic of the native-born. The same phenomenon applies to Danes and Swedes.

My account starts in the last decade of the eighteenth

century, because it was then that Scandinavia reached its nadir. At that time it comprised two recognisably embryo nation-states: Denmark and Sweden. Within Denmark's national boundaries was Norway; within Sweden's was Finland. In the next century, after rapid, kaleidoscopic changes, Denmark and Sweden were dismembered by European powers as part of a territorial carve-up following the Napoleonic Wars. The puzzled Norwegians and Finns then found themselves yoked in new constitutional creations; the Norwegians to Sweden and the Finns to Russia. For the rest of the nineteenth century, most of the indigenous inhabitants of Norway and Finland struggled for independence from their new and unexpected foster parents. In the twentieth century, as a result of Norwegian and Finnish pressure for devolution, the modern Scandinavian countries – Denmark, Sweden, Norway and Finland – emerged as sovereign nations in their own right, without the handicap of unwelcome and resentful appendices, and ready to try to recapture the lustre, if not the power, of their golden pasts.

This revised edition of the book ends with the nations of the region tossing about in the twenty-first century, and squabbling among themselves. Only in the twenty-first century have the 12,000 children born to Norwegian women during World War II who were fathered by occupying German soldiers dared to take their battle for compensation against Norway to the European Court of Human Rights. Norway's best known war-child (or 'whore child' as they were known), Anni-Frid Lyngstad migrated to Sweden to escape routine beatings and stigmatisation as a 'dirty little German'. Even as a pop idol in Abba, Anni-Frid Lyngstad never forgot this black spot on Norway's history.

And Sweden has turned out to be a special place in ways it cannot welcome. No other advanced democratic country has had its prime minister and its foreign minister slaughtered in the downtown of its capital, the 1986 murder of Olaf Palme being still unsolved. The painful memories of that murder were revived when Palme's protégé, Sweden's pro-European foreign minister Anna Lindh, was stabbed to death in NK, one of Europe's most glossy stores. By November 2003 the dead Swedish foreign minister merited 189,000 hits on Google's search engine in 0.26 seconds. The top report was that Swedish police had found the blood-stained trousers belonging to the chief suspect in her murder. During Sweden's presidency of the EU, Anna Lindh lined up with old Europe by vilifying George W. Bush as 'the lone ranger' for going alone in waging an unjust war on Iraq. While the pink panthers of the Swedish police force searched for DNA samples on the suspect du jour's trousers (Mijailo Miljailovic, a Swede of Serb origin, was said to hate Anna Lindh for backing NATO airstrikes in Serbia during the war in Kosovo in 1999), Swedish public opinion had already turned its back on Lindh and Europe, voting to keep the krona, because, as Prime Minister Göran Persson put it:

> I think we had a problem with the European development. You see, Sweden had a better development than Europe. And to convince the Swedes, who are a little bit Euro-sceptical, to shift the currency to the Euro in a time where we have a better European development than the rest of Europe, has been a too difficult task for me!

If the Swedes were Euro-sceptics, the Finns proved themselves paid-up Euro-enthusiasts, eagerly dropping the markka and embracing the euro. Finnish sophistication in foreign affairs and diplomacy was bred of long symbiosis with the Russian bear.

In the twenty-first century Denmark moved deliberately outside the magic circle of Scandinavian consensus. Asked by a *Le Monde* journalist why the Danes were the only people in Europe to support a war in Iraq, Prime Minister Anders Fogh Rasmussen went back to World War II for arguments: 'It's taken for granted that Denmark should adjust itself humbly, eagerly and passively to what the dominating European powers say ... But now this ends.' The Danish adventure began when the Prime Minister had a can of red paint thrown over his head in front of the world's incredulous media, and ended with Al Qaeda mistaking Norwegians for Danes and condemning Norway's foreign policy towards Muslims. Worried Danes feared that Denmark would revive its historical feud with Sweden, reclaim Norway and make a grab for Schleswig Holstein. One scared Dane wrote: 'Denmark's contribution to the liberation of Iraq from Saddam's tyranny is a bright moment in modern Scandinavian history. It stands in contrast against the attitude of Norway and Sweden, who would let the Iraqi people rot for our prejudice against America'. Other Danes cheered themselves with the image of their new crown princess, Mary Donaldson, pouting from the official website. On 8 October 2003 the Queen of Denmark officially gave her approval for Mary's marriage to Prince Frederik, heir to one of the most conservative monarchies in Europe. This Tasmanian law and commerce graduate had not even visited Denmark before December 2001. Prince Frederick's engagement to an alluring outsider was one bright omen for the third millennium when a new generation of Nordic citizens took over the running of their societies in a tricky and dangerous new world.

CHAPTER 1

The Ugly Ducklings

Scandinavia, unlike Greece and Rome for example, has no written records covering the last 2,000 years. Common sense and historical training are necessary to visualise what Scandinavia was like and how it was organised in the pre-medieval era, and archaeological evidence goes some way to filling out the picture. Among the first Europeans to notice Scandinavia was the Roman historian Tacitus. Tacitus, who had never been there, gave a pioneering description in 98 ad of the people living north of Germania: the Danes, Norwegians, Swedes and Finns. These men and women, who could not be said to have any recognisably modern form of state or idea of nationality, were nevertheless sufficiently homogeneous to be grouped together while existing separately. Although the origins of the Scandinavians are masked by time, and have always been the subject of disagreement and controversy, there is no doubt that from a linguistic point of view the Danes, Swedes and Norwegians were closely linked; the Finns were entirely separate. The closeness of the Danish, Swedish and Norwegian languages has allowed these three groups to understand and co-operate with each other. For the Finns the task has been much harder, despite their determination to be identified with Scandinavian attitudes, values and policies. So difficult is Finnish grammar and vocabulary that non-Finns have only rarely tried to master it, and thus the relationship between Finland and the other Scandinavian states has developed from the top, as a result of the efforts of statesmen and diplomats who have, as often as not, conversed in English or German or by using translators, rather than from the grass roots.

From Tacitus to the recent present there has been almost no ethnic dilution or enrichment of the Scandinavian race. Scandinavia has never been a melting pot. Even allowing for the recent liberalisation of immigration policies in the Nordic countries (with the exception of Finland) and the widespread acceptance of refugees, Scandinavia has remained racially stable. The geographic isolation and relatively large size of Scandinavia within the European land mass have combined with a harsh climate to deter migration to the north, and to keep Scandinavians inward-looking.

Scandinavia was far off the beaten track and produced little of value, so there was no incentive for non-Scandinavians to visit it, and until the Vikings made their spectacular efforts to break down the barriers there was little contact. The Vikings' victims gave them such a bad press that they have never lived it down. Despite the efforts of some scholars, who have pointed out the constructive aspects of Viking settlement, illustrated by recent archaeological digs at Wood Quay in Dublin and else-where, the Vikings have kept the reputation acquired from Irish churchmen and French poets who witnessed their destructive energy. The French described the Vikings as wild beasts who went by horse and foot through hills and fields, open places and villages, killing babies, children, old men, young men, fathers, sons and mothers, overthrowing, destroying, burning and ravaging. The Irish were equally comprehensive and rhetorical and characterised Viking behaviour as so bad as to be indescribable.

By the eleventh century, the Viking era, which began in 793 when the monastery of Lindisfarne was plundered, was over, and it was not until the late Middle Ages that Scandinavians were again to put a permanent stamp upon European culture. And at that time, as Professor T.K. Derry has observed, it was the Reformation which spread the most decisive changes among the people of Northern Europe and inspired the Scandinavians to make their presence felt. The Scandinavians were able to act in a more or less cohesive way as a result of the administrative unity of their region following a constitutional union in 1397. At Kalmar, in southern Sweden, Queen Margaret of Denmark persuaded Scandinavian leaders from Denmark, Norway, Sweden and Finland to settle their dynastic differences and unite under a single king. In a remarkable feat of balancing Queen Margaret used her position as the daughter of the King of Denmark and the wife of the King of Norway to promote Norwegian claims to the Swedish throne. The Kalmar union served the interests of a small clique, had no popular mandate and was destroyed by the barons who supported it when their interests changed in the 1520s. Sweden in 1523 repudiated Danish rule, and Scandinavia was redivided into two kingdoms of Denmark-Norway and Sweden-Finland. In the sixteenth and seventeenth centuries, the Scandinavian monarchs, the Danish Valdemars and Oldenburgs and the Swedish Vasas, conquered, colonised, arbitrated and directed European foreign policy on a scale equal to Henry VIII of England or Peter the Great of Russia. The strength and power of Scandinavia was illustrated by the Danish East India Company which acquired Tranquebar in 1626. During the next two centuries, however, a cycle of stagnation was established, as the rest of Europe caught up with Scandinavia and passed it. At the end of the eighteenth century, the kings of Denmark and Sweden ruled as absolute monarchs over kingdoms in decline. Christian VIII of Denmark had been crowned in 1766, and his Swedish neighbour and rival, Gustav IV, had ruled since 1792. The two royal capitals, and largest cities in Scandinavia, Copenhagen and Stockholm, were the same size as Glasgow, Edinburgh, Dublin, Liverpool, Manchester, Birmingham, Bristol, Hamburg, Brussels, Warsaw, Prague, Rouen, Milan, Turin, Geneva, Nantes, Bordeaux, Florence and Rome. Both capitals had populations of less than 120,000, were half the size of Moscow, St Petersburg and Vienna, a quarter the size of Paris and Naples and dwarfed by London, with its population of 1,250,000.

Copenhagen lay at fifty-five degrees north latitude on both sides of a narrow and deep sound that separated the small island of Amager from Zealand. The Danes occupied two clusters of islands. To the east, between the Skagerrak and the Baltic Sea, an archipelago of almost 500 islands stretched to Bornholm, eighty-eight miles east of the main group. A second string of islands, the Faeroes, was 700 miles away in the Atlantic, on the shortest route to Iceland and Greenland. To the south of Copenhagen were Schleswig and Holstein, two regions that, in 1460, had come under the authority of the Danish King Christian I. The Danish peninsula and archipelago was low-lying, and fertile clay loams produced an agricultural bounty that had the potential to turn Copenhagen into a large European trading centre. Across the Skagerrak from Denmark lay Sweden, the other great northern power. Whereas Denmark and Copenhagen were European in setting and manners, Sweden and Stockholm were unmistakably Nordic and the landscape unmistakably foreign. The extreme south of Sweden belonged geographically to Denmark, and the climate of southern Sweden was as equable as that of similar latitudes in Russia. But, as one moved north and west, the landscape changed, and the typically Scandinavian wilderness of lake, forest, mountain and river was habitable only under extreme hardship and with great skill. Central Sweden held Europe's biggest lake. In the forests full of birch, aspen, rowan, spruce and Scots pine were elk, deer, hare and, further north, the Arctic fox. Nature's greatest gift to Sweden, however, was mineral, not animal; the country had mountains in the north that were one third iron ore.

The effects of northern latitudes were bizarre and frightening to foreigners. From 26 May to 18 July, there was perpetual daylight in the northern areas of the Swedish-Finnish border. This gave a twenty-four hour growing season, but each miraculous germination was followed inevitably by a winter of permanent night, which threw the Swedes living north of the Arctic Circle into a state of perpetual depression. Ice formed along the northern shores of the Gulf of Bothnia (which separated Sweden and Finland) in November. Stockholm itself was not normally closed, but sometimes people could ski to Finland across the broken icefields. Finland had been a part of Sweden since the Treaty of Novgorod, but most of Finland's population knew and cared nothing for international treaties between relatively great powers, and continued to call Finland 'Suomi', which may or may not be connected to the Finnish word for 'swamp', *suo*. Certainly, no country in Europe was submerged by so much fresh water. There were tens of thousands of lakes, and forests of pine, spruce and birch. The bedrock of Finland was mostly part of the broad precambrian zone that stretched from northern Europe to southern Russia. The mean altitude of Finland was only 152 metres above sea level, and the country flat. Beneath sand-drifts, black peat and moss lay granite, concealed in much the same way as the intransigent character of the Finnish nation that was to emerge during the nineteenth century. A quarter of Finland lay north of the Arctic Circle, a third north of Iceland. Snow covered most of the country for months, the comparatively temperate areas on the latitudes of Åland, Turku and Helsinki having, on average, between 100 and 142 days of snow. The whole of Finland lay between sixty and seventy degrees north, on the same latitudes as the icy steppes of Siberia. To survive in the Finnish winter required ingenuity, adaptability and courage.

At the beginning of the nineteenth century, Norway shared

with Finland more than a common boundary north of the Arctic Circle. Both were soon to be transformed into subordinate regions within unequal unions, both were to serve two masters – the Norwegians were forced to bow to the Danes and the Swedes, and the Finns to the Swedes and Russians. In both countries, the nineteenth-century constitutional rearrangements would not expunge overnight the plantation ascendancy, and (as in Ireland at roughly the same time) the assumption of sovereign power by foreign states left the indigenous populations bewildered and confused, not knowing where to turn to assert national and individual identity.

Norway, like Finland, was a savage frontier rarely visited by outsiders: geographical determinism was seen at its most forbidding there. The mountains of Norway were composed almost entirely of primary rocks, more or less in the same form as when originally solidified and rarely overlaid with more recent formations. The gneiss, the oldest of these rocks, loomed in imposing pinnacles, 5,000 to 6,000 feet in height. There was scarcely any lowland and what was there was valley floor or small hill. South of latitude 67 degrees were Norway's glaciers, including the largest glacier in Europe, 515 square miles, which lay between latitude 61 and 62 degrees, and was an enormous roof of dazzling ice and snow, unbroken by moraines or crevasses. Within the Norwegian Arctic Circle intrepid geologists had already begun to investigate a landscape unchanged since the Ice Age.

At right-angles to the western mountains ran the fiords, in which the grandeur of the rock scenery was enhanced by cliffs, sometimes almost perpendicular and 3,000 feet high. The coast was indented on a smaller scale by 'viker' creeks, from which the Norwegian Vikings sailed out to spread terror and trade. The 'White Foreigners' (as their victims termed them to distinguish them from the Danish Vikings) began their period of exploration and conquest during the last decade of the eighth century and when, in 1070, their era was at an end, they had discovered Iceland, Greenland and probably Vinland. The Norwegian Vikings came from a country where water transport was virtually the only means of communication and their native fiords stretched for great distances into Norway's heartland. The Sognefiord, for example, ran 114 miles inland and was 4,100 feet deep in places. Glaciation produced sharp steps in the valley floors and hanging valleys provided Norway with an unsurpassed number of beautiful waterfalls. A warm North Atlantic current at the end of the Gulf Stream came across the ocean to the shores of Norway, providing the world's biggest temperature anomalies: average temperatures within the Arctic Circle were much higher than those 20 degrees to the south. The fiords were not penetrated by cold water from the open ocean and were always ice-free. On the banks of the fiords were strips of fertile and sheltered lands, which gradually built up a growing population with a summer life that was a blissful antidote to winter fogs, clouds and darkness. It was not, however, simply the (usually unfulfilled) hope of finding a noble savage that drove eighteenth century Europeans to look to Scandinavia. The north, despite its climatic defects, had growing strategic value. Napoleon's most important consideration when the modern history of Scandinavia began was the defeat of Great Britain. His strategy was based on a blockade, but the British, with their command of sea power and their native ingenuity, were easily able to continue to trade through ports that Napoleon was unable to control, some of the most important of which were in Sweden and Denmark.

Scarcely had the nineteenth century begun than the new European naval balance of power made itself felt: Britain turned its attention to the Danes, who had grown so prosperous from trade in grain and agricultural produce that concomitant social change was turning them quickly into a nation of freeholders.

But the era when Denmark's merchant navy could sail without obstruction around the coasts of Europe, or to the Danish West Indies, was over. When the Danish foreign minister, Andreas Peter Bernstorff, died in 1797, Danish sea power perished with him. It was left up to the British to bury it, which they did in Anglo-Saxon cold blood. Although Denmark joined the Second Armed League of Baltic Powers, which was set up with the motto 'free ship, free cargo' to protect neutral shipping by convoys during the Napoleonic wars, the British navy seized ship after ship in a bid to stop the Danish merchant navy helping the French.

The most dramatic sign of the new era was the ease with which a British naval force, commanded by Admiral Sir Hyde Parker, with Horatio Nelson as second in command, was able to force its way into the Baltic. In 1801, Admiral Parker anchored off Danish Elsinore and demanded permission to pass Kronborg castle so that he could sail to the Baltic. The commandant of Kronborg said that he could not permit a battle fleet bound for an unknown destination to pass his castle. So Admiral Parker waited until a favourable wind let him sail close in alongside the coast. Then, as the British ships passed, they bombarded the castle and the town of Elsinore, scoring only one hit on the town, which, the Danes were pleased to note, landed on the house of the British Consul. The Danish derision was short-lived. The fleet of their Russian allies was icebound in St Petersburg and could not come to their aid; the Danish navy was still in winter quarters in the harbour in Copenhagen, the crews on leave and their ships unrigged. With this tactical advantage, Nelson, who headed south towards Copenhagen and went into action with thirty-five men of war, had no hesitation in shooting a sitting duck. To try to counter their perilous position, the Danish fleet formed a blockade of floating batteries. But it was capable of firing broadsides from one side only, and its power to manoeuvre was limited to hauling and drawing on the anchor lines. The battle lasted five hours. British victory came after Parker signalled to Nelson to break off the fight. Nelson replied by putting his blind eye to the telescope.

In Denmark, the demoralising effect of the Battle of Copenhagen on 2 April 1801 was tremendous. Nelson met the Danish crown prince and accepted gifts under the quasi-chivalric norms of war. After an exchange of pleasantries, Nelson and the crown prince began to discuss the penalties to be extracted from the loser. The parley was interrupted by a message that Tsar Paul had been assassinated and that Alexander I was Emperor of Russia. Alexander I was pro-British and the Danes had six years of peace until 1807, when the Treaty of Tilsit changed France and Russia from enemies into allies. George Canning, the British Minister for Foreign Affairs, considered Denmark a potential danger and, when the Danes refused to give their navy to Britain, the British decided to assault Copenhagen with a land expeditionary force. This assault, in September 1807, was devastatingly effective. For three days shells rained down upon the city, streets were blocked by people attempting to flee, and the bombardment continued until most of the city was rubble. The British seized the royal dockyard and the naval storehouses. They made the Danish ships there ready for sea, destroying five vessels on their stocks. The whole Danish fleet stationed in Copenhagen was hauled out of harbour for the last time, having been loaded up with Danish property. Public opinion in Britain and Denmark was puzzled. Why had Britain acted with such vigour against a nation that was neither at war with nor unfriendly to them? The British forces destroyed much of Copenhagen. Civilians were killed and injured and watched their ancient capital go up in flames. Scottish infantry in kilts camped in the Tivoli gardens, and the Danes followed their monarch's choice and decision enthusiastically when thereafter Frederick VI backed Napoleon. A seven-year war followed and, at the end of it, when Napoleon was defeated in 1814, Denmark had to conclude peace at Kiel, losing Norway to Sweden and Heligoland to Britain. Norway was surrendered on 21 March 1814, at Eidsvoll Manor, where the Eidsvoll Constitution was signed, yoking Norway to Sweden and dissolving a four hundred and thirty-nine years' union between Denmark and Norway. Denmark retained Greenland, Iceland and the Faeroes and still owned small colonies in the tropics, the Virgin Islands in the West Indies, some trading stations on the coast of Guinea, the Indian trading stations of Tranquebar and Frederiksnagore, and the Nicobars.

Out of the dismemberment of the Danish nation came the literary response of three great Danes: N.F.S. Grundtvig, Søren Kierkegaard and Hans Christian Andersen, whose lives and writings were a mirror of the way in which the Danish people had to adapt to changed circumstances. Grundtvig was one of those Scandinavians who was met at the border. The north specialised in prophets who were almost exclusively honoured in their own land. In Grundtvig's case it was easy to see why. His outlook was parochial and nationalistic and his repetitive and dull style worked against the interest of his ideas. Grundtvig's Danish chauvinism was the product of experience abroad, the crushing pressure of other European states on Denmark's borders, and the educational system in Denmark at the beginning of the nineteenth century.

Nikolaj Frederik Severin Grundtvig was born in 1783. In the Napoleonic era, education in Denmark was classical, with a garnish of the principles of the enlightenment and eighteenth-century rationalism. Grundtvig, who graduated at the University of Copenhagen with a theology degree in 1801, revolted against what he had been taught there, being particularly hostile to the classical idiom, observing that there was no coherence between Roman and Nordic thought, unless one regarded the educated elite as a group of Romans who were intent upon having the rest of the world as slaves.

Grundtvig visited England in the summers of 1829, 1830 and 1831. On his first visit he went no further than London, and spent most of his time in bookshops and the British Museum. On his second visit he went as far as Exeter, Bristol and Oxford, and during his third visit he spent time at Trinity College, Cambridge, where, he said, he felt more at home than he would have been at Copenhagen University. But Grundtvig was impressed with more than the Cam, the Granta and the Backs. The Cambridge influence on his thought showed in his belief in laissez-faire in economics and his conception of the ideal university. Like many observers swept off their feet by their first contact with a foreign culture, Grundtvig was inclined to idealise what he saw: he said that what he chiefly admired in England was the free activity, the masterly grasp of the useful and the clear vision of what was honourable, not an impression that would have occurred to everybody. Inspiration across the North Sea led him into a life of public service. He played a leading role in the constitutional reform movement of 1848, and was one of the principal organisers behind the foundation of the folk high school movement, which grew in importance as the century progressed and is the foremost reason for contemporary interest in him.

The key figure in Grundtvig's strategy for educational reform was the Danish king, Christian VIII. But the conjunction of events that brought the 1848 revolutions to Europe exhausted Christian VIII, who died in the middle of a constitutional crisis. The sequence was neatly described by Hans Christian Andersen, who, by 1848, was a polished courtier. When the king suffered from insomnia, for example, it was Andersen who was summoned to read him a fairy story. Andersen had a ringside seat at the burial of the ancient privileges of the monarchy in Denmark and the establishment of democratic representative institutions. Andersen's own life was a fairy story that became increasingly grim. He had a perfect existentialist background: his grandfather went mad; his mother was an illiterate washer-woman who had an illegitimate child before she married Hans's father two months before Hans's birth. Andersen recalled that his father, who had fought in the Napoleonic wars, spent most of his life dissatisfied and daydreaming on his cobbler's stool, thinking about the validity of religion. In the evenings things brightened up when Hans's father declaimed Holberg's plays and *The Thousand and One Nights*. But generally speaking he never smiled, except when he was reading. Once he had tears in his eyes when a university student came for a pair of boots, showed the cobbler his books, and talked about everything he was learning. 'That was the way I should have been let go,' said the old cobbler, who then kissed his little son and was silent for the whole evening.

The great Scandinavians seemed particularly cursed with eccentric or unsympathetic fathers. Young Hans waited until he was fourteen, broke open his clay piggy bank and amid its ruins found the coins that took him off to Copenhagen where he hoped to work in the theatre. But Hans was not suited to an actor's role. His voice was breaking and, like the Ugly Duckling, he was extremely unattractive. He gave up the idea of a life on the stage and studied and matriculated at the University of Copenhagen. Matriculation was a degree that any man who sought a state position had to have, but for Hans Christian Andersen matriculation was a licence to write. Andersen wrote a play that was accepted by the Royal Theatre in April 1829, ten years after he arrived in the capital hoping for a job. The play, *Love on the Nicholas Tower*, was a hit. His student friends nearly tore the theatre down applauding their young hero, the crown granted him a travelling scholarship (a widespread custom at the time designed to promote indigenous talent), and Andersen set out to see Denmark feeling that life lay bright before him.

From Denmark, Andersen travelled south through Paris,

where he was much taken by the paintings in the Louvre. Late in summer 1833 he sought refuge in the Jura, and there he drew and wrote lyric drama. In the early nineteenth century Scandinavians were fascinated by the mess in southern Europe. Andersen, for example, often said how much he longed for a filthy Italian town, which was so characteristic, just the thing for a painter – the narrow dirty streets; the grey, grimy stone balconies with stockings and underwear on them; windows out of order, one up, one down, some large, some small, mamas sitting there; lemon trees with yellow fruit hanging over the wall. Northern Italy, where the streets were clean, regular and formal, he could not stand. But the picturesque – goats, the small peasant boys, the vineyards and the exuberant enthusiasm for rocky stone angels and crosses complete with Jesus – fascinated him. He looked out for rundown inns and reed huts where he was able to smell and touch thistles, wild figs and pyrethrums, and his paintings on Capri of the ruins of Tiberius' villa and his sketches of an amphitheatre, with vineyards, orange and olive groves and fishermen's huts, were some of the ancestors of French impressionism, and helped to define Scandinavian society by being its antithesis.

In the civilised countries outside Southern Europe Andersen was a lionised house guest. He traded on his popularity and starred in the London season of 1847, in which he had cult figure status, and his children's stories were applauded as serious artistic works. Andersen was a snob and a salon democrat: he was upset to see the Copenhagen bourgeoisie march on the royal palace to demand a new constitution from Frederick VII. Hans had shot rabbits with Christian VIII, but the barrels of the Danes were destined for sterner targets in the years ahead and Andersen was to find himself harnessed to the cause of Danish nationalism.

One of Andersen's earliest critics was the philosopher Søren Kierkegaard who, with a superb sense of the futility of human existence, took Andersen's book *Only a Fiddler* as a subject for his own first work. Kierkegaard, who described Grundtvig as 'a lot of nonsense', soon grew to disparage Andersen as 'a European coach tourist' and threw himself into the real business of living, being one of the first existentialists. Kierkegaard was born in 1813, the seventh and youngest son of his father's former housekeeper. His problems began when his father, Michael Kierkegaard, in a spectacular act of defiance given the topography of Denmark, stood on a high point on a Jutland heath and cursed God. God's reaction was slow but comprehensive. Michael was liberated from peasant poverty by an uncle and had decades to regret his action, which he felt sure would destroy his soul. As a young man Søren tossed in his theological studies at Copenhagen University and gave himself up to the bohemian life of a writer. He was a short, spindly hunchback with a rasping high-pitched voice, and became a feature of Copenhagen's high street, wandering up and down, smoking cigars, carrying a cane, fighting and mixing with a raffish circle of friends from the demi-monde. But beneath the dandy exterior, Kierkegaard never came to terms with his birth and his father's longevity, and manifested what came to be accepted as a stereotype of Scandinavian anxiety. His fundamental human experiences led to an acute nervous breakdown. By a tortuous connection of unrelated data Kierkegaard concluded that since almost the whole large family had died shortly after his birth, except his father (who lived to be 82), his father's morbid religiosity served as a graveyard cross to remind the child of the futility of human endeavour. The fact that 'Kierkegaard' meant 'churchyard' in the Danish language reinforced his sense of doom. His dread was pathological in its intensity and destroyed his chance of ordinary happiness. He never married, throwing his energy into writing, but his literary relics, thirty books and a two-thousand page journal, established him as one of the most important philosophers of the nineteenth century, particularly on account of his masterpiece *Either/or*, which was published in two volumes in February 1843. Kierkegaard argued in it that one had to choose between two different attitudes to life – the aesthetic and the ethical. It is difficult to summarise existential argument, particularly since Kierkegaard delighted in paradox and believed that after his death no one would find in his papers a single explanation of what had filled his life. Kierkegaard himself argued that the truth could only be understood by someone who struggled for his life upon 70,000 fathoms of water. It is agreed, however, that Kierkegaard made a great contribution to Christian ethics through his attack on Hegel and his belief that what was required was the transformation of the life of man.

At a non-existential level, the representatives of the Danish working class pondered, during the 1840s, on another unsatisfactory duality: the way in which the constitutional reforms foreshadowed by the flow-on of the July 1830 French revolutions had been stifled by the crown. Although public discussion of political issues had grown during the 1830s, and a Liberal Party existed, Christian VIII, who, as King of Norway in 1814 had helped to frame Norway's free constitution, did not seem disposed to grant the same privilege to his Danish subjects. But Christian VIII died in January 1848, and the Liberals in Denmark obtained constitutional reform from his successor, after a demonstration in March had given notice of the directions of public opinion. Frederick VIII replied to the demonstrators, publicly renounced absolutism and planned a representative government led by A.W. Moltke as prime minister. In the new Danish ministry were leaders of the Liberals, D.G. Monrad, O. Lehmann, and A.F. Tscherning, who described himself as a friend of the peasant-farmers.

On 23 October 1848, a national assembly convened and drew up a new constitution, which was signed into law on 5 June 1849. Under the new arrangements, Denmark was given a parliament consisting of two chambers, the Folketing and the Landsting, the members of the former to be elected for eight years by indirect vote and the latter for three years by direct vote. The position of the crown was that absolute monarchy was overthrown. Thus what the French people got by revolution in 1789, the Danes achieved by a constitutional rearrangement fifty years later, when the absolute monarchy of the crown was replaced by a constitutional monarchy nominally responsible to the two houses of parliament. Of course, the tenor and substance of government remained largely unchanged. The influence of the crown in daily affairs (apart from the role of the sovereign during wars as an arbiter of foreign policy) was considerable for some time after the alteration of the external forms of power.

Sweden, in the first four decades of the nineteenth century, was as disturbed as Denmark. As an ugly duckling, Sweden was pushed about the farmyard and forced to gather scraps. The crucial turning point for Sweden came in April 1805, when Russia and Great Britain entered into their alliance against France. During the same year Sweden and Austria joined the group. Foreign policy in Sweden was the prerogative of the king, Gustav IV Adolf, but he did not pause to think why it was that a great and powerful nation like Britain interested itself in an alliance with such a relatively small one as Sweden, nor to ponder the results of miscalculation if the war turned out badly. Other Swedish foreign policy makers were to be much more cautious in the future, and Swedish neutrality during two twentieth-century world wars can be traced back to nineteenth-century experience.

In the event things did turn out badly. Napoleon defeated the Russians and the Austrians at Austerlitz, drove the Austrians out of southern Germany and, while Austria sued for peace, the Russians retreated. Troops from three nations – Sweden, Britain and Russia – attacked Hanover with similar disastrous results: the Swedes were forced to retreat to Pomerania, and the British and Russians evacuated their forces. After intense diplomatic lobbying in 1806, Prussia joined the anti-French front, but Napoleon defeated the Russians at Jena and Auerstadt, and once more was in command of Europe. The Swedes were left alone in the events that followed. In Pomerania, Swedes attacked French troops in 1807 with heavy losses. As a tactical ploy, the Swedes requested a ceasefire, which Napoleon granted on 18 April 1807, only to have the ceasefire broken by the Swedish king on 2 July 1807.

The French retaliated and crushed the Swedish forces, over-running Pomerania on 13 July, Napoleon having earlier, on 8 July, signed three treaty instruments with Alexander I: a peace treaty, separate and secret articles, and a treaty of alliance.

The Treaty of Tilsit was a milestone in world diplomatic history. It had all the ingredients of duplicity essential to a great international agreement. Ostensibly, the treaty was signed in order to stop the war between the two major European continental nations. Tradition has it that Alexander I and Napoleon initialled it as they floated on a raft in the River Neimen. Alexander was charmed by Napoleon's Corsican blarney, and the two monarchs agreed publicly that Russia should accept French hegemony in Central and Western Europe, that two new states, Warsaw and Westphalia, should be created, and that Prussia's size should be reduced.

The aim of the treaty was to encourage Britain to accept Russian mediation for an end to the war with Napoleon. By a strict timetable, the British were expected to give their answer to Russian diplomats before 11 August. If Britain did not accept Russian mediation, Russia agreed to join the French in an operation designed to crush their former ally and to seize its imperial and colonial possessions. The ducklings were about to lose their farm: under article five of the Treaty of Alliance between Alexander I and Napoleon, it was laid down in French that if Sweden did not close its ports to the English, recall its ambassador from London, and declare war on England, the two emperors would attack Sweden and constrain Denmark to declare war.

British trade again was the target of the proposed enlarged blockade system, but it is probable that the devastating wider effects on all the Scandinavians were never contemplated. It has been generally accepted by historians that Gustav IV Adolf was mad. Madness is the usual term to describe his state of mind during the Napoleonic wars, and the term is used clinically rather than pejoratively. There have been no attempts to exculpate him on the grounds of rare disease, nor to rehabilitate his image in the spirit of the medical revisionists who have worked on George III's reputation. Gustav IV Adolf rejected advice, kept his legitimist and religious hatred of Napoleon, which had been fanned by French emigres in 1803–4, kept the vast 'subsidy' paid to him by the British crown, and refused to change sides. On 21 February 1808 his hopes that swamps, poor roads and lakes would prevent a Russian attack on Swedish Finland were dashed. The Swedish-Finnish Army collapsed before a Russian offensive. When spring came, Sweden tried to counter-attack in southern Finland and won some victories that would be insignificant were they not the occasion for patriotic verse subsequently composed by Johan Ludvig Runeberg. The turning point came in May 1808, when the vital fortress of Sveaborg was surrendered by General Klingspor, the officer entrusted with frontier security. The best that could be said of him was that he had two chins, one eye and half a heart.

Gustav IV Adolf lost Finland and his crown. A revolution against him began in Varmland in March 1809, led by General George Aldersparre, but before the march on Stockholm was finished, General K.J. Aldercreutz had seized the king, dethroned him and sent him into exile to write explanatory memoirs showing how he had the greater interest of Sweden at heart and would have triumphed if he had had a chance to play a

Norwegian trump. During May 1809 the Russians occupied Åland and were poised to attack Stockholm. The British advised their Swedish ally to make peace, to which the Russians agreed in September. The peace treaty was signed at Hamina, and Sweden lost Finland and Åland. The eastward expansion of Scandinavian culture, which had begun with crusades in the twelfth century, ended abruptly.

Wearily the Swedish Riksdag met to elect a new ruler. They chose to reject some Danish princes. A small group of junior Swedish officers, not entirely having given up hope of a new conquest of Finland, negotiated the candidature of a marshal of the empire, Jean-Baptiste Bernadotte, making Charles XIII King of Sweden in name only. In this they hoped to please Napoleon, on account of his long lost love of Desirée, Bernadotte's wife. From the autumn of 1810 Bernadotte (who took the Swedish title Charles XIV John), against the wishes of many Swedes, began to direct Swedish foreign policy in opposition to Napoleon, who was not surprised. In 1809 Napoleon described Bernadotte as an intriguer whom he could not trust: he had nearly lost him the battle of Jena, was mediocre at Wagram, and did not do what he might have done at Austerlitz.

By 1811 the Franco-Russian alliance was dissolved. In 1812 Napoleon concluded a treaty with Prussia and Austria to fight Russia, and on 24 June 1812, 600,000 troops under the emperor invaded Russia. Moscow was captured and it burnt in September. The Grand Army retreated in November and December. Once again European alignments were reversed. In January 1812 Napoleon had seized Swedish Pomerania, which antagonised the pro-French faction at the Swedish court and made it easier for Charles XIV John to continue his pro-Russian policies. Charles XIV John considered that Sweden could not benefit from war against Britain and Russia, so with the Pomeranian issue as the *casus belli*, the Swedes changed sides, knowing well that Britain and Russia both favoured the idea of

Norway passing from Denmark (Napoleon's ally) to Sweden. Charles XIV John joined an alliance with Russia in April 1812, with Britain in March 1813, and with Prussia in April 1813. He was to be given a prime role in the destruction of Napoleon's power. Britain agreed to supply subsidies and naval assistance for the acquisition of Norway, and Sweden in return promised 30,000 troops for mainland operations. Neither Britain nor Russia helped with the conquest of Norway, and Charles XIV John accordingly, at first, declined to keep his part of the bargain. By August 1813, however, he was head of an army of 160,000 and went into action against the French. Although he knew no Swedish, he had learned Swedish military history and kept his 30,000 Swedes in reserve. Charles XIV John quickly defeated Marshal C.N. Oudinot and Marshal Michel Ney but, instead of advancing to the Rhine after the battle of Leipzig, broke off to assault the Danes in Schleswig-Holstein to help cement his claim to Norway.

Alexander I never forgave Napoleon for the confidence trick involved in obtaining his approval to the Treaty of Tilsit. The invasion of Russia and the devastating aftermath were traumatic triggers of Russian imperial francophobia. Hatred of Napoleon and extreme mortification at his own youthful gullibility made Alexander I inordinately fond of Charles XIV John, and so although Clemens Metternich tried to restrict Swedish aggrandisement on the defeat of Napoleon, the Treaty of Kiel which ended the war was, by and large, drawn up in Sweden's favour. It was a truism of war in both the nineteenth and twentieth centuries that to lose in battle was to lose in territory. Denmark was a plump duckling and it is surprising that there was so much left of it after the carve up: the Danish people were even compensated with Pomerania and Rugen for the loss of Norway, proportionate relief for Norway's contribution to the Danish debt.

The Treaty of Kiel was signed on 14 January 1814. By its

provisions Frederick VI of Denmark renounced his sovereignty over Norway in favour of the Swedish monarch. The Norwegians responded by rejecting this arbitrary severance of their ancient connection, declared their hostility to Sweden and determined that they would be masters of their own fate. The Danish viceroy, Prince Christian Frederick, led the struggle against their Scandinavian eastern neighbour and the will of the great European powers. Prince Christian Frederick was heir-presumptive to the crown of Denmark, and without difficulty was persuaded to govern as regent of Norway, until representatives of the Norwegian people could meet at Eidsvoll and draw up a constitution.

The Eidsvoll Assembly was a medley of forty-seven officials, thirty-seven peasants, sixteen town representatives and twelve men from the army or navy. This group were determined to make a permanent constitution. The Eidsvoll Constitution which the assembly drew up in 1814 replaced the administration that had grown up under the royal laws of Danish autocracy, and it was based as nearly as possible on the American constitution and French revolutionary constitution of 1791, containing the idea of limited monarchy and a separation of powers. Norway was declared to be a free, independent and indivisible realm governed by a limited form of monarchy. The executive and judiciary were separate from the legislature, the former consisting of ministers nominated by the king and having no say in the deliberations of the Storting Parliament which was provided with the fundamental powers of passing laws and levying taxes. The Storting was divided after election into two houses, the smaller (being a quarter of the whole) was given the historic name Lagting, being set up to revise the bills proposed by the larger division, or Odelsting. In the event of disagreement, the two houses were to sit together and a two-thirds majority could then pass the bills. Finance matters were to be dealt with jointly. Ministers were liable to impeachment for crimes and were to be tried by members of the Lagting and the Supreme court together.

The electoral system was representative but not democratic. The vote was restricted to officials, townspeople who owned valuable premises, and farmers who owned their farms or held a lease of not less than twenty-five years. Election was indirect, through representatives chosen by the primary electors, as under the French constitution of 1791. The peasants, who constituted eighty per cent of the population, were given a minimum of two-thirds of the seats. The party system was discouraged, members were required to be residents of the area that they represented, and came to the capital for a single session at three-year intervals, although the king might summon a special Storting if he desired. Under this system, the king imposed ministers upon the people, and the people imposed laws and financial measures upon the king. The king was given power to hold up a bill until it had been assessed by three successive Stortings, and this was to cause difficulties as the nineteenth century proceeded. A pro-Swedish party, headed by Wedel Jarlsberg, had little support in the assembly at Eidsvoll, and the constitution contained a clause (that helped to save Norway in 1940) entitling the king to govern from abroad.

On 17 May 1814, members of the National Assembly put their signatures to the constitution and on the same day elected Prince Christian Frederick, King of Norway. The independent monarchy, unlike the constitution, lasted for a very short period. War broke out between Sweden and Norway on 29 July 1814. It was a short war, lasting less than a fortnight, but Swedes and Norwegians died in it, and despite the efforts of historians to minimise its effects, the psychological legacy was to prove a considerable handicap to pan-Scandinavianism in the future. Charles XIV John himself took command of the Swedish Army in July 1814 and marched across the frontier with an army superior in all respects, apart from the justice of their cause. For generations Norwegians would not forget that Sweden's last great military adventure was against its Scandinavian cousin. The war was ended by the Convention of Moss on 14 August 1814. The Swedish regent recognised and accepted the new Norwegian constitution, and Christian Frederick summoned a Storting to meet in October. He then resigned, and set sail forthwith for Denmark, over which he ruled as Christian VIII between 1839 and 1848. The Storting (not without reluctance) affirmed the principle of union with Sweden and, on 4 November, the king of Sweden was elected to the vacant throne of Norway. The Norwegians, however, continued to observe 17 May as the true date of their national regeneration, which to a large extent was the result of the far-sighted expertise of W.F.K. Christie, the secretary at Eidsvoll and the first president of the Norwegian National Assembly.

Since the abdication of Christian Frederick, the Norwegian ministers had governed Norway, and Charles XIV John tactfully avoided any allusions to the rights which he might have temporarily acquired nearly a year before under the Treaty of Kiel. Charles XIV John and his son, Oscar, bound themselves to observe the constitution, and in 1815 the Norwegian and Swedish parliaments ratified the agreement for the administration of the two countries by an Act of Union. The act naturally was differently interpreted in Stockholm and Christiania. Swedish public opinion considered that Sweden had acquired a new territory in compensation for the loss of Finland to Russia, but the Swedish monarch was often impartial in his dealings with the two countries that he governed. There were, however, potential constitutional problems. The king, as head of the executive, controlled the foreign policy of both his kingdoms. Norwegian councillors were excluded from membership of the legislative body which passed laws on foreign affairs. The king was principally resident in Sweden and he was represented in Norway by a viceroy who, until 1829, was

Swedish. To make matters worse, it soon became obvious that although the Norwegian Parliament might choose to become increasingly liberal, democratic and reformist in its reflection of social change, executive power resided in a bureaucracy appointed by the crown.

Amid financial chaos and the collapse of the Norwegian shipping and timber industries as a result of the Napoleonic wars, the Bank of Norway was established in 1816. The currency was devalued to a tenth of its nominal value, subsequently a thirtieth, and a silver tax was introduced. Norway was a primarily agricultural country. Its leading town, Bergen, was relatively prosperous because of the rich fishing industry. But most peasant farmers lived in medieval poverty. Their houses were window-less, and although the stone hearth in the middle of the floor gave way gradually during the century to an iron stove near the door, living conditions were cold, dark and smoky. Most houses were single storey and during the winter cattle wintered in their stalls, without light or standing room, huddled together to give maximum warmth. They were lifted out as skeletons when spring came, their droppings being shovelled out on to the fields. The situation in Norway resembled that in Ireland, where there was a population explosion and multiplication of small tenancies. And, like the poor Irish, many Norwegians were victims of alcoholism, as the Storting, moving towards freedom of trade, gave permission to every farmer to distil brandy. Spirits thus became cheap, poisonous and disastrously accessible to a population that had to cope not only with drunkenness but also leprosy.

In the depressed social and economic climate, which even a relatively liberal constitution could not assuage, the 1830 revolution in France gave an impulse to radicalism. The most significant political development after 1830 was the emergence of the peasants as a force in politics. Two-thirds of the seats in the parliament under the Eidsvoll constitution had been allocated to the peasant electors, and in 1833 the Norwegian farmers had their first majority in the Storting.

The Norwegian peasantry focused their attack on the crown. They persisted with their celebrations of the accession-day of the deposed Dane, Christian Frederick, which Charles XIV John took, not unreasonably, as an unsubtle demonstration against himself and the power of the Swedish crown. On 17 May 1829, the Swedish viceroy ordered soldiers to charge a group of celebrating Norwegians. And so 'The Battle of the market place' was incorporated into the anti-Swedish canon of the Norwegian independence seekers. Charles XIV John's popularity with Norwegians reached its lowest point in 1836, when he dissolved the Norwegian legislature against its will, only to find the latter retaliate by impeaching and fining one of his ministers. Oscar, the son of Charles XIV John, who became king in 1844, behaved in a more conciliatory fashion, to find that his generosity was used as a lever to extract yet more concessions. Oscar allowed the Norwegian name to be placed first on documents concerning Norwegian internal affairs, and the merchant navy flew both flags. The Norwegians, however, objected to the mark of the Swedish union being superimposed on the Norwegian merchant ensign, and that, and peasant opposition to government expenditure, became the chief matters of discord. A typical attitude of the peasants was that ministers should not be permitted to sit in the parliament because they would control the elected representatives of the people instead of the people controlling the representatives. No peasant entered government before 1844, and the civil service then, as now, was able to manipulate parliament through its inside knowledge of the administration; the bureaucracy was a self-perpetuating clique that reproduced itself generation after generation.

A similar situation existed in Finland, with the pressure of the nationalists directed against a foreign monarch, in the Finnish case the Russian tsar, who was at first magnanimous in victory. The tsar himself came to Finland. He travelled to Porvoo in March 1809 with great ceremony, taking with him a throne embellished with the symbol of the double eagle. Beneath an autocratic canopy Alexander established Finland as a grand duchy, not a province of the Russian empire. He endorsed the Lutheran Finnish religion, even though it was not the same as that practised in most of Mother Russia, and said that Finnish laws could continue to be implemented within the grand duchy. The administration of Finland was put in the hands of the Finnish Senate and the Committee for Finnish Affairs was set in St Petersburg, with a Russian governor-general, in much the same way as the British, under the Act of Union, established a lord lieutenant in Dublin. The new Russian government of Finland faced difficulties with language. Swedish was the language of government in Finland, as it had been since 1523. So the governor-general did not waste his time attending the Senate, and for a time Finnish affairs were conducted in the same spirit that had existed before the Diet of Porvoo. After 1809, the Russian tsar had the same powers as the Swedish king he replaced. This meant that the rights of subjects under Swedish custom were retained by the Finns, although they lived in a grand duchy of the Russian empire. The autonomy of the grand duchy was manifest in the Diet, and in an important provision all matters concerning Finland were submitted directly to the emperor. Moreover, the territories ceded to Russia after eighteenth-century wars and peace treaties in 1721 and 1743 were restored to the grand duchy in 1811.

Russian interest in Finland in the nineteenth, as in the twentieth century, was primarily strategic. The incorporation of the grand duchy was a guarantee of the security of St Petersburg, which Peter the Great had founded after his conquest of Karelia, Estonia and Livonia at the beginning of the eighteenth century.

Russian strategy was to use control over Finland to guard the approaches to St Petersburg, and to defend it first from the Sveaborg fortress on the islands at Helsinki's harbour entrance, and, later, at the western extremity of the grand duchy, in Åland, where the fortress of Bomarsund was developed to extend Russian protection almost to the harbours of Stockholm.

As strategic issues grew in importance during the nineteenth century it is hardly surprising that the tsar strove to reorganise, reshape and redirect the energies of the administrative institutions of Finland. In 1823 Governor-General A. Zakrevsky abolished the Committee for Finnish Affairs and submitted problems to the tsar personally, by-passing the secretary of state for Finland. When Alexander I died in 1825, Zakrevsky insisted that the Finns take an oath of fealty to his successor, but since he named the incorrect successor (Constantine, whereas Nicholas I became emperor) the Finns were content to continue in the spirit of the grand duchy guaranteed by Alexander I. Nicholas I did not disturb the status quo by convening the Diet, which was not called until the 1860s.

The growth of the Finnish economy in the early nineteenth century was slow, but it was put on a sound financial basis after the establishment of the Bank of Finland in 1811. The Bank of Finland issued Finnish rouble currency until 1860, when a separate currency was printed, the mark. For a moment or two things had looked brighter in Finland after the Russian takeover. Russia was, after all, a much larger country than Sweden, and more cosmopolitan in its outlook. St Petersburg had been a magnet for enterprising Europeans since the days of Catherine and Peter the Great. Finland benefited, as did Sweden, from the migration of talents from the tsar's court. It was a case of 'go west, young man', and in the west lay Finland. One of the first to branch out was the Scottish toolmaker James Finlayson. Finlayson visited the rapids of Tammerkoski in 1819 and asked the tsar if he could establish a factory in Tampere. The tsar agreed, and the economic development of Finland was given a push as Finlayson was granted land along the rapids and money to begin the production of tools and machines operated by water power. By 1828 Finlayson was producing cotton and woollen cloth, the Finnish textile industry had begun and Tampere was set on the road as the industrial centre of Finland and, for a later generation, the home of social democracy and the left. In 1833, Finland launched its first steamship, the *Ilmarinen*.

The new Helsinki, which replaced the old Swedish capital of Åbo, was the greatest monument to Russian benevolence. Helsinki was burnt to the ground in 1808 in one of the periodic conflagrations that wooden buildings were subjected to in that era. The reconstruction of the city was begun by Johann Albrecht Ehrenström, who set out the new town with straight roads and open squares on the contemporary idiom. He also invited Carl Ludvig Engel to Helsinki and in 1824 Engel succeeded Carlo Bassi as controller of public works. Engel died in the 1840s, but by the end of the decade Helsinki was transformed into the largest city in the north designed on a single plan. Considering its tiny civilian population of 4,000, it was extravagantly provided with notable public buildings centred around the senate square, the university, the library, the esplanade and the quays.

However much Alexander I might regard Finland as an area in which he could experiment with the idea of constitutional monarchy, and however pleasant conditions might be in a new capital, the articulate middle-class nationalists of Finland were not satisfied with the subordinate status of Finnish culture in the grand duchy. In Finland, Finnish language and literature took third place to Swedish and Russian. This unsatisfactory state of affairs was difficult to overcome as there appeared to be no Finnish culture to speak of. The collection and compilation of a unique Finnish cultural heritage was the first prerequisite of the development of a sense of national identity and worth.

Finnish patriots recognised the importance of philological

research, which they conducted in the remotest part of eastern Finland on the border of Russian Karelia. In 1835, after twenty years compilation and collection, under the leadership of Elias Lönnrot, the *Kalevala* was published in the Homeric epic style. The word 'Kalevala' was a poetical name for Finland, and was translated as 'land of heroes'. The *Kalevala* was used by those who set out to promulgate the artistic superiority of Finnish language and culture over that of the conquering nations, Russia and Sweden. It was exclusively and aggressively Finnish, allowed no foreign encroachments in style, vocabulary or content, and was the chief vehicle for the expression of Finnish romantic nationalism and the inspiration of the Young Finns, as their determination to cast off the yoke of foreign cultural imperialism grew. The only full nineteenth-century translation was into Swedish, in 1841, so the *Kalevala* had the added magic of being accessible only to the initiated who could speak and understand the unique syntax of the Finno-Ugrian language, which was incomprehensible to most Indo-Europeans, as it contained virtually no borrowed words and was based on different grammatical principles than most of Finland's neighbouring languages.

Thus while the Russians built, and expatriate social life flourished among the garrison citizens of the new capital, the seeds of revolt had been sown by the takeover of the country. J.L. Runeberg personified those who resented the inclusion of Finland into Russia, and he began to compose a cycle of verses to celebrate the legends of Finnish resistance to Russian conquest and government. It was no accident that during 1848, the year of revolutions, Runeberg's poem *Our Land* was set to music, and it developed into the country's national anthem. 'Our Land' was not, unfortunately, everybody's choice.

Many Finns, and other Scandinavians, were forced by poverty to leave their homes and take their lives in their hands by sailing to foreign shores. There was a long tradition of exploration and colonisation of America, and some went as far as Australia. King Gustav II Adolf sponsored a series of Scandinavian migrations as he attempted to bolster Swedish prestige by establishing a colony in America during the seventeenth century. In 1638 a party of Swedes and Finns migrated to Delaware. The Scandinavian migrants were accompanied on their odyssey by their pastors, who contributed a vein of moral solace to the desperate struggle for a livelihood in the early years of settlement. In the nineteenth century a stream of Danes and Norwegians joined the Swedes and the Finns, changing the face of America and depopulating their own countries. The first Norwegians emigrated to the United States on the fifty-four foot sloop *Restauration* in 1825. Fifty-three of them arrived in New York, sold their ship, and moved to Orleans County where, helped by Quakers, they began to farm, moving out to the prairies of Illinois in the mid-1830s. Emigration began in earnest in the 1840s, and by the end of the century almost 400,000 people of Norwegian birth were recorded on the United States' census.

'America fever' swept Scandinavia during the nineteenth century, and during the nineteenth and early twentieth century, over 1,000,000 Swedes emigrated. 'Cousin' and 'American' became synonyms. Almost one in five emigrants came from southern Sweden, and the province was all but depopulated. By the time the United States closed the door, 350,000 Finns had emigrated. Danish migration did not start until the 1850s, when Mormon missionaries enticed their first Danish settlers to Utah. Before 1848 the migration of Scandinavians was not considered dangerous to the survival prospects of the northern countries. But it was a symptom of deep-seated social and economic problems that seemed insoluble on native soil.

Despite the ominous wastage caused by emigration, by the end of the 1840s Scandinavia was breaking out in all directions. The ugly ducklings were gaining more feathers, and growing fatter and more self-confident, although they were still vulnerable prizes for someone else's table. The next two generations, however, were to concentrate on new issues, of which the most important was the question of devolution. The Danes tried to fight off a campaign for liberty in the two grand duchies attached to their kingdom, in the face of liberal public opinion that supported assistance to romantic nationalism. And Norwegian and Finnish nationalists, in the period after the 1848 revolutions, saw the fight for democracy as part of the struggle for national independence, and held firmly to the concept of individual liberty within autonomous national boundaries, free from the sovereignty of their masters, the Swedes and the Russians.

CHAPTER 2

Out of the Doll's House

While each of the Scandinavian countries followed a unique path of development in the last half of the nineteenth century, and many of the themes of their history – devolution, for example – continued well into the new one, there was an organic unity in the period from the 1848 revolutions in Europe until the 1890s. After a brief encounter with pan-Scandinavianism, romantic nationalism triumphed. Although the centuries of greatness that had made Scandinavia a cultural unity were not forgotten, the people living within the various Scandinavian countries began to assert their cultural identities. In a world exposed to the Darwinian doctrine of evolution, survival of the fittest meant that the weakest would go to the wall – in the north as well as in the Galapagos. To survive in the next century, Scandinavians believed, one had to assert one's cultural uniqueness. Each of the Scandinavian countries sought liberation, or responded to the demands for freedom. If Sweden and Denmark identified with Henrik Ibsen's character Torvald, reluctantly letting his spouse go, Finland and Norway were on the side of Nora, determinedly walking out.

Denmark's internal and international situation was an example of the way in which the new forces of self-determination were interrelated both in domestic politics and foreign policy. The Danish radicals' struggle for constitutional reform within Denmark was closely connected to the attempt of German nationals within Denmark's borders to achieve self-determination and end the political connection between Schleswig and Holstein. The Napoleonic war had radicalised German nationalists, and German speakers believed, by 1848, that the time was right to break the constitutional link that had existed since the Danish King Christian I became the ruler of both duchies in 1460. Christian I was elected by the nobility of Schleswig and Holstein and obtained a charter of privileges affirming that Schleswig and Holstein were in an indissoluble association. To the romantic nationalists of the nineteenth century no such thing as an indissoluble association existed. The rival dynastic claims to the duchies weakened the claim of constitutional legitimacy. The population of Schleswig was Danish in the northern countryside, German in the south, and mixed in the northern towns and the centre. The difficulty with language, which was the central focus of discontent, had not been an issue before the nineteenth century. Since the fifteenth century the language of southern Schleswig had been German, and of northern Schleswig Danish; government was carried on in German. But in a development of the new German nationalism (which had budded after the German Confederation was formed in 1815) the recorder in the Schleswig Assembly refused to take down a speech in Danish by a pro-Danish deputy, and the matter came to a head.

The Danes lost their Schleswig–Holstein possessions in two phases. The first crisis began with the 1848 revolutions in Germany, when German nationalists, fighting the battle of the common man, overlaid democratic demands with a claim for their northern border states. This was an area of 6,000 square miles, which contained the strategic and important towns of Kiel, Schleswig and Flensburg, and which was divided by the River Eider.

On 8 July 1846, Christian VIII had confronted the two

groups of protagonists, Danish and German, by publishing an open letter in which he re-asserted the integrity of Schleswig–Holstein, proclaimed Schleswig a part of Denmark but, in a deliberately ambiguous oversight, did not define the succession laws in the case of Holstein. When Frederick VII became king on Christian's death in January 1848, the German majority in both duchies demanded incorporation in the German Confederation, and their cause was taken up with democratic enthusiasm by the radicals of the German 1848 revolution. In March 1848 a provisional government at Kiel proclaimed independence. Frederick VII declared the union of the duchies dissolved and began a campaign against the revolutionaries by stating his determination to tie Schleswig to Holstein. The parliament of the German Confederation asked for Prussia's help and the Prussian armies quickly marched through Schleswig, even entering Jutland, before agreeing to a truce. King Frederick William IV of Prussia was acutely aware of the irony in his conquest, the popularity and success of which was based in part on anti-monarchical sentiments that he did not share. On 23 February 1849 the Danes warned Prussia that the peace treaty would not be renewed unless concessions were made to the Danish point of view. Fighting continued in April. Again the Prussians marched through Schleswig and into Jutland, and were only stopped by diplomatic pressure from the British, Russians and French.

In all there were two years of negotiation, three outbreaks of war and three armistices in the first phase of the Schleswig-Holstein dispute. During the revolutionary war, the Danes won only one skirmish, the Battle of Isted. This victory was enough to give them a respite, and the Danes reluctantly signed a treaty that ended the war for a decade. The treaty was underwritten by the great European powers, Lord Palmerston being particularly keen to maintain what was left of the Danish mainland as one property, and the treaty was signed in London on 8 May 1852 by Denmark, Sweden, Great Britain, Russia, France, Austria and Prussia. Behind it was the expectation that Danish integrity would be a permanent element in the European balance of power. The biggest problem to be solved – succession – appeared in 1850. The duchies were claimed as his potential inheritance by the Duke of Augustenborg, but he nobly stood aside in favour of the popular choice of the major European powers, Prince Christian of Glucksburg.

After the treaty, Schleswig's administration was re-established with royalist Danish-minded civil servants being appointed to administer the province. Thirty of the revolutionary leaders were exiled. The Danish government decreed that the language in the northern part of Schleswig was to be Danish, in the southern part German and, in no-man's land, where the two languages mingled, it was decreed that Danish language should be used in schools. Prussia and Austria objected to the new democratic constitution of Denmark being applied to Schleswig on the grounds that this would bind Schleswig more tightly to Denmark than to Holstein. Radicals pointed out with great effect the irony of the Danes gaining constitutional reform as a result of the revolutions of 1848, and at the same time preventing democracy and national self-determination for Schleswig and Holstein.

During the next decade, the German Confederation, of which Holstein was a member, grew stronger, and German public opinion demanded the incorporation of Schleswig into the German orbit. The Danish government rashly decided to settle the question by incorporating Schleswig into Denmark, allowing it to share equally in the country's political democracy, and thereby, they hoped, killing any demand for home rule. This involved Denmark in breaking the peace treaty, extending the authority of the Danish government to the River Eider, and separating Schleswig from Holstein. The Act of Parliament to permit this was passed on 13 November 1863. But, history repeated itself in a most unfortunate way: in the midst of the constitutional crisis King Frederick VII died before he had signed the bill. Christian of Glucksburg, Christian IX, succeeded him (according to the provisions agreed upon earlier in London) but the situation was complicated and made more tense by Christian's deliberation for three days before he decided whether to sign the new act.

The Danish act was a violation of the treaty, and the Duke of Augustenborg, whose father had earlier renounced all his son's rights, had himself proclaimed duke of a united Schleswig–Holstein. Otto von Bismarck, Prussia's Minister of State, subsequently supported the Duke of Augustenborg and persuaded Austria to join forces. The triumvirate presented Denmark with an ultimatum demanding that the Act be repealed, the government in Denmark resigned, a new one was formed, and the Danish army withdrew from Holstein to demonstrate that it had no desire to hold on to a member state of the German Confederation. The Danes then faced war as they took up a defensive position on the southern border of Schleswig, along the thousand-year-old border defence embankment.

On 1 February 1864, the Austro–Prussian Army crossed the border at the River Eider and marched northwards under General Friedrich Wrangel. The Danes withdrew from their ancient defence to a more easily held one. Public opinion in Copenhagen demanded the dismissal of the general who supervised the retreat. The Prussian Army was equipped with breech loading rifles: the Danes were still using muzzle loaders. Not for the last time, the German artillery was more modern and vastly superior to that of its enemy, being able to fire across a wide fiord and score hits behind earthworks which the Danish Army hastily occupied. Pan-Scandinavianism, whose romantic literary output was increased at the time of the Schleswig war, had no effect beyond the assistance of a few Norwegian and Swedish volunteers fighting on the side of the Danes. Denmark stood alone and the Germans soon controlled the whole of the Schleswig–Holstein provinces.

After the defeat of 1864 a conference in London came to the conclusion that the best the British and their allies could hope for was that Prussia's fortunes might be transient, and that international conjunctions might change to enable Denmark to recover Schleswig, or at any rate the northern clearly pro-Danish part of the province. However, with Prussia's military victories over Austria in 1866 and France in 1871, German power was established in the heart of Europe, and the Schleswig–Holstein issue seemed permanently settled.

While Denmark was to struggle for national survival, the big events for its three greatest sons – Grundtvig, Kierkegaard and Andersen – were personal and centred on such things as an unhappy love affair or a quarrel with a parent. Andersen fell in love with Riborg Voigt and Jenny Lind. Kierkegaard was jilted by Regine Olsen who sailed from Copenhagen to the Danish West Indies, which her new husband governed. But the character of their general response was conditioned by their political circumstances. No artist (although Kierkegaard tried) could avoid the momentous changes in Denmark that followed the revolutions of 1848 and the wars with Prussia over Schleswig-Holstein. Kierkegaard's response to the three-year war over Schleswig-Holstein was naturally existential. He complained that his manservant, Anders, had been called up for active service. At the same time he made a classic attack on the new democratic constitution of 1849, observing that of all tyrannies a people's government was the most agonising, the most fatuous, absolutely the ruin of everything great and sublime. It was fortunate that Kierkegaard never lived to see social democracy or the Russian Revolution, as he

concluded his diatribe by remarking that a people's government was a true image of hell, for even if you could endure its
torments, the tyranny of democracy did not allow you the
comfort of being alone.

Grundtvig, on the other hand, was a Dane with a political
message, expressed most forcibly in anti-German terms. For
Grundtvig, the word 'German' was a term of abuse. He
observed that it was 'a high German notion' that life was
explainable even before it was experienced. Grundtvig believed
that whenever such German ideas were incorporated into the
educational structure all schools became workshops for
disillusion and death, where 'the worms live high at the
expense of life itself'. This he rejected, maintaining that if the
school, as an educational institution, was to realise its potential
for benefiting life, then it should not give the highest priority
to purely intellectual activity and to its own institutional status
but set as its chief goal the task of helping solve life's problems.
The idea, said Grundtvig, that those who constituted the
nucleus of the people – agricultural workers, large and small
independent farmers, skilled manual workers of every trade,
sailors and businessmen – did not need any training other than
that which was gained behind a plough, in a shop, climbing
the mast of a vessel, or in a place of business might be all right
for barbarians and tyrants. But the idea had never been acceptable to the Danish king or to the people because it ran contrary
to their Nordic way of thinking. The people of the Nordic
countries were never enslaved by foreign invaders. 'I have
striven,' said Grundtvig, 'impelled by Nordic vigorousness
to liberate myself from this whole foreign and spurious way
of thought.'

He strove so well that he was elected to the Constitutional
Assembly in November 1848 and complained that the ideals
of the folk high school, which had been accepted by the
sovereign, should be neglected by his successor. He bewailed

the fact that a high school project, which Christian VIII had established during the last years of his reign and devoted his very last thoughts to, had been buried with the king in his grave. Grundtvig recalled that the king had intended the high school to open the door for greater freedom and scientific study than was hitherto practised in Copenhagen, and should provide an opportunity for all young people, regardless of class or occupation, to acquire a better foundation for the study of their mother tongue. He argued that the Danish folk high school should provide better instruction in subjects about Denmark and everything Danish than that which had been available through any publicly sponsored educational opportunity. His object was to provide an educational institution for all young people. The school was aimed at awakening the national consciousness of young Danes, nourishing their love of country, instructing them in related areas at an early age, and teaching them, whenever feasible, that regardless of their social rank and occupation, they belonged to one people, and as such had one mother, one destiny and one purpose.

H.C. Andersen, although he was not such an obvious romantic nationalist, joined Grundtvig as a recruiting sergeant, using his reputation in England to publish an important and influential anti-German letter in the *Literary Gazette*. In his propaganda piece, Andersen began by observing that politics were not his business: poets had another mission. But when convulsions were shaking the countries so that it was almost impossible to stand on the ground without feeling it in the very ends of fingers, even poets had to speak. The war in Denmark was carried on by the entire Danish people, said Andersen, and was one where noble-born and peasant, inspired by a righteous cause, placed themselves voluntarily in the ranks of battle as enthusiasm and patriotism filled and elevated the Danish nation. Andersen went to Sweden between 1848 and 1851 and carried on personal diplomacy with King Oscar I, but apart from a token Swedish force which landed on Funen, nothing, in military shape, came of pan-Scandinavianism. For, while in the mid-nineteenth, as in the mid-twentieth century, people in Britain were behind Scandinavia, and governments praised the northern liberal idealists, all shrank for as long as possible from giving more than moral aid.

The loss of Schleswig and Holstein brought about the downfall of the Danish National Liberals. In 1866 a conservative administration drew up a new constitution that was thermidorian in its tone. General suffrage was retained for the Folketing, but the landowners and large taxpayers were given power in the Landsting, and as a result parliamentary politics polarised on chamber lines, with a reformist lower house at odds with the upper house until 1872, when the left secured a majority in the lower house and insisted that the king select a ministry containing their representatives. By 1884 there were even two Social Democrats in the Danish lower house, which had eighty radical members, and the king and Conservatives were forced in 1877 and 1885 to declare a 'provisional budget' when the lower house refused supply, a procedure out of step with the spirit of parliamentary democracy that had been hailed so optimistically after 1848.

One of the most indignant propagandists for the Danes in the Schleswig-Holstein conflict, and the working class in their struggle against reaction, was the Norwegian author Henrik Ibsen, who tried to ring out a 'Marseillaise of the North' when he watched the Prussians march into Berlin with trophies they had taken from Schleswig. Although in his early years he was the most celebrated victim of Danish cultural imperialism, Ibsen burned with indignation, bitterness and passion over the way his fellow Scandinavians had let down Denmark. Ibsen described Denmark as a smaller brother being beaten up by a German bully, who went unmolested.

By the time of the Schleswig-Holstein war Ibsen was on

the way to being acknowledged as one of the great dramatists of Europe. He had been born at Skien, on 20 March 1828, and supported himself from the age of fifteen, first as an apprentice and then as an assistant at a chemist's shop in Grimstad until 1849, when he prepared himself for the matriculation examination, which he took in 1850. His first published work was some minor poems, but he then wrote a verse drama, *Catalina*, which was inspired by the revolutionary spirit of 1848 and the Latin text he was bound to study for his matriculation examination. His next work, the dramatic poem *The Burial Mound*, was performed at the Christiania Theatre. In 1851 he was appointed to the Norwegian Theatre, which had been established in Bergen, and worked there as a dramatic author and then as a producer. In summer 1852, with a grant from the theatre, he went on a tour to Copenhagen and several German cities to study art and literature. By 1854 he had written a couple more historical dramas, which had been performed in all the theatres in Norway, as well as in Copenhagen, and at the Royal Theatre, Stockholm. His full-length play, *The Vikings at Helgeland*, appeared in 1858 and was reviewed favourably in Denmark and Sweden.

Ibsen resigned from his appointment at the Bergen Theatre in 1857 and accepted the post of artistic director at the Norwegian Theatre in Christiania, an appointment he held until the theatre went into liquidation. In 1858, he married the daughter of the Dean of Bergen, not being debarred as the father of a bastard, but as his expenses were greater than his salary (300 specie dollars a year) he had to leave the town in debt. The liquidation of the theatre meant a loss of more than a hundred and fifty dollars to him, as well as his regular employment. He said of it: 'to live exclusively from literary employment in this country is impossible.' He had debts of nearly five hundred dollars, saw no prospect of improving his position and felt obliged to make provisional preparations to emigrate to Denmark, feeling that 'to leave my native country and to give up what I had hitherto regarded, and still do regard, as my real career, is an inexpressibly sad step for me to take'. Ibsen was a careerist and not an existentialist. The first product of his twenty-seven years abroad was *Brand*, completed in Rome in 1865, a polemical outburst against Ibsen's sworn enemy – complacent and stultified Norwegian provincialism. Since the hero of *Brand* took as his motto 'all or nothing', Ibsen was asked if *Brand* was a representation of Kierkegaard. Ibsen replied that when he wrote *Brand* he had an empty beer glass with a scorpion in it standing on his desk. From time to time the creature became sickly so Ibsen threw a piece of soft fruit to it, which the scorpion attacked furiously emptying its poison into it, and then grew well again. Ibsen asked whether there was not something similar to that about 'us poets', but said that it was a complete misunderstanding to imagine that he had described the life and career of Søren Kierkegaard in *Brand* as he had read very little of Søren Kierkegaard and understood even less.

Throughout the period 1848–90 Ibsen explored the dramatic metaphors of European reform and the uniqueness of Norwegian life. During the 1870s he was forced to consider the role of the state and the role of government and, in 1871, believed that the state had to go. Ibsen said that he would join a revolution if it could undermine the concept of the state and set up free choice and spiritual kinship. In an anarchistic mood, Ibsen pointed out that the state had its roots in time, and that greater things than it would fall. Even religion would fall. There was nothing eternal, he argued, either about moral concepts or the forms of art: 'who will guarantee me' he asked, 'that two and two are not five up on Jupiter?'

With social questions uppermost in his mind, Ibsen began to write and publish a series of social plays, the first, *Pillars of Society* in 1877, the next, *A Doll's House* in 1879.

Whatever mathematics existed in the heavens, Ibsen could not avoid involvement in the national romantic movement, and it was during the composition of *A Doll's House* that Norwegian nationalists asked him to lend his weight to the campaign for a pure Norwegian flag. Ibsen replied churlishly that as far as he was concerned the mark of union could remain, but what ought to be taken away was the mark of prejudice and narrow-mindedness and shortsightedness and subservience and unthinking trust in authority, so that every individual could sail under his own flag. Ibsen thought it was not his job to make himself responsible for the liberty and independence of the state, but to awaken as many people as possible to liberty and independence. He returned to the creation of *A Doll's House*, the play that made him famous, in which the heroine showed how a woman could not be herself in a society that was exclusively male and judged feminine conduct from a masculine standpoint. These ideas, which stirred passions a hundred years later, were sensations in the nineteenth century. On 4 December 1879, *A Doll's House* was published in Copenhagen and the response was electric. Critics pointed out that it ended on a note of inexorable calamity, pronouncing a death sentence on accepted social ethics, as the heroine, Nora, left her husband, Torvald, and walked out on him on Christmas Eve, leaving the children asleep in their beds. By February 1878 *A Doll's House* was being performed in five different theatres in Berlin in three separate translations. In one it was played as *Nora*, with an ending preferred by the German theatre manager. In this version Nora did not leave the house but was forced by Torvald to the door of the children's bedroom. A few lines of dialogue followed, Nora sank down at the door and the curtain fell. Ibsen described the German alteration as 'a barbaric outrage against the play' and became embroiled in controversy over the implications of his work for social reformers.

Towards the end of the century Ibsen turned to the working

class. On 14 June 1885 he addressed a workers' procession in Trondheim, saying that only nobility of character, mind and will could liberate public life. The transformation of social conditions, which was happening in the rest of Europe, was largely concerned with the future status of women and workers. Ibsen was hoping and working for that.

Two years later, on 24 September 1887, at a speech in Stockholm, Ibsen said that it had been claimed that he too was in the vanguard of things and had helped to create a new age in the land. Against this, he believed that the age in which they stood could be described as a closure, from which something new was being born. He believed the scientific doctrine of evolution was correct about the spiritual elements of life and that the time was coming when political and social concepts would cease existing in their present forms, and that from these two a unity would emerge containing within itself conditions for the potential happiness of mankind.

Ibsen's musical counterpart on the world stage was Edvard Grieg. Grieg was the most famous representative of the Norwegians in Bergen who had emigrated from Scotland. His Scottish ancestor came to Norway in 1746 after the battle of Culloden. His mother was herself a musician, and gave her son instruction from the age of six. Grieg's musical career began in earnest when in 1858 he played some of his juvenile pieces to Ole Bull, who persuaded his parents to send him to Leipzig Conservatory. The Grieg family were delighted with Bull's sponsorship, for Bull was a folk hero and a symbol of the new Norway that had broken free in 1814. Significantly, it was in 1848 that Bull had tried to found a Norwegian national theatre (as distinct from those performing almost only Danish plays) in Bergen, and had engaged the then almost unknown young author named Henrik Ibsen as house playwright and producer. Bull visited America several times, losing his money and almost his life in an attempt to establish a Norwegian colony in

Pennsylvania under the name of 'Oleana'.

The real centre of musical, intellectual and artistic life for Norwegians was not Leipzig, however, but Copenhagen. Most Norwegians of the urban professional and business classes had close connections with Denmark, and many of them believed the cultural ties between the two countries should never be broken. It was understandable that Grieg should feel attracted to Denmark, and he moved to Copenhagen, where he arrived with work that was pronounced trivial by his teachers. In Norway Grieg had been on excellent terms with the local Hardanger fiddle players and enjoyed imitating their traditional style on his violin. What was trivial to the metropolitan power was vital to the national romantics, as Grieg found when he met Rikard Nordraak in Copenhagen in 1864. Nordraak was a national romantic looking for the distinctly Norwegian in literature, ballads, mountain scenery, traditional costumes, festivals, and, above all, folk song and dance. He and Grieg journeyed to Italy, the goal of so many Scandinavians, where there was sun, a low cost of living and plenty of company for northerners who wanted to relax with fellow Scandinavian authors, artists and musicians. Indeed, one of the tourist attractions for Scandinavians in Rome was the familiar sight of Ibsen drunk.

A decade earlier one of the main debating points had been the conflict between the national romantics and the pan-Scandinavians. The national romantic movement did great service to Norway by pointing out and preserving what they could save of Norway's medieval and Viking heritage. The Norwegian historian P.A. Munch worked on a history of the Norwegian peoples in which he stressed the uniqueness of local culture. He also drafted the text of an appeal to save Trondheim cathedral which, at the end of the 1850s, was in danger of demolition. But by 1871, following a series of lectures at Copenhagen University by the Danish author and critic,

George Brandes, there was a major reorientation of social, political and literary thought in Norway in the direction of romantic nationalism. Ibsen stood apart as usual, and was more concerned with royalties. Grieg went even further, saying that *Peer Gynt* represented a romantic nationalism he was thoroughly sick of, as it was 'full of cow turds, norse-norsehood, and be to thyself enoughness'. In 1874 the Norwegian government gave Grieg a life annuity, designed to enable him to give up teaching and conducting and devote himself to composition and, two years later, *Peer Gynt* was performed with Grieg's music at Oslo in February 1876 in the absence of both the dramatist and the composer. The performance was repeated thirty-five times within the year. Ibsen was living abroad and Grieg was living in Bergen, which many Norwegians regarded as a German Hanseatic town and not really part of Norway.

Peer Gynt, despite Grieg's reservations, made his name. It showed that he was not merely a composer of trifles. One contemporary critic claimed that it was possible that Ibsen's *Peer Gynt* would live only through Grieg's music, which had 'more poetry and artistic intelligence than the whole of Ibsen's five-act monstrosity'. Grieg worked as a journalist for the local newspaper, *Bergens Posten*, commenting on Richard Wagner's *Ring*, where the obvious connection between Nordic and northern mythology could not help but get into the consciousness of even the most detached enthusiast for romantic nationalism. Grieg observed that Wagner wanted his medieval Teutonic hero to be 'primitive Germanic', but he could not help thinking that if a Scandinavian with Wagner's gifts were to work on the myth of Sigurd, the atmosphere would be better conveyed.

The tour of Germany and immersion in Wagner's greatest music reinvigorated Grieg's creative zest, which had been dimmed by the death of his parents and his reduction to a jobbing teacher of music; despite the critical success of

Peer Gynt he was still underemployed. He stayed near the Hardanger fiord during the summer of 1877 and began to work in quiet solitude, creating in musical form fiddle fairies, troll hills, and Norwegian dances. The critics often described this work as lacking organic development, the product of a laborious talent barely concealed by all manner of affectations especially in harmony, lacking invention, being tasteless, frivolous, all under the cloak of Norwegian nationalism. George Bernard Shaw, a great supporter of Ibsen, was not so enthusiastic about his fellow Norwegian. The great dramatist, who made the debate about 'Ibsenism' the centre of literary controversy in London in the 1890s, spoke for most people when he described Grieg as a musical grasshopper compared with musical giants like Wagner.

There was more to Norway in the late nineteenth century than high artistic endeavour. Under the Swedish administration of Norway, the ministry of the interior was supported by the peasants in parliament to fund public road building to link the mountainous interior at as many points as possible with the fiords. The main feature of the new roads was the English macadam surface and the reduction of the gradient from one in five to one in twenty by zigzagging up the mountain sides; this public works programme would pay off in the twentieth century, after the Norwegian tourist boom began in the 1890s. The first railway was established between Oslo and Eidsvoll in 1851–54 following the overland winter haulage route that brought timber to the Oslo sawmills. Robert Stephenson was engineer and English capital was provided. In 1854 a cheap postal service was introduced, conducted chiefly by steamers along the fiords and, with the inauguration of the telegraph service, the timber and fishing industries increased their productivity. During the late nineteenth century Norway was badly hit by the transfer of orders to shipyards working in steel technology. The use of iron and steel instead of wood made it less easy to fill market demands in the shipping industry. The traditional methods of constructing what was required on the shores of fiords was becoming useless as sail was superseded by steam, and the changeover required a capital expenditure beyond Norway's capacity. Oslo's loss was Glasgow's gain. By 1890 Norway had fallen back from third place to fifth in world tonnage owned, and of that tonnage about seventy-five per cent were sailing ships, considered obsolete everywhere in the world but in Finland. In 1876 Plimsoll visited Norway and the Plimsoll line was introduced, which led to a further temporary diminution of Norwegian influence in mercantile marine business in the world. Nevertheless, over the period 1873–95 shipping profits covered ninety per cent of the deficit caused by the excess of imports over exports.

In 1848 in Norway, there was a sporadic revolutionary spin-off from the 1848 European revolutions. The leader of the Norwegian left was Marcus Thrane, whose biography sounds similar to that of an Ibsen character. In his early childhood his father had been found guilty of misappropriating funds from the Bank of Norway, of which he was a director and chief cashier. Thrane visited France in 1838, spending two months in prison as a vagrant. He visited London and in May 1848 published newspaper articles that advocated self-determination as the best solution to the Schleswig-Holstein problem. He was appointed editor of the local newspaper in Drammen, and successfully organised the workmen there and in Oslo until after eighteen months' work, there were 273 associations with 21,000 members. They demanded manhood suffrage and held a meeting in Oslo that coincided with a parliamentary session. The Working Men's Association pressed for shorter working hours, abolition of trade monopolies and the provision of smallholdings through government action to reduce the competition for employment. The Association was put down, however, after riots, and Thrane spent three years in prison waiting for trial. When he was sentenced to a four-year prison term, one hundred and thirty-three workers were convicted with him, and after he was released in 1858 he seized the chance to emigrate.

A turning point in the Norwegian struggle for independence came in 1861 when at the head of the ministry in Oslo was placed the highly successful minister of the interior, Frederik Stang. He remained for nineteen years and achieved notoriety by his eventual acceptance of the persistent Swedish demand for a joint committee to revise the terms of the union. The Swedish proposals amounted to a full recognition of the existing inequality, such as that the foreign minister of Sweden acted on behalf of both countries and that the king's court was established in the Swedish and not, except for brief intervals, in the Norwegian capital. But to recognise the Swedish proposals would have been to recognise that Norway's position was that of a junior partner in the union. The Swedish proposals were defeated in the Storting by ninety-two votes to seventeen and marked the rise of a new generation of nationalists in Norway and their organisation in party form by Johan Sverdrup. The administrative post of Statholder was abolished by Oscar II as a gift to the Norwegian people on his accession to the throne after the death of Charles XV in 1872. A year later, in 1873, Stang was styled as minister of state for Norway, whereas the previous top-ranking member of the Norwegian ministry had been the senior of its three representatives in the Swedish capital, the minister of state in Stockholm. The old arrangement had implied that the centre of authority was to be found where the king was, the new that it lay in Oslo.

In January 1859 Sverdrup formed an alliance with Søren P. Jaabak, the leader of the peasants. In 1859 Sverdrup and Jaabak agreed on a reform programme that included the abolition of the ancient servitude under which farmers had to provide free post horses for officials on their journeys about Norway. But the first big change in the constitution of 1814 occurred when the meetings of the Storting were made annual instead of triennial. This proposal came from the ministry, which hoped for a quicker transaction of business as a main result. As a constitutional amendment it required a two-thirds' majority in the Storting. Many peasants thought annual sessions were too frequent and likely to bring them under too much ministerial influence. But Sverdrup convinced them that it would be better, and the consequences were that parliament had better control of the budget, more political interest in the constituencies, and there was a better chance of organising administrative structures within political parties.

In the 1880s the quarrel continued between the left, the right and the crown over the question of the seating of ministers in the Storting. Eventually, after the repeated passage of legislation, King Oscar claimed that his veto was absolute, and not merely suspensive. Sverdrup replied by passing a resolution on 9 June 1880 that asserted the supreme authority of the Storting over the ministry and demanded that they should promulgate the constitutional amendment. Stang refused to do this, and he therefore resigned.

The Sverdrup Liberal Party represented their success as forestalling a royal coup. The political opponents of the Liberals were dealt with by impeachment. King Oscar was forced to agree that the will of the Storting majority could be resisted only by force of arms, and on 2 July 1884 Sverdrup and other Liberal leaders took their seats in the Storting as the king's ministers. In this dramatic crisis responsible government was established in Norway. It remained the practice that ministers be chosen from outside the Storting in many cases, which they then attended by virtue of their appointment. But a new provision was introduced giving ex-ministers the privilege of standing for election in any constituency despite the usual residential qualifications.

Norwegians resisted the principle of universal military service, which was made effective in a new army law. At the same time an official grant was made to the rifle clubs – a sort of equivalent to the French National Guard or Irish Republican Army – which had rallied so conspicuously to the support of the Storting. By the end of the nineteenth century the Norwegian rifle clubs had a membership of 30,000, two-thirds of whom were no longer liable to be called up for the army, and a stock of 15,000 army rifles, perhaps to be used in a war against Sweden.

After 1848, there were dangerous personal and national rivalries everywhere in Scandinavia. While Norway's major literary figure, Ibsen, gained an ill-deserved reputation as a champion of women's rights, his young Swedish neighbour and rival, August Strindberg, was intent on sticking his knife into what he described as the old troll's back. With a singular appropriateness Strindberg set out to tear down Ibsen's hero women, and point out how the Darwinian laws of evolution and natural selection inevitably meant that men would triumph over women. Sweden in the nineteenth century was a man's country. It provided immense natural resources and a block-busting determination to exploit them. It was no accident that Alfred Nobel set up his first high explosive factory in Sweden and named 'dynamite' after the Greek god of power. Having been deprived of first rank national status in the sphere of European territorial aggrandisement, the Swedes turned to economic development, and their Germanic thoroughness and the Protestant work ethic soon made their economic miracle unique in the north, then in Europe, and finally, in the twentieth century, in the world.

Strindberg, Sweden's most famous nineteenth-century son, was born in 1849. He studied occasionally at Uppsala, writing his first major work, *Master Olof*, in 1872. *Master Olof*, like Strindberg, was at first rejected, and Strindberg, his sense of bitterness growing, worked as a librarian. He met and married a Swedish-Finn, Siri von Essen, and their love affair, marriage, divorce, and custody wrangles were the sources of Strindberg's dramatic inspiration and the bitterness of his views on the battle of the sexes.

Strindberg's masterpiece, *Miss Julie*, a naturalistic drama played out in the period it took for the action to unfold, broke away from every dramatic convention. Real objects were not props on the stage. Like Ibsen, Strindberg worked in taboo areas. The heroine, her menstrual period coinciding with midsummer eve, flirts with her father's butler, Jean. Jean, an expert seducer, lies to Miss Julie about his love for her. Miss Julie, however, is convinced of it, but almost immediately afterwards regrets her impetuosity. She attempts to coax a renewed declaration of love from Jean, but all Jean is prepared to do is to suggest that they set up a hotel in Switzerland where Miss Julie could act as bait for customers, buy a count's title in Romania, and live happily ever afterwards. It soon becomes apparent that Jean is insincere. He is, after all, engaged to Kristin the cook. Miss Julie, in a horrendous sequence of revelations, points out how she has been brought up as a man, but lacks manly resolution and, in the end, after a gruesome moment when Jean chops the head off her pet bird on the kitchen table, walks off the stage and cuts her throat with Jean's razor.

Miss Julie was more than Strindberg's wish fulfilment over his disastrous dealings with women. It was a specific attack on Ibsen's activity in espousing the feminist cause, and a modern parable on the Darwinian theory of evolution, where nature was red in tooth and claw.

The Darwinian model seemed particularly appropriate in

Sweden. Survival of the fittest meant that the weakest went to the wall and became extinct. In the battle of the sexes no amount of role swapping, or women clad in men's clothing, would disguise the fact that men were stronger in Scandinavia. Nothing could prevent the Finns, Danes and Norwegians from recognising that natural selection had favoured Sweden. Sweden had the best natural resources, and there were no substitutes for abundant mineral resources in nineteenth-century economic development.

In the constitutional setting, the battle for superiority took place in 1866 between the chambers of the Swedish parliament. The Parliament Act of 1866 introduced by Louis de Geer abolished the four estates of nobles, clergy, burghers and farmers and established in their place a bicameral legislature. From that time the Swedish parliament began to develop a modern legislative look. The modern Swedish constitution came into existence in 1809 when the powers of king and parliament were separated. It was hoped in 1809 that parliament would be reformed, but this did not happen for another two generations, when the Parliament Act of 1866 became as much a landmark in Swedish parliamentary history as the 1832 Reform Act in England.

Until 1866 the estates functioned with a medieval pageantry that would have done justice to the court of Louis XIV, with the four estates in the hands of the representatives of the nobles, the church, the stock exchange and the town hall. The four chamber system of parliamentary government was unwieldy, and in 1857 joint sessions of the whole parliament were introduced with members (up to 1860) being permitted to attend debates and address the parliament in their capacity as ministers of the crown. The catalyst for Swedish parliamentary reform in the 1860s was the appointment of Louis de Geer to the council of ministers in 1858 and his subsequent appointment as chancellor and minister of justice.

Louis de Geer pointed out to the king, Charles XV, that a rational system of parliamentary representation had been adopted in Europe and it seemed time to bring about a reform in Sweden where the injustice of leaving the right to levy taxes with four estates, two of which were privileged, might in troubled times lead to the gravest consequences. De Geer was so determined to replace the estates with a bicameral legislature and a general franchise that he followed the normal procedure of threatening to resign if he did not get his own way. King Charles XV was initially inclined to adopt delaying tactics by putting the matter off while he considered whether or not to dismiss de Geer. After discussion with Napoleon III in France, however, Charles began to consider that it might be to his advantage to associate domestic and parliamentary reform with a forceful foreign policy. This idea was rejected by de Geer. De Geer rented a villa near Skansen in central Stockholm in 1864 where, during the summer, to appropriate background noises from a small zoological garden, he drafted the new Parliament Act which established the authority of a two-chamber system. Parliament was to meet annually on 15 January with extraordinary meetings being summoned for special purposes at the request of the king. Previously there had been no special date for meetings of the parliament and the introduction of annual sessions was an important innovation.

Elections were to take place in September, every three years, and the triennial elections were for the two chambers. The term 'first chamber' was preferred to 'upper chamber' because the chambers were to have equal status. But the election of members to the first chamber was for nine years, and to be eligible men had to be over thirty-five, and to hold real estate of 80,000 crowns taxable value. The electorate of the second chamber was to consist of men entitled to vote in local elections who, for at least five years, had leased farm property of a taxable value of 6,000 crowns, or paid taxes on income of at least 800 crowns a year, on the theory that ownership of real estate gave a man more of a stake in the country than income from other sources. Members of the second chamber were required to be at least twenty-five years old.

The intention of the 1866 Parliament Act was primarily political, to change the system of representation, but parliament in its turn was affected by social changes that resulted from Sweden's industrial revolution. Although there is no question of the importance of 1866 in Swedish history, there was no immediate social upheaval as there was in France after 1789. It was characteristically Swedish to accomplish as effectively by bureaucracy what the French achieved with a guillotine. In abolishing the clergy estate, the Parliament Act reduced the authority of the Lutheran church in political affairs. But to call the 1866 Parliament Act a victory of the middle-class or of liberalism is to give a misleading impression of Swedish political development. The age of liberalism in a political sense had not arrived – the urban middle-class upon which it depended was still small in numbers.

The ideologue of Swedish liberalism was Adolph Hedin, a writer greatly influenced by French culture and aware of political developments in Britain and the United States. Although he disliked British imperialism, he was more inclined to look westwards than to Sweden's southern neighbour, Germany. The enthusiasm for Britain has always been balanced in Sweden by an equally influential group who favour German models and connections. Hedin's *Fifteen Letters*, published in 1868, pointed out how much the 1866 Act failed to be a victory for democracy, and that a crusade was necessary so that political reform could filter down to allow some system of social reform. Like all pamphleteers, Hedin spread his net widely. He attacked the prerogatives of the crown which gave it power over some economic legislation, and argued that economic legislation should, like civil legislation, be enacted by the king and parliament jointly and not by the king alone. He opposed the nomination of the speaker by the king, and examination of the competence of members of parliament by the executive. He also opposed the power of the church in Sweden, claiming that the regulation that 'all servants of the crown had to be of the true evangelical faith' was a limitation of religious freedom. He argued that Norway ought to be treated as an equal partner in the union and recognised that the failure of the Swedish crown to treat Norway as an equal in diplomatic affairs was the chief source of friction between the two countries.

In the middle of 1867 Hedin founded the new Liberal Association and at the end of 1868 a Liberal Party was formed in the second chamber as the ideal of reform could not be trusted to the farmers. Under the parliamentary leadership of A.V. Uhr, the new Liberal Party proposed universal suffrage for men and women over twenty-one and many other prog-rammes that shocked both chambers. After a year or two the party disintegrated. By 1898, however, the Liberals had produced a monster petition of 364,000 signatures – 66,000 of which were said to be by people with the franchise – arguing for the estab-lishment of universal suffrage for parliament for all persons over twenty-one.

If the forces of natural selection were epitomised in the development of Swedish parliamentary liberalism, they were personified in Alfred Nobel. Nobel's father, Immanuel, moved to St Petersburg in the 1830s, partly to escape creditors and partly because opportunity had knocked. When Immanuel arrived in St Petersburg, he put his inventive genius to the construction of land and sea mines, and the Russian Army set him up with a factory where he produced gun carriages and machine tools. In 1842 Immanuel was sufficiently prosperous to send for his family, who joined him, travelling from Stockholm to St Petersburg. Alfred had received no formal education but his father had sent him to Paris where he had studied chemistry. In the 1840s he began to experiment with highly explosive nitro-glycerine. When 300 pounds of explosive that was being prepared for a tunnel excavation exploded in his laboratory, five people were killed, including his youngest brother, Emil. Distraught, Immanuel died of a stroke. Nobel took the disaster philosophically, observing, however, that one could not expect an explosive substance to come into general use without waste of life, and he set about trying to solve the problem not of explosion but of detonation, so that he could make nitro-glycerine more stable as a high explosive. Although Alfred Nobel is chiefly remembered as the inventor of dynamite, in reality his invention of the blasting cap should, from a purely technical point of view, be placed well ahead of dynamite.

Immanuel Nobel's mines were used at sea during the Crimean War in 1854, and with such success that his factory was expanded by the Russian government. Nobel's brothers made fortunes from oilfield developments. With family capital Nobel moved his small backyard factory to a large lake in central Stockholm which, under Swedish law, was beyond the jurisdiction of the city of Stockholm, and formed the Nitro Glycerine Company. Then he found a site for a plant to replace his floating factory at Vinterviken, where the world's first high explosive factory opened in March 1865 and immediately boomed as new mines and railway tunnels were opened by it. Orders came from Germany, Belgium, Finland and Norway. He also successfully set up a plant in Vienna. The French War Ministry appointed a commission to study the use of nitro-glycerine for military purposes, and nitro-glycerine was used in Italy and England shortly afterwards. By 1865 the Swedish patent mania was underway, and the Nobel company illus-trated the difference between gun powder explosions and nitro-glycerine by setting up large-scale civil engineering blasting projects.

It was not long, however, before a petty criminal blew up a ship with the first home-made nitro-glycerine time bomb. There were a chain of such explosions in the mid-1860s in Australia, the United States, Panama, Norway and Belgium. Undeterred, Nobel worked on and in 1867 manufactured dynamite, a solidified version of nitro-glycerine and an absorbent clay. The word, 'nitro-glycerine', was removed from the labels in advertisements of the Nobel firm and a new mixture was patented under two names, one indicating power and the other harmlessness: 'Dynamite' and 'Nobel's Safety Powder'.

The mixture of kieselguhr and nitro-glycerine, which produced dynamite, was highly explosive but relatively safe to handle. It soon became popular, but there were technical problems. The dilution with inert kieselguhr diminished the explosive force of the nitro-glycerine and so Swedish miners preferred to use liquid products. The new invention was also liable to sweat and exude dangerous drops of liquid nitro-glycerine. Nobel solved this problem by inventing blasting gelatine or gelignite, the colloidal solution of nitro-cellulose (gun cotton) and nitro-glycerine. Gelignite was the ideal high explosive for engineering purposes, slightly more powerful than nitro-glycerine, insensitive to shock and resistant to moisture and water. Moreover, it could be used for submarine blasting, and its production costs were low. Nobel's biggest factory in the UK was at Ardeer in Scotland, which later became the nucleus of Imperial Chemical Industries (ICI).

On his death, Nobel left an estate of 33,000,000 Swedish crowns, an immense private fortune, for the formation of a fund from which prizes would be awarded to inventors in physics, chemistry, physiology, medicine, literature and to the person who did the most or the best work to promote fraternity between nations by the abolition or reduction of standing armies and by the holding and promotion of peace congresses, the most worthy to receive the prize whether he was a Scandinavian or not. Nobel described his political views as 'moderate social democrat', the socialist part consisting of the fact that he was strictly against inherited fortunes, thinking that no one should have anything that he had not earned. He believed in private initiative, and his ideal form of government was a system where there was a dictator elected from among a number of provincial ones. Because of his treatment at the hands of public opinion after his explosive manufacturing disasters, he was opposed to free speech and a free press and unsympathetic to democratic innovations in the Swedish constitution.

Nobel invented the atom bomb of the nineteenth century but constantly tried to illustrate its peaceful uses. One of his most successful large-scale engineering projects with the new explosive was to blast out some of the granite rocks obstructing development in Helsinki harbour. He held a demonstration in the Finnish capital to show future customers the potentials of his discovery. The Finns watching could scarcely have had a more devastating demonstration of the cataclysmic forces that were, in the next generation, to tear apart Mother Russia and free the grand duchy to rule itself.

In 1863 the first meeting of Finnish popular representatives since the Diet of Porvoo was held. The same day that the Diet opened in Helsinki there was a large military parade: 20,000 Russian troops paraded in front of the tsar, accompanied by his foreign and defence ministers and the lord of the admiralty. In his speech to the Diet, the tsar observed that the operation of the Finnish Diet would show that free institutions were no danger to a people who worked to improve their country. And in the opening period of Alexander II's reign, a liberalisation of Russian policy allowed the embryonic expression of Finnish public opinion, accompanied by subtle changes of policy directed at an improvement in Russo-Finnish relations. In the 1860s, the administration of Finnish affairs was largely in the hands of liberal-minded Russians, anxious to display Finland as a good example of what could be achieved, even in an autocracy.

The 1860s and 1870s showed liberalisation in many respects, and such important and influential Finnish families as the Mannerheims felt no odium in serving the tsars. Evidence of this was provided by the decision of Carl Gustaf Mannerheim, who was to play a determining role in Finland's twentieth-century history, to join the Russian Army. The Mannerheims had been ennobled in 1693 by Charles XI of Sweden, and there was little doubt that a place was waiting for Carl Mannerheim at the top of society. His family might have come out of a Tolstoy plot: his father was preoccupied (like Nobel) with a French mistress, Mannerheim himself was expelled from the Finnish corps of military cadets for a number of offences and, since as a result of his pranks a Finnish military career was impossible, in 1887 he left to seek his fortune in St Petersburg, signing himself 'Gustaf, the apostate'. The apostate served two years at the Nikolayevskoye cavalry school, joined a line cavalry regiment, and spent the 1880s trying to find a vacancy in the Chevalier Guards elite corps.

By 1848 most Finns recognised that the Napoleonic wars marked the end of Sweden and Denmark as great powers and illustrated the rise of Russia to regional dominance. But the Finns did not anticipate the changes in Russian policy towards the grand duchy that occurred as Russia began to find its interests threatened during the second half of the nineteenth century. In 1858 the tsar imposed censorship on Finland, a recognition of the extent to which the Finnish grand duchy was a safe harbour for dissidents in the empire. Many important Finns left their homeland after 1858, a loss to their mother country and a gain to their new land. Among the most famous was the explorer Adolf Erik Nordenskiöld, whose adventures in the 1870s (when he was feared lost on a voyage from the Atlantic along the coast of Siberia to the Bering Strait) gained as much world headline space as the feats of Livingstone and Stanley. Nordenskiöld was a Swedish Finn (married to Gustaf Mannerheim's Aunt Anna). He was taught by J.L. Runeberg at the Borgå Lyceum, took a doctor's degree at the university in Helsinki, and was destined for the chair of mineralogy had he not decided to seek refuge in Sweden, where freedom of expression was guaranteed, at least for the Swedes.

Although the Russians tried to keep the lid on expressions of incipient nationalism, they recognised that the economic development of Finland was necessary for strategic purposes, a policy given point by the Crimean War. In 1855 a joint British and French naval force attacked Sveaborg and, although unable to take it, destroyed the main headquarters' buildings by bombardment. So the public works that led to easy transport of troops and strategic materials were begun. The Saimaa Canal was finished in 1856, and vital railway links made between Helsinki and the Finnish provinces in 1865 and Kuopio in 1889. Simultaneously, the Finns continued to build up their sense of national identity. *The Seven Brothers*, Alexis Kivi's masterpiece and a milestone in the history of the establishment of the Finnish cultural identity, was completed in 1870, the same year that the rail link was opened between Viborg and St Petersburg. The Russian administration was well aware of the paradox of its efforts. It had educated and advanced a group of Calibans, and Russia's profit was that they knew how to curse. The ramshackle bureaucracy of the Russian administration could not keep the lid on the demands for social reform, however, and hand in hand with new prosperity and a sense of national purpose went the growth of working-class political movements, from their beginning in 1883 with the establishment of the first labour organisation. Not only the working class, but more importantly the liberal middle class, held Russian autocracy in contempt.

Alexander II's popularity was such that he was four times the victim of attempted assassination and, in 1881, it was fourth time lucky. Not lucky for Finland, however, as his successor Alexander III was even more determined to continue his Russification programme.

In 1889 the process of Russification achieved constitutional force as, on 15 February, Finnish laws were placed under Russian control. Alexander III explained that he was prepared to allow laws relating exclusively to the internal affairs of Finland to continue to operate, but any laws affecting the general welfare of his empire would be made by Russians alone. The law-making programme of the Finns was small, but the implications for the future were clear. Finland was about to lose its status as an autonomous grand duchy and be absorbed into Mother Russia. In the next decade this programme of Russification and its antithesis, the Finnish drive for national self-determination, intensified.

CHAPTER 3

The Age of Vampires

In the 1890s the pace of life in Scandinavia quickened. Events in the last decade of the nineteenth century moved with a speed and a consequence not paralleled until the Gorbachev-period reforms a century later. And as in the Napoleonic era, the pressure and pace of change was conditioned by the foreign policy priorities and decisions of the great powers who took, as had become customary, little account of the views of Scandinavians. Since the Franco–Prussian war, Germany had been a united and threatening force in the Baltic area. So to oppose the new might of Germany the British Foreign Office encouraged a Franco–Russian entente as a counterbalance. In response, Russia strove to stamp out fifth columnists within its borders, and Germany worked underground to encourage the spread of liberalism. Finland was the cockpit of this clandestine conflict. Subversive elements, hostile to the Russian government, built up lairs and hides in Finland, for the comparative liberalism of life west of Lake Ladoga meant that arrest was not so likely, and pamphlets urging the overthrow of tsarist autocracy could be printed and distributed much less dangerously.

The Finnish experience was a portent. The nineties were not always gay for Scandinavians. On the contrary, except perhaps in Denmark, Scandinavians everywhere were subject to bloodsuckers of one kind or another. Both in spite and because of the international situation, some Scandinavians tried desperately to make the end of the century a belle epoque. Many Scandinavians escaped to Italy, Germany and France, where they experienced the dizzy hedonism of decadence in Paris, Hamburg or Rome. Some tried optimistically to take back the redolent aniseed smell of absinthe with them and packed bottles in their baggage when they took their seats on the North Express and turned for home. But the bitter bouquet of wormwood did not last at the sixtieth latitude. Vodka was more suitable. Madness, nervous breakdown and anarchy within the Scandinavian community were as much a part of the period as the art of Aubrey Beardsley in London or the presence of Oscar Wilde in Paris.

In foreign affairs, Finland's blood was sucked by Russia, and Sweden was a vampire which fed on Norway. The cultural benefits of the vampire age were enormous to posterity, even if they were not appreciated by the artists in their infernos. The 1890s was the vampires' decade; Bram Stoker published his gruesome tale *Dracula* in 1897. But before then the paintings of Edvard Munch and Strindberg's *Miss Julie* showed that the occult blood enthusiasts were flourishing in the north. The 1890s saw the efflorescence of a group of Scandinavian bohemians who could be relied upon to out-drink and out-produce any other group of artists of the period while symbolising by the subject matter of their creative output some of the major social changes of their era. Henrik Ibsen, August Strindberg, Akseli Gallèn-Kallela, Edvard Munch, Edvard Grieg and Jean Sibelius all showed by their works the torment in Scandinavia as Finland groaned under the pressures of Russification and Norway struggled to release itself from the Swedish union.

There was little enthusiasm for the ideals of pan-Scandinavianism in the 1890s. In fact, the chances of

Nordic co-operation were at their lowest ebb, and nowhere was the introspection of the Scandinavians more apparent than in Denmark. After the issues of the Schleswig-Holstein period, the 1890s was a period of relative calm for the Danes who resisted the vampire cult that absorbed the energies of the other three Scandinavian nations. During the 1890s the Danish composer Carl Nielsen illustrated through his works the essential calmness of the Danish people at a time when the greatest excitement for the Danes was to be gained by strolling around the lake in the Tivoli gardens on Sunday and watching the royal family being rowed past to the sound of military bands. The age of Kierkegaard, Grundtvig and Andersen was over. The Danes did not doubt where power lay in their region. The Franco-Prussian war had shown it all too clearly.

In Denmark as elsewhere in Europe, the 1890s saw the growth of working-class political movements. Pressure from the left took the normal course in European parliamentary democracies by focusing on a demand for increased state aid to the disadvantaged. Bismarckian schemes for Danish conscription and free orange juice were accompanied by calls for plans to help the aged, support for votes for women, reform of the legal system and the right to organise in free trade unions with the aim, among other things, of securing a limit on the hours of work. And in 1890, for the first time, two Social Democrats were elected to the Danish Parliament to spearhead the attack of the left.

In 1891, a new poor law was passed that ended some of the bizarre practices that had grown up in the nineteenth century: the auctioning of pauper children, the practice of forced marriage to reduce the ratepayers' budget, and the restriction of some civil rights that poor law beneficiaries had forfeited hitherto when they became wards of the parish. A Sickness Benefit Act was passed in 1892. In 1899, a new Primary Education Act and a Small Holdings Act showed how and where the pressures of the left were succeeding. The Small Holdings Act of 1899 was a piece of pioneering land legislation insofar as it allowed for the support of the state to help small holders purchase larger allotments.

For all the flurry of social reform, many Danes considered that life in Denmark in the 1890s was boring. A brief flicker of general interest lay in such issues as whether a new co-operative slaughterhouse would be a success or whether Danish exports would be destroyed by the new technology of refrigeration which enabled the transportation of huge quantities of New Zealand and Australian meat into Europe. Many Danes wondered whether the old days were not better, despite the terror of the bombardment of Copenhagen and the frenzy of the defence of the old Danish Viking positions during the Schleswig-Holstein wars. Whatever the Danes in the factory or on the farm might have felt about the glories of the past, for the political masters of Denmark the watchword was neutrality. The Danes had got where they were in 1890, dismembered, by a series of wars in which they were at a hopeless disadvantage. The turning point came in 1894, when the radical wing of the Venstre Party agreed to a reduced annual conscription on the understanding that all Danish governments ought to seek neutrality as their main foreign policy objective.

In domestic politics the enhanced power of the working class showed in the decision during 1896 of the Employers Association to band together to resist the growing strength of the trade unions. Two years later, in 1898, members of the Danish trade union movement sank their differences and joined together in an Association of Trade Unions. The main battle-lines were drawn for the conflict between capital and labour in the coming century, with neither group of protagonists content to rely on the security provided by the as yet embryo state to protect its interests. The clash came in 1899. The strike weapon of the workers was countered by a classic lockout strategy, which ended with 40,000 Danish workers barred from work for four months.

Social reform was an issue not only in Denmark, but also in Sweden. The 1890s saw the class struggle intensify. At the turn of the century it was obvious that constitutional reform had not ended poverty and exploitation. There was a ruling class and it was called just that: 'överklass'. When they went to church the poor were assigned the rear pews. They tipped their hats deferentially and referred to their betters in the third person, although they were addressed by the personal 'du'.

A study of urban workers in Stockholm in 1895 found that 17 per cent lived in one room with no kitchen, 42 per cent had one room and a kitchen and 26 per cent achieved the Swedish dream of two rooms and a kitchen. Most Stockholm workers spent twelve hours at work each day. Membership of the upper class in Sweden was largely the prerogative of the higher echelons of the bureaucracy. Most of the bourgeoisie aspired to join the civil service for the security, prosperity and power it conferred, and the young aspirants both suffered and enjoyed the masochistic middle-class pressure of being unable to afford their ambitions. Family members ate dry French bread and sipped soup once a week, buoyed up by the thought that the bread winner could expect an annual invitation to the royal castle, or to a royal ball. As a nation at that time, the Swedes were described by their contemporary critics as the greatest social climbers since Cinderella. This phenomenon was recognised throughout Europe. It was no accident that Jacques Offenbach in *La vie parisienne* cast two Swedes, Baron Gondremarck and his wife, in the comic roles of greedy, gullible foreign tourists.

The urge to better oneself was understandable considering the relatively low standard of living. It was a product of difficult times in the nineteenth century and made all the more imperative by the new ever-widening opportunities that seemed to beckon some but not all the inhabitants of Sweden, by no means then an egalitarian society. The most sensitive and durable illustration of the new climate of opinion was the way in which Swedish graphic arts demonstrated cosy domesticity and rural virtues. Carl Larsson personified one Swedish view of the end of the century. He was born in May 1853, and as a small boy lived in a slum apartment in Stockholm's old town. Armies of cockroaches and other vermin came out of holes in the walls, not that there were many walls. The Larsson flat was one room and a kitchen. His mother often cried and his father often raged. In misery and squalor Larsson determined that the way to success was through the gallery doors and, after charity elementary school, became a prizewinner at the Academy of Arts in Stockholm. In 1880 he obtained a grant to study in Paris. From Paris, Larsson moved to Grez, where he lived in a commune of Swedish open-air painters and developed a style using water colours that was admirably suited to his languid scenes of Swedish life. Larsson married a fellow Swedish artist, Karin, in Grez in 1883 and by the 1890s was back in Stockholm painting a series of pictures of their children and family life. Larsson explained that long before his later children were born he had learned that it was a rich man's world. 'I had realised that I must make money. The memory of the hardships and miseries of my early years and that awful Stockholm slum made me deter-mined that Karin and our children should know happiness and security, and I have tried to make the happiness and security shine out in all the pictures I have made of our home and family.' He succeeded. In the 1890s he received a commission to decorate the National Museum in Stockholm with murals. He completed the task in 1897, made sure that he was paid, and bought a farm called 'Spadarvet' and a neighbouring one for his parents.

There was, of course, anxiety as well as happiness and serenity for Carl Larsson. In one untypical self-portrait, Larsson painted himself as a haggard gloomy ghost, distorted and unrecognisable, his head against a background of black scrawling forcefield lines. Remembering the slum misery of his childhood and despite his prosperity, Larsson was never at ease with his father. He was able to paint his way out of his class background, but for many Swedes such poverty was the catalyst for the conflict between capital and labour, and took the institutionalised form of a fight between the social democrats and the ruling class.

The size of the gap between the higher and lower classes explained the bitterness of the clash between the Social Democrats and the groups who engrossed power. The first Social Democrat meetings in Sweden were held on the eve of the vampire age, in 1881, and the Social Democratic Party was founded in 1889. Social democracy began in the 1890s, the same decade that saw the formation of the Swedish Confederation of Trade Unions in 1898. The employers were quick to realise that the conjunction of the radical socialist ideology provided by the Social Democrats, along with the demand for smörgåsbord necessities from an organised trade union group (which could give, besides financial support, a mass backing to the intellectuals), would lead to great social structural changes. And since these structural changes were bound to be against their interests, the employers organised in retaliation as the Swedish Confederation of Employers, but not until 1902. The 1890s was the decade of the common man in Sweden. At the beginning of the 1880s there were only 9,000 trade unionists but, by 1900, 66,000 had joined, an equivalent of 25 per cent of all industrial workers. In 1898 the Swedish Confederation of Trade Unions organised itself on a tripartite system, which lasted unchanged until 1968. It operated through a congress, a representative assembly, and an executive committee secretariat. The congress was the fundamental decision-making body of the Swedish Confederation of Trade Unions, met every five years and was made up of three hundred delegates from member unions. The National Co-operative Association was organised in 1899 in the same spirit of collectivism.

Despite the pressure for change in the 1890s, the high policy makers in Norway and Sweden were preoccupied with the struggle of the Norwegians to end the Act of Union. Thus, while one vampire to the Danish working class was the bourgeoisie, a sentiment shared by the working class in Norway and Sweden, the worst bloodsuckers to all but the most conservative Norwegians were the Swedes. Norway's relationship with Sweden became more and more strained as the Swedes resisted Norway's attempts to get increased representation on a committee that helped draft foreign policy priorities.

The Norwegian attack on the Act of Union focused on control of foreign affairs. The Venstre Party went into an election in 1891 on the platform of the establishment of a separate Norwegian consular voice, and their efforts were supported by the electorate who returned sixty-five members. The attempt to set up a Norwegian foreign ministry involved an attack on the powers of the Swedish king, who used his constitutional right to veto a bill from the Norwegian parliament aimed at a unilateral declaration of independence in the foreign affairs field.

In the 1890s there was a complicated interplay of political manoeuvres. In 1891 the radicals of the Venstre, led by Johannes Steen, had a majority in the parliament. After the Swedish king's veto in 1893, they adopted the tactic of going into opposition and leaving a conservative minority ministry in charge under Stang from 1893 to 1895 until a coalition was formed in the face of increasing friction between Norway and Sweden. The Norwegians protested against the king's veto by withholding a token proportion of the Norwegian payments towards the costs of the monarchy and diplomatic representation. On three occasions they passed a bill to create a Norwegian flag without the mark of union with Sweden on it. On its third passage in 1898, the bill became law without the approval of the king.

The Swedes reacted to the Norwegian demands in much the same way that the British reacted to the republican Irish. Bolstered by the support of conservative Norwegians, the Swedish General Staff produced a war plan, and the Swedes threatened the Norwegians with armed force if they did not drop their claims to independence. Professor Oscar Alin, from the vantage point of his history chair at Uppsala, led the Swedish backlash, and pointed out that while Norway benefited from the union through the tariff advantage it received, its contribution to the upkeep of the realm was disproportionately small. Alin concluded that Norway could have equal status in the union when it provided equal financial support to the administration and defence of the country. In response, the Norwegians began to fortify their boundary and ordered four ironclad battleships, two in 1895 and two in 1898. The oral tradition recalled that it was only two generations earlier that Swedish troops, led by their Bernadotte monarch, had killed Norwegians in an act of war.

Among the Norwegians who rallied was Ibsen. At a turning point in Norwegian history Ibsen returned to Norway where he settled in 1891. He continued to work there on the happiness of mankind, unabashed by the criticism he received. Ibsen may have left Norway drunk, but he returned sober to find that he was damned for pandering to the decadence of the era. The 1890s saw the universal acceptance of Ibsen's work. One perspicacious critic attributed Ibsen's European success to the way in which he had systematically created a drama of abnormality. As long as Ibsen's works remained healthy, said one reviewer in the *Morgenbladet*, they remained unnoticed abroad. But once his plays had the right undertone of pessimism, godlessness and despair, they were fitted to satisfy the contemporary craving for sensation and titillation. And never was sensation and titillation more sought after than in the 1890s, and nowhere was Scandinavian decadence more paraded than in Ibsen's play *Hedda Gabler*, where the curtains were drawn on the action and no ray of natural light fell on the actors. Ibsen explained to his audience that his main aim in *Hedda Gabler* had been to create the heroine's character. Her masculinity was extreme. Hedda eventually shot herself with her father's pistol when no man seemed likely to match her fiery spirit or her sexual libido.

Hedda Gabler was the last in the long line of Ibsen's plays that aimed to shock as well as entertain the audience. Its plot was melodramatic and unconvincing unless the audience willingly suspended disbelief. Hedda, a general's daughter, returned from the obligatory sun-tour holiday in Italy where her husband, Tesman, was a historian more interested in the local archives than he ought to have been on his honeymoon. His infantile sexuality is illustrated by Ibsen through Tesman's relationship with his aunts. During the course of the play, Hedda is shown as a femme fatale, with a string of rejected lovers panting after her. One of them shoots himself after a manuscript he has written in competition with Hedda's husband is destroyed in a fit of Freudian pique by the heroine.

The reaction of audiences and critics varied. Oscar Wilde was sent into a fit of terrified pity by it. Strindberg, although unhappy with its style and construction, saw *Hedda Gabler* as a vindication at last of his views on the works of the Norwegian dramatist. In a typical metaphor of the 1890s, Strindberg crowed that *Hedda Gabler* showed that Strindberg's seed had actually fallen into Ibsen's brainpan and grown to such an extent that Ibsen carried his semen and was his uterus – a positive variation on his less polite observation that Ibsen was a decrepit old troll whose shit would rebound on him. Recognition of Ibsen was not confined to Scandinavia. In 1896, *Peer Gynt* was first staged in Paris. George Bernard Shaw, who saw this production as a milestone in humiliation of the English stage, remarked that Paris had beaten London to produce a work that had the same effect on the imagination as *Hamlet, Faust* or *Don Juan*. Ibsen, who had been described by his critics as unnatural, preposterous, brainsick, nauseating, morbid, unwholesome and ghoulish, had arrived in the 1890s.

As a lion of the time, Ibsen was in demand as a public speaker, especially by those groups who found that his plays reinforced their iconoclasm. But he generally teased them. On 26 May 1898 he spoke to the Norwegian Women's Rights League in Oslo, saying that he was not a member of the Women's Rights League, that he had never been tendentious in anything he had written, and that he had been more of a poet and less of a social philosopher than people seemed inclined to believe. Finally, he thanked them for the honour of being said to have worked for the women's rights movement as he was not even sure that he knew what women's rights were. Ibsen was disingenuous. His realistic 'problem plays' put Norwegian literature in the vanguard of European drama and were a touchstone of social change. Havelock Ellis introduced a volume of Ibsen's works containing *Pillars of Society* and *Ghosts*. Karl Marx's daughter, Eleanor, played Nora at a private read-ing of *A Doll's House* and translated (badly) *An Enemy of the People* and *The Wild Duck*.

Despite the rise of working-class movements, and the impact of the new theatre of social pathology, the most important issue of the 1890s was the struggle of the Norwegians for devolution. For obvious reasons Scandinavian historians have played down the extent of the crisis over the ending of the union between Sweden and Norway. The bitterness of the factions brought the two neighbours to the brink of war. In the event, the union was dissolved peacefully, but the probability of fighting between Swedes and Norwegians was not ruled out in the 1890s. Ibsen was dragged into the controversy as one of the symbols of Norwegian independence. After all, his son Sigurd was the chief protagonist of those who called for an independent foreign office in Norway. With his experience in the Swedish-Norwegian Consular Corps, Sigurd was the most likely candidate to lead such a new department should the Norwegian left be able to wrest control of their international relations from the grip of the Swedish monarchy.

Grieg, who was a mild man and not given to hyperbolic gestures, applauded Ibsen's attack on Norwegians; the two most famous sons of Norway were both disgusted that the Norwegian nation had sunk so low that it would not rise to drive 'the Swedish enemy' out of the land. In the 1890s Grieg was too sick to use a rifle if Sweden had carried out its threat to suspend the Norwegian constitution and war had broken out. He said that he was, however, strong enough to go into battle with a pistol, and to let himself be carried off to prison by the Swedes in a gesture of martyrdom that would bring world public opinion on to Norway's side. Despite his intense nationalism and hostility to the Swedish union, Grieg was not a blind Norwegian artistic chauvinist. As one of the organisers of the 1898 Bergen music festival Grieg insisted that a national music festival ought to allow Norwegian music to be performed under the best possible conditions, and it was all the same to him whether this involved Norwegians, Germans, Japanese or Dutchmen. He restricted the performance of his works in the festival, concentrating on works that had gained a reputation in Norwegian literature, and on the composers whose contribution in their own country to the advance of the Norwegian musical life seemed to entitle them to be represented.

To Scandinavians the 1890s were the end of the era of nineteenth-century liberalism. The ideals that the thinkers of the enlightenment, the revolutionaries of 1789 and 1848 and the constitutional reformists had struggled for seemed lost. The Swedish hold on Norway and the Russian grip on Finland were Nordic instances of a worldwide threat to liberty. The Dreyfus case was the first in a long line of examples of Scandinavian concern for injustice outside their region. With no concern for his lost market, Grieg abandoned foreign royalties and performances by attacking the French after the events in October 1894, when Captain Alfred Dreyfus, a Jewish officer on the French general staff, was courtmartialled for treason and imprisoned on Devil's Island. Grieg took part in the press campaign against the authoritarian anti-semitism of the French Republic. He published a blast at the French in the *Frankfurter Zeitung*, and for the rest of the decade he was threatened with kicks if he ever appeared in Paris again. In the meantime the French replied in kind. Grieg was stigmatised in a masterly stream of abuse as a green-eyed poor bohemian who walked the streets of European capitals giving his five francs of art in the good houses; in another burst of mixed metaphors, he was described as a genial photographer who swam in obscure fountains.

The dispute had more than symbolic interest. It illustrated the gap between the Scandinavian intellect and the Romance frame of mind, besides showing the insensitivity with which Scandinavians took upon themselves the role of conscience of the western world. For, by the 1890s, the western world was forced to look again in Scandinavia's direction. In keeping with the daring and innovative reputation of the north, a Scandinavian explorer captured the world's attention. In 1892 Fridtjof Nansen laid before the Royal Geographical Society in London a plan that was condemned as suicidal by the orthodox but successfully completed in 1896. Nansen proved that Polar ice drifted from Siberia towards Spitzbergen by constructing a ship, the *Fram*, which was lifted, but not crushed, by ice after Nansen had deliberately let it be caught. The *Fram* expedition took from 24 June 1893 until 13 August 1896, and in that period Nansen performed heroic scientific feats, leaving his ship to explore the terrain in dog sleds and kayaks and spending a winter in a stone hut roofed with walrus hides, eating, among other things, polar bears, and using blubber as fuel.

However it was not an explorer but an artist who personified the Norwegian vampire spirit of the 1890s. Edvard Munch burst through the front doors of the world's art galleries and salons during the 1890s, and became infamous following an invitation by the Berlin Artists' Association to join in the celebration of their fiftieth anniversary as part of a large international exhibition. The scene in Berlin was stolen by the Norwegians. Twenty-nine of them were invited to exhibit, only to find their paintings seized after the organisers were convinced that the Norwegians were 'an anarchic clique of impressionist terrorists'. The artist to stand out was Munch. On 5 November 1892, he opened an exhibition of fifty-five paintings which closed a week later in one of the biggest scandals in Germany's art history. Such a thing had never happened in the fifty years' history of the Artists' Association, but pictures like Munch's had never been exhibited, as the radical German art of that time was naturalism. The exhibition was attacked by newspapers and art historians, and Munch was described as brutal, formless, crude, grotesque and depraved. Anton von Werner, on behalf of the boots and uniform painting supporters of the establishment, declared that the exhibition was a mockery of art: it was filthy and vile, and so he declared it closed, amid shouting, whistling and, in the end, fist fights, as the younger artists tried to leave the room and their pugnacious elders barred the way. Munch remarked that all the uproar was really a pleasure, adding that a better advertisement would have been hard to obtain. He expressed his amazement that something as innocent as painting could cause such excitement.

Munch's family was a part of the Norwegian bourgeoisie. It had produced army officers, clergymen and an historian, P.A. Munch. Munch's father was an army doctor, and the children in the evenings read, under an oil lamp, the works of Walter

Scott, as well as P.A. Munch's *The Legend of the Gods and Heroes* and *History of the Norwegian People*. The family was poor. Munch's mother and his favourite sister, Sophie, died from tuberculosis. In Paris when he heard of his father's sudden death, Munch said that he lived with the dead, his mother, his sister and his grandmother. Sophie's death in 1877 was a traumatic experience for him, then a shy and sensitive fourteen year old. *The Sick Child*, which he painted over and over again, was based on his experience, and he commented that illness, insanity and death were the black angels who kept watch over his cradle and accompanied him all his life.

Munch reacted against the bourgeoisie by embracing impressionism. He despaired that the people who viewed impressionist paintings did not understand that there could be the least wisdom in momentary impressions, that a tree could be red or blue, that a face could be blue or green. They knew that was wrong. From their childhood they had known that leaves and grass were green and that skin was pink. They could not understand that anything else could be sincere. It had to be humbug and done in carelessness or madness, most probably the latter. They could not get it into their heads that his paintings were done in earnest, in suffering, that they were the product of sleepless nights and that they had cost blood and nerves. Munch, who obviously expressed himself better in paint than in words, took the time to note that if you were drunk and saw two noses, you had a duty as an artist to paint two noses and also a crooked glass, if a glass looked crooked. If you were trying to get at something you had felt in an erotic moment, when you were hot all over from the act of love, you had at that moment found a motif and could not present it exactly as you would have seen it at some other time when cold. Munch's most famous painting was *The Shriek*, painted in 1893. It expressed the shock and the overpowering feelings of anxiety, abandonment and endless loneliness that gripped

Munch as he watched a sunset. He explained that he walked down a road with two friends. The sun was going down, the sky turned blood red and he felt a breath of sadness. He stood still, deadly tired. Over the blue-black fiord and town lay blood and tongues of fire. His friends went on ahead, but he stayed behind trembling with anxiety. He felt a great shriek in nature. Munch, with a typical reflection of the spirit of the age, sketched an illustration for Baudelaire's *Les Fleurs Du Mal* in 1896. In 1896 Sigmund Freud had published his thesis on neurosis, and neurosis loomed over the 1890s like a nightmare. Munch's portrait *Puberty* (1894–95) was graphic comment on the new era. The decadents generally cultivated the obscure, the sick and the subconscious mentality, and Munch painted skeleton after skeleton.

Not surprisingly, Munch got on well with Strindberg, although they teased each other mercilessly. Strindberg, whenever possible, repeatedly tripped up Munch with his walking stick, and Munch retaliated by pretending not to know how to spell Strindberg's name, and by ornamenting a lithograph of Strindberg with a portrait of a woman whom Strindberg saw as a vampire. Munch's paintings show how deeply he was affected by Strindberg's view of women as bloodsuckers who drained the creative force out of men. Munch explored this in several representations of metamorphosis during a kiss on the nape of the neck, when the figure kissed lost its human characteristics, and in his *Frieze of Life* series, in which he painted three roles of women: virgin, whore and nun. When *The Three Stages of Women* were exhibited in Christiania, the police were summoned and letters to newspaper editors called for a boycott of Munch's work. In a catalogue entry of one of his exhibitions, Strindberg drew the viewer's attention to an aspect of *The Kiss*, saying that 'in the fusion of the two beings the smaller seems to be on the point of devouring the larger – as is the habit of vermin, microbes, vampires and women'. Demands for women's suffrage might have been in the air, but in the era of Bram Stoker such artists as Munch reflected a different reality.

German visitors who were invited to Munch's exhibition in 1895 saw his works displayed in Berlin. The curious paid an entrance fee of one mark, and, when they strolled off the Unter den Linden into number sixteen, into the Ugo Barroccio gallery, were given a catalogue that gave Edmund Munch double billing with Axel Gallèn. Axel Gallèn, who later Finnicised his name to Akseli Gallèn-Kallela, was the bridge between the Scandinavians and the Finno-Ugrians. His artistic training had its roots, like that of Munch, in a Paris studio, where he worked in a coterie including Toulouse-Lautrec, Gauguin, August Strindberg and Carl Larsson. Gallèn-Kallela adapted his internationalism to the spirit of Finland which, in the 1890s, was decidedly decadent. When one of the Finnish nationalist leaders died in 1893, Gallèn-Kallela thought nothing of setting up his easel in the morgue, although whether the widow was pleased with the likeness has not been recorded. The Finnish national epic poem, the *Kalevala*, exercised a powerful influence over Gallèn-Kallela, and in 1897 he painted a number of monumental *Kalevala* paintings. Gallèn-Kallela was also a nature worshipper and in his landscapes and portraits of Finnish peasant life he captured something of the Finnish spirit of desolation and melancholy so appropriate to the 1890s.

The Finns, as Gallèn-Kallela's paintings showed, were a non-Aryan people, and quite different physically from other Scandinavians and the Russians. For hundreds of years Finns had derived their laws and institutions from Sweden and even on the eve of Finnish independence in 1917 half the Finnish landowners and middle class spoke Swedish. When Alexander I annexed Finland under the Treaty of Tilsit, he promised the Finnish estates that he would respect Finnish institutions and laws. In 1869 the Finns gained further ratification of their rights when Alexander II confirmed the special relationship between

Russia and Finland and the tsar ruled Finland not as emperor but as grand duke. Until the twentieth century the grand duke organised the government of Finland through his viceroy, the governor-general. The governor-general was always Russian and, accordingly, spoke no Swedish and left the day-to-day administration of the country in the hands of senators with local knowledge.

The Senate itself prepared laws and ordinances, which the grand duke submitted to the Diet of Four Estates: the nobility, the clergy, the representatives of the middle-class, and the peasants. As a result of constitutional reforms made in the middle of the nineteenth century, the Diet, to a limited extent, could initiate legislation. After 1869 fundamental laws could be made, altered, explained or repealed only on the representation of the emperor and grand duke with the consent of the estates, thus differentiating Finland from Russia, where the tsar's powers were unlimited. Finland was not only a grand duchy with unique privileges under the tsar, but also an oasis of economic prosperity in the Russian desert. Between 1812 and 1866 its population more than doubled to reach 2,300,000 and the revenue of Finland grew at a much greater rate than that of Russia. But in 1890, when the Finns contributed seventeen per cent of their revenue for military defence, the Russians gave twenty per cent. Many Russians understandably complained about this and also protested that on the railways of the Finnish grand duchy the Swedish and Finnish languages and currencies alone were used – and that such an affront took place daily within one hundred miles of St Petersburg.

Alexander III was a cork in the pan-Slavist tide. He attacked Finnish autonomy and, in January 1890, began the vampire decade by appointing three committees, sitting in St Petersburg, to iron out the differences between the Finnish and the Russian customs, postal and coinage systems. In June 1890 the Finnish postal service was 'assimilated' as the existence of the new telegraph invention was obviously a strategic weapon that could not be left in control of non-Slavs. In May 1891 the Committee for Finnish Affairs in St Petersburg was abolished. The press was censored and compulsory use of the Russian language was extended into the recalcitrant grand duchy. Alexander III's masterstroke was to create a committee of six Russians and four Finns to interpret grey areas in the constitution. But his death and the accession of Nicholas II on 1 November 1894 caused a temporary lull in the first attempt at the Russification of Finland.

In the honeymoon period (which normally accompanied the accession of even the Russian tsars) the Slav grip on the Finns was relaxed: whereas 216 press articles were suppressed in 1893, only forty were suppressed in 1897. In 1898, however, General Kuropatkin was appointed the Russian Minister of War, and the vampire sank its fangs in deeper. There is no doubt that many Finns thought Russia's difficulty was Finland's opportunity. The Russians felt as the British did over Ireland: that their satellite was potentially hostile to the military needs of the empire and ought to be brought into line to contribute more to imperial defence. Kuropatkin and the pan-Slavs convinced the tsar that it was strategically dangerous for the Finns to have an autonomous military system. There was one Finnish member on the military committee to the Russian General Staff, and he protested against the Imperial Manifesto of 3 February 1899. Under this the Finnish Diet was told that although Nicholas II wished to leave purely Finnish affairs to the consideration of the Diet of the grand duchy, he warned his subjects that there were other matters bound up with the needs of the whole Empire that could not be left to the Finns. As the Finnish Constitution, being a modified offshoot of a medieval Swedish one, had not envisaged the concept of imperial integrity as it was interpreted by Nicholas II in the 1890s, the tsar decided to reserve to himself the final decision on which laws came within the scope of the general legislation of the Russian Empire. His manifesto showed that in the twentieth century, about to dawn, the Finnish Diet would be reduced to a consultancy role.

The next Sunday the Finns went into mourning for their constitution. The gradual increase in devolution and the growing power of the left-wing in politics in Denmark, Norway and Sweden (and in the rest of Europe) were evidently not to be shared by the Finns. The statue of Alexander II was a meeting point for those who detested the policies of his grandson, Nicholas II. In February ski runners set out to all of Finland's remote villages to gather a petition against Russification. Within five days, 10 to 15 March 1899, 529,931 names were signed. Since the marks of illiterates were rejected, that must have encompassed virtually all Finns who could read and write. Not for the last time the support of world liberal opinion went with a Finnish deputation who took their case to the heart of Russian government. Among the Scandinavian intellectuals who supported the Finnish stand were Henrik Ibsen, Fridtjof Nansen and George Brandes. Outside Scandinavia Emile Zola, Theodore Mommsen, Anatole France, Joseph Lister, Herbert Spencer and Florence Nightingale expressed their hope that the Finnish cause would be sustained. But Nicholas II refused to receive the petition, ordered the bearers home, and his governor-general, Bobrikov, began the suppression of newspapers as a first step to the Russification of Finland in which the merging of the Finnish and the Russian civil services was a key element.

The 1890s was a period of great cultural and political excitement. Everyone knew that the old age was dying and that a new century would begin a new era. The fierce determination of the Russians to extend the use of Russian language into the Finnish administration illustrated to the Finns the success of their opposition and the importance of the struggle. The Finns set out deliberately to identify their culture with that of Western Europe and rejected pan-Slavism in every field they could.

One of the centres of resistance to the new hardline tsar's regime was Fazer's café in the Helsinki city centre. Fazer was a Finnish success story. By the 1980s the firm had an annual turnover of over US$200 million. There was a time when Fazer was the third most well-known name in Finland, preceded only by Svinhufvud and Mannerheim. It was in the 1890s that the Fazer family spread its wings and nourished revolution on a diet of coffee, macaroons, biscuits, cakes and sandwiches in a patisserie and coffee house that was, at times, the nineteenth-century Finnish equivalent of the Jacobin Club. The Fazer family came to Finland via Russia, like Carl Ludwig Engel and James Finlayson and Alfred Nobel. The Fazer family were Swiss and the family name originally contained an extra consonant. Eduard Peter Fatzer left Switzerland for Finland in 1844. His sons were successful in a variety of fields. Frontier Finland was open to talent. Edvard Fazer opened a concert bureau in Helsinki and was one of the cultural revolutionaries who promoted the international awareness of Finland as an important and significant cultural frontier by pushing the theatrical stars of Russia through the Finnish door to the west. It was the Fazer agency that organised the major breakthrough in ballet in the twentieth century: the performance of the Diaghilev *Ballet Russe* at the Theatre du Chatelet, in Paris on 18 May 1909. Thus a Finnish entrepreneur, using his grand duchy's proximity to St Petersburg and contact with the west, was responsible for the great cultural injection given to the arts in the twentieth century by the stars of the Russian Ballet, Vaslav Nijinsky and Anna Pavlova.

Edvard's brother, Karl Otto Fazer, was apprenticed as a young man of eighteen to a French confectioner, M.G. Berrin, in St Petersburg. Fazer finished his apprenticeship in 1886 and travelled to Berlin and Paris as a post-graduate student in the appetising field of confectionery. At that time the Russians, Finns, Swedes, Norwegians and Danes imported their chocolate from Suchard in Switzerland. In the pre-revolutionary days before 1917, to found a chocolate firm was to be in on a boom. It was as good as a gold or nickel mine and Karl Fazer rode the crest of the wave. A prestigious architect drew up plans for a huge innovative art nouveau building, a monster tribute to the Finnish appetite for sweets. Despite the constitutional problems, for the Finnish upper class, at least, the living was easy: the importers of the French champagne Perrier-Jouet advertised daily throughout the 1890s to an appreciative local audience.

'Karl Fazer's Konditori' opened on 16 September 1891, selling confectionery, ices, over twenty sorts of cakes, tea bread, and specialising in balls and wedding buffets for *fin de siècle* Finns. Fazer's became the Finnish equivalent of the Central European café although, being limited to Helsinki, it never obtained the revolutionary potential of the ubiquitous Irish pubs. Students met at Fazer's over a glass of port wine and plotted the overthrow of the Russian yoke. Less dangerously, the women of Helsinki began a long tradition of emancipated chats over coffee. For the 56,000 Finns in Helsinki in 1890 the rigours of climate and Russification were softened by toffee. Caramels brought the Finns the associations of *A Thousand and One Nights*. They represented escape to the warmth of the south, and Karl Fazer fed this appetite with combinations of chocolate, hazelnuts, cream, strawberries, eventually even diversifying to marmalade and macaroons in a labour-intensive industry (largely employing women), which went from strength to strength. Ironically, the provincial proximity of Helsinki to the great capital of St Petersburg gave many Finns a taste for luxuries they would never have dreamed of under a Swedish empire.

One of the representative Finnish beneficiaries of the burgeoning but threatened grand duchy was Gustaf Mannerheim. Mannerheim, who was living in St Petersburg at the time, spent his evenings in visits to the ballet. The 'model mercenary', who was to be the 'future hangman of the Finnish revolution' (as one of his more jaundiced critics described him), personified the successful careerists of the Finnish nobility whose affection for the better things in life blinded them to the increasing oppression of the Russians.

In the 1890s Mannerheim was strikingly handsome, six feet four inches tall, beautifully dressed, and he stood out as he went through his duties as a member of the Guard of the Winter Palace. Mannerheim married Anastasia Arapova in 1892, the daughter of a former chief of police in Moscow. The marriage reduced Mannerheim's debts, for, as has been unkindly observed, Anastasia's fortune was more attractive than her features. Although his family regarded marriage to a Russian as further example of Gustaf 's apostasy, they need not have worried. The marriage barely survived the decade before Anastasia, having broken both legs in an accident, left her husband for the south of France, never to return. Mannerheim was close to the apex of tsarist power. He was chosen for his striking and charismatic presence, but not his linguistic ability, to be one of the four Chevalier Guards officers who attended the throne during the coronation ceremony of Nicholas II. He was by then a heavy drinker who rarely refused a toast but managed continued sobriety – a useful accomplishment in the 1890s.

This characteristic, but few others, was shared by Mannerheim's equally precocious countryman Jean Sibelius, born in Hämeenlinna, a garrison town, on 8 December 1865, two years earlier than Mannerheim. Sibelius inherited from his father a taste for lonely pub-crawling, gregarious drinking parties and a disregard for the principles of domestic economy. When Jean was eleven, his mother enrolled him in the town's Finnish Grammar School. This Finnish-speaking school was a pioneering venture. Most grammar schools' secondary education was conducted in Swedish, and the decision on his mother's part to bring him into early contact with the Finnish language opened his eyes to the inspiration that came from Finnish mythology as enshrined in the national epic, the *Kalevala*. At home the Sibelius family spoke Swedish, but both cultures and languages flourished side by side. Indeed, Runeberg was Sibelius's favourite poet. Sibelius also read Strindberg's *Red Room* in his last year at school, and his response was, 'Strindberg tore everything to shreds and I adored this.' In the 1880s Sibelius had violin lessons with the Hämeenlinna military bandmaster and was an enthusiast for both the Scandinavian tradition of Grieg and the Russian influence of Peter Tchaikovsky.

Sibelius was enrolled as a law student at the Tsar Alexander University of Helsinki (as it was then called), but he was uninterested in study to such an extent that a book he left on his desk (hoping for inspiration) was exposed month after month until the open pages turned yellow. His family bowed to the inevitable and a career in the musical world was accepted.

The 1890s, like the 1960s, saw a huge gap between the generations. The younger writers reacted strongly against the romantic lyricism of Runeberg and read modern authors such as Zola, Ibsen and Strindberg. Sibelius was very attracted to *Therese Raquin*, but advised his fiancée not to read *Nana*. The young of Helsinki applauded Ibsen for daring to represent syphilis in *Ghosts*, but their elders were appalled. Those art galleries and salons still dominated by conservative tastes came under heavy fire from the younger painters who took French artists as their models. The rift between the generations was also reflected in the political situation. From his residence on the southern esplanade, the Russian Governor-General Bobrikov kept a careful watch on the political cross-currents and skilfully played off the Finns and the Finno-Swedes against each other. Finland's privileged position within the tsarist empire was watched with growing distaste by the pan-Slav nationalists in

St Petersburg, and an anti-Finnish campaign was launched in the Russian press. But Finland had been loyal to the tsar since the days of Alexander II, and Sibelius's university years (1885–89) were unclouded by economic problems or politics to such an extent that he went to riotous parties which continued for two or three days at a time.

The turning point for Sibelius came when he married and spent his honeymoon collecting folk songs in Karelia. His journey should be judged against the general background of Finnish artistic circles in the 1890s. More than fifty years had elapsed since the *Kalevala* had been published and by the 1890s the time was ripe for artists, poets and musicians to create something original but in its spirit. Sibelius was not alone in his expedition into inner Karelia. Gallèn-Kallela spent his honeymoon there as did Igor Stravinsky, on the eastern side of the border. The spirit of the *Kalevala* and the upsurge of interest in Karelia were two dominant features of the Finnish cultural scene in the 1890s. They were not isolated phenomena, but ran parallel to the preoccupation with symbolism and primitivism and the development of art nouveau on the continent.

During the spring of 1893 the students of the Viipuri Student Corporation at Helsinki University planned a series of historical tableaux from episodes in Karelia's past; Sibelius was the obvious composer to ask to write the incidental music. The tableaux were to be performed during the autumn and the proceeds were to go towards projects that would strengthen Karelia's cultural ties with the rest of Finland. The students thought an artistic defence was the most effective way of meeting Russian cultural penetration. The idea of the tableaux appealed to Sibelius as it gave him opportunities to combine and interweave Finnish and Swedish elements, since Viipuri castle, in which many of the tableaux were set, was the eastern bulwark of Finland during the Swedish period.

The pageant took place on 13 November 1893 and proved

an excellent way of circumventing tsarist censorship. What could not be put directly into words on the stage or in the press could be hinted at in a stage pageant. The Helsinki press described the curtain rising, showing Finland, a virgin holding a shield with a lion in one hand, her other arm draped around a young Karelian woman who stood close to her as if inviting protection. At the end of the first performance the public rose to its feet and joined in with the national anthem.

National romanticism and the promotion of Finnish identity had to be set aside in the struggle for a living. In 1896 Sibelius and his drinking partner and fellow musician Robert Kajanus were competitors for a music teaching post at the university. Kajanus attacked Sibelius in a public polemical exchange hoping that Sibelius's friendship would be unaffected. He was a poor psychologist. Sibelius thought such behaviour from a friend was contemptible. The university consistory recommended Sibelius's appointment, but the decision lay in the hands of W.C. von Daehn, the secretary of state for Finnish affairs at St Petersburg, who was also chancellor of the university. He sensed the majority feeling in the ruling party was not in Sibelius's favour, and the university decided that it needed a reliable, practical musician rather than a temperamental young genius. Accordingly, von Daehn overruled the appointments committee and the consistory and appointed Kajanus. In typical Machiavellian fashion one of his staunchest opponents afterwards wrote to von Daehn saying that he felt that Sibelius's work, which had a thoroughly national imprint, was of sufficient quality and importance for him to be guaranteed some kind of minimum subsistence, more than was usual with artists. Sibelius lacked any feeling for practical affairs, and a state pension of 3,000 marks and some smaller support from time to time would enable him to continue his work and enrich national art. Accordingly, at the end of November 1897, the Finnish Senate approved a recommendation to the tsar that Sibelius be given an annual award. For ten years he was granted 3,000 marks, after which it was turned into a permanent pension for life.

In the 1890s, Sibelius took little active part in political life, but he was caught up, reluctantly, by the growing struggle of the working class for political rights and composed a workers' march. Sibelius pleaded artistic detachment, and even at one point tried to be classified as Russian in order to place his works with the Russian publisher Belaiev, who also printed the works of Rimsky-Korsakov and Glasunov. In *The Workers' March*, work was seen as the will of God, and when it was published in 1896 in a workman's calendar, the Finnish working-class movement had yet to hoist the banner of socialism. Sibelius jotted in his notebook: 'Flirting with the workers, worse than currying favour with the upper class. One has to crush so much of your own potentiality.'

Sibelius threw his energies, however, into the public protest movement in November 1899 when the Finns held a fund-raising gala designed to support (with typical Finnish sense of humour) 'the Press Pension Fund'. The Russian secret police were not deceived. The celebrations lasted three days and included a performance at Helsinki's Swedish Theatre of work by Sibelius, which later became part of *Finlandia*, the tone poem that asserted the unique cultural identity of Finland.

By 1900 it had become clear that the mere passage of time during the nineteenth century had failed to provide answers to the most pressing problems faced in Scandinavia. A scientific revolution had overturned old orthodoxy and paved the way for a new liberation of the human spirit. But the growth in applied sciences, such as chemistry and engineering, had less immediate benefits than might have been expected. Certainly in Denmark, the experiments with controlled fermentation at the Carlsberg brewery improved the lot of beer drinkers everywhere. But a feeling that more negative than positive results were pending as a result of scientific discoveries led to general questioning of the idea of inevitable progress. The beneficial effects of applied scientific and industrial research were not always accepted by a grateful public. Scandinavians were quick to grasp the grim fact that the most spectacular use of applied science in the north had been Nobel's invention and patent of dynamite and detonators. And so it seemed to be everywhere. Social theorists devised new explanations and solutions to explain and alter human behaviour, only to have noble ideas perverted by anarchists, as surely as the Swedish populariser of dynamite blew up his young brother.

The 1890s marked the end of a century that had failed to establish working democratic representative institutions. The Norwegians had hoped that the democratic ideals proposed at the Eidsvoll Manor talks would have been developed. The Finns had hoped that the grand duchy status that they achieved after the Diet of Porvoo bound Russia to treat Finnish aspirations with sympathy and tact would not be abrogated. But in the 1890s the struggle for national self-determination intensified, and the reciprocal counter-attack of the metropolitan powers in Sweden and Russia closed a circuit that inevitably led to more resistance, more repression, and so on. The Finns and the Norwegians were acutely aware that the power to change their societies lay outside their borders. In the eighteenth century, Finland's capital was Stockholm, and Norway's Copenhagen; in the early twentieth, despite progress in decentralisation, the focus of power for the Finns and the Norwegians was in St Petersburg and Stockholm. If social reform and national self-determination were to be the watchwords of the new twentieth century, the status quo had to be altered.

The Finns also knew that by the 1890s there was, in Russia, a group that planned to overthrow the state by force. As a part of the planning strategy, the Russian Revolutionaries drew on Finnish nationalism and patriotism to recruit members to their cause. Those Reds who tried to manipulate patriots and nationalists to overthrow the state caused fratricidal anguish. Both the Finns and the Norwegians believed that the attempt to create a new society, in which there would be a radical change in the balance of power away from the middle class and in favour of the workers, would be met with force, both externally from the metropolitan powers, Russia and Sweden, and later internally by the efforts of the bourgeois White Guards.

All these momentous political issues were hammered out in a period of re-appraisal in which the new orthodoxy was finally overthrown. Religious belief had helped to bring the peasant communities in rural Finland and Norway together, but with the new pressure for education as part of a social welfare reform programme, Darwinian theories undercut accepted values. In the new century, the rural peasants were to react against anarchism and socialism by embracing right-wing radicalism, most notably in Lapua, where their religious zeal was converted into a pietist revolt against socialism. The urban working class had little tradition of religious observance, and were open to the counter claims of Marxism. The middle classes saw their cherished values and institutions challenged, ridiculed and turned on their heads on the stage with devastating effectiveness by Strindberg and Ibsen.

In the 1890s the workers also appreciated revolutionary theatre. Enthusiasm for Grieg and Sibelius was not exclusively reserved by the middle-class intellectuals who understood the nationalism implicit in their music. Members of the ruling class, whether they were bureaucrats, investors, factory owners or higher servants of the crown, were confused to find that national self-determination was not to be the end of the matter, and that when the metropolitan powers were swept aside so, in all probability, would be the last vestiges of privileged minority rule.

In the 1890s, the Scandinavian ruling class consoled itself, as it had on the eve of the French Revolution, with champagne, theatre, tourism and the good life. Mannerheim's too-expensive seat in a box reserved for Chevalier Guards at the St Petersburg ballet was as much a political statement as Munch's painting *The Shriek*. In the new century a conjunction of forces was to compel all the protagonists to sink their differences or to rearrange their ideologies, and to look back on life in the 1890s as a touching aberration, before a new battle with trolls began.

CHAPTER 4

At War with Trolls

The twentieth century was the dawn of a new era in Scandinavia, marked at the international relations level by the continuation of the independence movements in Norway and Finland. The Finns reasserted their national identity at the first opportunity, the Great International Paris Exhibition of 1900. In the Finnish pavilion the Finns produced an exhibit for Paris that was unique and outrageously nationalistic. The Finnish pavilion was made of huge blocks of stone, castellated windows at ground level and a steeply pitched roof. The roof line was broken by a series of short flag poles and the whole surmounted by a huge tower which had more than faint suggestions of the Middle East, blended with art nouveau touches. The door to the pavilion was guarded not by classic figures of antiquity but by the bears and squirrels that expressed Finnishness through the country's fauna. There was nothing like it in Paris and little like it in Finland, but as a means of drawing world attention to the uniqueness of Finnish culture it was an overwhelming success. The pavilion was the first joint effort of the three major Finnish architects of the twentieth century – Hermann Gesellius, Armas Lindgren and Eliel Saarinen – who shared more than a common view on the intrinsic worth of the unique Finnish environment, and built not only the Finnish pavilion that caused such a ripple in Paris, but also their home and studio, which they constructed in an idyllic setting on a lake on the outskirts of Helsinki. It was to Finnish architectural style what the Red House of William Morris was to the English and the embodiment of the Finnish romantic movement. They also designed the Finnish National Museum between 1906 and 1912. Lindgren was director of the Helsinki School of Arts and Design and the inspiration of a younger group of architects led by Lars Sonck. The furniture in the Finnish pavilion was designed by Louis Sparre. Akseli Gallèn-Kallela decorated the building with frescoes in which he tried to create the atmosphere of medieval stone churches and castles and designed a rya tapestry rug called *The Flame*, in which the beauty and the harmony of the texture, shapes and colours reached a technical and artistic mastery. Since other national exhibits had the solid facade and architectural imagination of European bank buildings, the Finnish pavilion stood out. It was summed up by *Le Figaro* as strange and charming.

The Russians did not find it so. Prince Tenishev was appointed by Nicholas II as commissioner for the exhibition, and he had orders to stop any manifestations of Finnish separatism. But the label 'Section Russe' at the entrance of the Exhibition Hall only served to emphasise the Finnish claims for grand duchy status.

During the next two decades the demand of the Finns was to change into a claim for independence. The Finns rubbed the message in with a performance of Sibelius's work by the Helsinki orchestra which performed in a chauvinistic spirit under the baton of Sibelius's old rival Robert Kajanus. The orchestral tour was intended to show the flag at the time when leaks from the Russian administration revealed a plan to introduce Russian as the official language of the grand duchy, and it had great propaganda value. Its artistic success was more questionable and Sibelius preferred to forget it. Most of the time he was drunk and sulking; since he was unpaid he refused to conduct or perform and did nothing more than step on to the stage to receive applause. Not that there was much. In Stockholm,

Sibelius was desperately sick after drinking too much absinthe, and his hangover was not improved when the performance of his First Symphony started in a tent, recently vacated by a circus who had left behind some hay and horse manure. A gloomy Sibelius found out in Copenhagen that the Russian censor had closed down the *Nya Pressen* newspaper. In Cologne there were only ten paying customers in the audience to hear Sibelius's work for an orchestra one hundred strong. And when 'the Finnish Grieg' arrived in Paris he was too low in spirits to meet any of the other famous composers. The final blow to Sibelius was to find that the organisers of the Finnish pavilion, though daring in the architectural and decorative arts, were not prepared to risk being closed down in Paris by calling his stirring patriotic music *Finlandia* and had opted for the ambiguous compromise *La Patrie* instead. Grimly Sibelius set about crossing off 'Russe' from the concert tickets and replacing it with 'Finlande'.

When Sibelius and the Helsinki Orchestra returned to Finland it was a changed country. The war with trolls was on in earnest. Finnish national identity was of international concern. While the Swedes exploded their jelly in the form of gelignite, the Finns ate it, and in both cases those with influence and importance in Europe were forced to look in the Scandinavian direction. Fazer's *Finlandia* jellies were supplied to King Edward VII's Coronation in 1902, and each box of jellies carried thereafter a picture of King Edward's crown. The recipe for the green jelly speciality was an old Russian one and came from St Petersburg. But while the Russians were happy to give the Finns their jelly recipes, they would not give them their freedom. In July 1901 the triumvirate Tsar Nicholas II, Governor-General Bobrikov and War Minister Kuropatkin acted on the foreshadowed threat of February 1899: they imposed military conscription in Finland and dissolved the Finnish Army of 6,000. With its abolition in 1901, the indigenous Finnish officer corps died, leaving the army of the future in the divided hands of such Finnish born officers in the Russian Army as Mannerheim, and those of the Jaegers who fought for Germany in World War I. Kuropatkin's plan allowed for Russian officers to command all detachments, and even non-commissioned officers were required to speak Russian. The conscription legislation was passed in defiance of all Finnish representative institutions, and artists like Sibelius put their signature to a petition against it, as did many Finnish civil servants, who were charged with running the bureaucracy in what was becoming a classic example of indirect rule. The conflict exposed a deep split in the Finnish community as forces hardened to resist the Russification programme in quite different ways. The Finnish nation split into two groups, the Compliants and the Constitutionalists. The Compliants were led by richer farmers and the clergy, and preferred to be called the 'Old Finns'. They believed that it was a fact of life, in the north as elsewhere, that the great powers were unyielding, and considered that for tactical reasons it was better to bend before the wind rather than be snapped off by a gale. The Old Finns were also political conservatives and believed in a harmony of interests between sovereign and people. They looked backwards to Alexander II's reforms and predicted that Nicholas II, if appeased, would begin to see the wisdom of co-operation rather than conflict.

The Constitutionalists, on the other hand, took their stand on their interpretation of the Diet of Porvoo, which had guaranteed Finnish autonomy. They organised an underground resistance to the Russian call-up on the lines of the Kagal movement of the Jews who were persecuted in Russia. They argued that the conscription law was illegal, and that their resistance to it was therefore lawful. They published a 'Citizens' Catechism' that was based on the idea that those who complied with the tsar were as dangerous as the carriers of the plague in medieval times.

The dispute caused internecine bitterness that threatened to overshadow the issue of national independence. The Russian secret police helped both parties and, with typical Finnish stubbornness, the battle lines hardened. Compliants took the jobs of Constitutionalists who had been dismissed from their government departments for refusing to carry out the new conscription laws. Families broke into factions and shopped at different shops, banked at different banks, and sent their children to different schools.

Nicholas II was happy with a one per cent realisation of his Finnish conscription target. He understood the difficulties in making the Finns, accustomed to herrings, eat blinis. But even one per cent proved difficult. The system was based on a lottery, but most refused to buy a ticket and to register. The leaders of resistance were the most vulnerable: the students at the university. Likely candidates for recruitment began to emigrate, and it was soon clear that the Russian bear had broken its teeth on a Finnish rock. The attempt to conscript Finns was abandoned and a financial contribution levied from Finland in lieu. The Finnish Army was not reconstituted before World War I and, when the Russo-Japanese war broke out in 1904, only career soldiers like Gustaf Mannerheim served in the Russian forces as combatants.

Although the attempt at Russification through conscription failed, Nicholas II continued to press for control of Finland through the courts and the senate. The language of the senate was changed to Russian, which meant that Bobrikov was able to direct proceedings more expeditiously. The takeover of the judicial system was more complex. In Helsinki a demonstration held against the Old Finns' power in the Senate was stopped by Cossacks. The Turku Court of Appeal promptly indicted the Russian governor, who had called in the Cossacks, and as a result Nicholas II purged the Turku bench of all but his supporters. At the same time the Finns established what some Russians saw as an underground army of national liberation, led by Konni Zilliacus. Bombs were exploded. Arms were imported. Plans for a rising were hatched. Governor-General Bobrikov was charged with the responsibility of maintaining order. In April 1903, Bobrikov was given dictatorial powers to deal with the threats in Finland. He used his authority to close down businesses, ban organisations, and to deport individuals from Finland either abroad or to uncongenial locations in the Russian empire. Most of the leaders of the Constitutionalists were dismissed from their positions, banished, left for Sweden, or closed their mouths. Bobrikov was assassinated on 16 June 1904 by Eugen Shauman, a young civil servant. Shauman shot himself immediately after-wards, and was elevated to hero status. Sibelius's morbid, melan-choly and hypochondriacal patron, Baron Axel Carpelan, noted with satisfaction in his diary the details of Bobrikov's wounds: he had been shot three times, once in an epaulette, once in the throat, once in the stomach.

When Finland's attorney-general, E. Soisalon-Soininen, was murdered by an assassin aiming to deplete the ranks of the Old Finns, the murderer's barrister was Per Svinhufvud, who was to become one of the leaders of the nation after independence. Not that there was anything unusual about the use of assassination as a means to hasten change; it was the era of political murders in Russia and some Finns began to adopt Russian models in this respect also.

In 1903 the Finnish Labour Party adopted Marxism, and the working-class movement in Finland began to adopt a more radical stand on the need for speedy social change than the Swedes, Norwegians or Danes. Members of the Finnish working class were encouraged by foreign policy developments which helped to undermine the stability of Nicholas II's regime. On the eastern border of Russia, the Japanese, not content with defeating the Russians in war, acted as agents behind the Russian lines and paid for the consignment and shipment of arms to Russia's enemies in the grand duchy. The arms consisted of three tons of explosives, 15,000 rifles and 2,500,000 rounds of ammunition. They were shipped from England, where three vessels, two yachts and a small steamer, the *John Grafton*, set sail for the western isles of Finland. The *John Grafton* was eventually run aground and scuttled by its crew, but the arms were carried off in order to fuel the armed rising, when it came, against the Russians, the Finnish bourgeoisie, or both.

The Finnish left equated political victory for the working class with national victory of the Finns over the Russians. During the 1905 revolution, Helsinki workers took strike action in the last days of the Russian general strike. In reply Nicholas II rescinded the 1898 manifesto and admitted its illegality, but the battle lines were too strongly defined for a return to the status quo to satisfy the left in Finland. For them the independence war was a class war and inevitability was on their side. In 1906 Finnish Red Guards, led by John Kock, again called a general strike in support of the men of the Russian garrison of Sveaborg who were in mutiny against their officers. The White Guards were organised in response and civil war was narrowly averted by the comprehensiveness of the rout of the left.

After the 1905 revolution, Nicholas II granted some measure of parliamentary reform to the Finns, and the grand duchy held elections for a one-chamber parliament created by Nicholas II, for the tsar was able to push through the old four estates a comprehensive reform of the parliamentary system that no one else had the power or authority to do. The old regime debated the reason for the new parliament before the elections. Mannerheim sat in the Estate of Nobles as head of the baronial branch of the family from February to June 1906, but did not take part in the debate, considering the demand for a unicameral system and universal suffrage absurd at a time of general ferment. A committed servant of Nicholas II, he had been promoted to colonel in the field, having fought in Manchuria and been exhilarated by the battlefield atmosphere in the war against the Japanese.

Mannerheim's reservations were of no account. The tsar gave his assent to the reform bill, the old Diet rose for the last time, and elections were held. The effects of the election results were as stunning as the results of the 1906 election in Edwardian Britain: the Social Democrats won eighty seats, the Old Finns fifty-nine, the Young Finns twenty-six, the Swedish People's Party twenty-four, the Agrarians nine and Christians two. After the elections Nicholas II counter-attacked the Finnish positions. In order to defeat those who opposed his policies, in 1908 the tsar repealed the Diet of Porvoo and set up a ministerial council. On 30 June 1910, it was enacted that all laws concerning Finland had to be passed by the Duma when they were, as Russian legislation defined them, matters of imperial concern. In 1912 a Parity Act was passed that gave Russians equal citizenship with Finns when in Finland and in August 1914 when World War I broke out, Finland was in constitutional terms a part of Russia governed by the Russians, a state of affairs applauded by the liberal west since it was in their foreign policy objectives to strengthen Russia for the coming war against Germany.

One Finnish state of mind was personified by Sibelius. His 1900 performance in Paris was a warning to the Russians that the menacing cloud of pan-Slavism could not overshadow the uniqueness of Finnish culture and a mark of the determination of the Finns to resist incorporation into an empire with which they were out of sympathy. By 1917 Sibelius had taken the next emotional step: he made a commitment to Germany in the war in the hope that the defeat of Russia would be followed by self-determination for minorities within the Russian empire. Accordingly, in 1917 he composed the choral work *The March of the Finnish Jaeger Battalion* for male vocalists. This work, which has not been much performed in Finland, and was wisely published anonymously, glorified the efforts of the 2,000 Finns who enlisted in the kaiser's army to fight under the

'Hunter Regiment' banner against Russia as the 27th Royal Prussian Light Infantry.

Sibelius's affairs in the twentieth century went from bad to worse in tune with the fate of the Finnish people. Supported by the generosity of his friend and fund-raiser, Axel Carpelan, Sibelius left for Italy after the 1900 tour, as, like Ibsen, he preferred to create in the warmth of the south. He composed the Second Symphony and, in 1908, visited the United Kingdom, and made concert tours of Sweden, the Baltic States, France and Germany. But by 1914 he wrote music in a pessimistic mood, and his health seemed to parallel the political scene: a tumour had been found in his throat. Sibelius was returning from the United States when World War I broke out, and was affected at once when his status in Germany changed from that of popular composer to enemy alien. He was barred from a concert in Sweden by the Swedes who feared reprisals when he would not consent to be billed as a Russian composer. Sibelius's misfortunes were shared by Gallèn-Kallela, who left his studio-home and did not return until the 1920s. The mood of Sibelius's Fourth Symphony, which was inspired by a period in the nineteenth century when the peasantry were so poor that they ate tree bark bread, was mirrored throughout Finland until the two Russian Revolutions in 1917. At Karl Fazer's, for example, the war year 1914 dictated new conditions for the Finnish economy of which they were then but a small part. The war at sea stopped imports necessary for confectionery, and such luxuries as chocolates and jam, which Fazer depended on, were rationed.

The internal situation in Finland during the war years of 1914–17 was very fluid, as divisions formed within the Finnish community groups seeking different means of obtaining Finnish independence, with different ideas on how the country ought to be governed, and in whose interest, once independence was achieved. The Marxists, who were as inspired with the potential of revolutionary political behaviour after the 1905 revolution in

Russia as they were disappointed by the results in Finland, were the most cohesive. The Finnish left was organised to be ready to seize power on behalf of the working class, once the next revolution came, as they believed it would, such was the inevitability of history and dialectical materialism.

When the February 1917 revolution broke out, Finns prepared for a blood-bath, but Russian autocracy disappeared before the eyes of the Finns with astonishing speed. In short order the workers in St Petersburg struck, Nicholas II dissolved the Duma, key sections of the military forces mutinied, a soviet of workers' deputies met, a provisional committee of the Duma was formed, and Alexander Kerensky became Minister of Justice. One of Kerensky's first priorities was border security. Finland had, briefly, been the haven for liberal politicians fleeing the secret police, and its strategic importance could not be over-estimated.

A most disturbing feature was the growth of private armies. Although they began as secret societies, Civil Guards, by mid-1917, were prepared to combine their resources to fill the power vacuum caused by the withdrawal of police and military power from Finland. Finland shared a land frontier with Russia and had to be calmed. Kerensky visited Finland to try to reassure the Finns and gain support for the provisional government. But it was through Finland, and to the famous Finland Station in St Petersburg, that Lenin travelled, and by early November 1917 the Bolsheviks were victorious.

To celebrate, the Finnish working class responded with a general strike. Sibelius prepared for the worst. His sympathies, when he expressed them, had been notoriously anti-Russian and his villa 'Ainola' was in a Red area. The call for a class war was felt as keenly in Helsinki as in St Petersburg. The left considered that if the fruits of the Russian Revolution were to be tasted by the working class in Finland, they had little alternative but to attempt a military coup. The Social Democrats lost their majority in parliament in October 1917 and, on 15 November, parliament, which had been debating the issue since midsummer, granted the Finns independence and self-government on the obvious grounds that the powers of Nicholas II had by then ceased to exist and had therefore reverted to the state. Per Svinhufvud led the cabinet, which was non-socialist, and on 31 December Lenin recognised the legitimacy of Svinhufvud's regime – the first head of state to do so. Earlier, on 5 December 1917, Lenin directed himself to the Finnish question in a speech he made to the all Russian Navy Congress, saying that if the Finnish bourgeoisie brought arms from Germany to use against the workers, the Bolsheviks offered the latter a union with the Russian toilers. In a burst of hyperbole Lenin said that the bourgeoisie could carry on a contemptible and petty brawl over frontiers; the workers would not quarrel on that score: 'We are now – I am using a bad word – conquering Finland, but not in the way in which the international plunderers – capitalists – do it. We are conquering Finland by the fact that while letting men live in a union with us or others we at the same time support the toilers of all nation-alities against the international bourgeoisie.'

In 1917, Russia was devastated by war with Germany and the Finnish Reds had to be content with rhetoric. At that point (at least) Russia's borderlands were not threatened by the Finns. Naturally the Red Guards were not satisfied with the status quo, feeling their class interests threatened to such an extent that life under Svinhufvud and the bourgeoisie was as intoler-able as it had been under Nicholas II and Bobrikov; the left turned to revolution. By January 1918 blood was frozen in the gutters of Helsinki, and the capital city of the new nation was in Red hands.

The civil war was the fundamental issue in Finnish politics during the 1920s and 1930s, and divided Finnish society, as the troubles did in Ireland, for at least three generations. It began formally on 28 January 1918 when Red Guards in southern

Finland revolted. Simultaneously Civil Guards commanded by Mannerheim (many of whom had never heard of him) attacked Russian troops in Ostrobothnia. Strict constitutional legality was on the side of the Whites. Svinhufvud stayed in Helsinki when civil war broke out, but members of the Finnish senate, who established a legitimate government in Vaasa, directed the White effort. The key figure in the civil war turned out to be Mannerheim. At the outbreak of World War I he was a popular Russian officer serving in Poland. He was part of an aristocratic circle who spent their leisure hunting roebuck. As commander of a guards regiment, Mannerheim was in regular contact with Nicholas II, and took part in shoots at the imperial hunting lodge near Warsaw. On 18 October 1912 he had been appointed a major-general, and when the Austro-Hungarians declared war on Russia on 6 August 1914 he was one of the most senior Finns in the Russian Army. He quickly had his hair cut short, grabbed the travel bag he normally kept packed against the possibility of manoeuvres, fought in Galicia and the Carpathians, was decorated leading his brigade, and transferred to command the 12th Cavalry Division. His division was ordered to Romania and he was on short leave in Petrograd when the revolution in March 1917 broke out. He visited Nicholas II and Alexandra at Tsarskoye Selo in mid-February, and narrowly escaped arrest by the revolutionaries who were looking for officers to punish. Because of his bearing, rank and uncompromising patrician air, he was particularly vulnerable. After a night at the ballet, he watched the revolution begin from the Hotel de l'Europe on the corner of the Nevsky Prospect. On 14 March the famous Order No. 1 that reduced the power and authority of the officer corps was issued by the Soviet. Mannerheim's career as a Russian officer was over.

Mannerheim was in a nerve-wracking and exhausting situation until the call to save Finland came. He had no illusions about whom he was saving Finland for – when deputies from the Soviet Army arrived to discuss his future he had all the chairs except his removed from the room where he interviewed them. Transferred to the reserves after the unsuccessful Kornilov revolt, he did not leave the Russian Army until after 6 December 1917, when Finland declared itself independent. As a young man, Mannerheim left Finland apostate; he returned a middle-aged refugee. He was unable to get a Finnish passport – the Bolsheviks controlled movement in and out of Leningrad – and when he did arrive back in the country of his birth, he found that the Finnish bureaucrats in Helsinki, sceptical about his identity, would not issue him with a bread ration card. His fortunes changed dramatically, however, when he was forced to prove his Finnishness as commander-in-chief of the Finnish government forces, having been chosen for the role by a small group of Finns involved in the leadership of the national revolution.

By the time of the civil war Mannerheim's political philosophy had toughened. He said that he preferred to die with a sword in his hand than be murdered by the Bolsheviks. When he arrived in Helsinki in December 1917, he learned of the military preparations that had been made for him by the activists. He also claimed (in an indirect tribute to either imperial Russian security, or imperial Russian ignorance) that he did not know of the existence of the Finnish Jaegers. Mannerheim's last command, the Sixth Cavalry Corps in Transylvania, had been the culmination of a thirty-year career of distinguished service to the Russian crown, a lifetime for a lesser, normal man. But Mannerheim had several more lives to lead. He was not only a soldier but a statesman. He knew that the civil war could be won only with outside help and that this was only likely to come from Germany. He also understood that the use of foreign mercenaries would leave such great divisions that, if the use of German troops was not subject to strict conditions, Finland might win the war but lose the peace.

Mannerheim came into conflict with the Svinhufvud cabinet whose aim was victory at any price. Svinhufvud was so determined to secure power that critics argued he was prepared to mortgage Finland to the kaiser in perpetuity. Mannerheim's first task was to recall the Finnish Jaegers from Germany, but whereas he wished to keep leadership and fighting in the civil war in Finnish hands as far as possible, Svinhufvud travelled to Berlin, where he got the help of a German relief expedition of 10,000 troops under the command of General von der Goltz. Mannerheim, who was a prima donna cavalry officer, refused to continue to direct the war effort unless the German troops were under his control. Mannerheim's suggestion was turned down and the civil war was fought with massive German assistance. The Finnish Jaeger battalion was, however, among the most bloodthirsty of Red hunters.

In the plans of the right-wing revolutionaries for a 1917 rising against Russia, it was crucial to have more arms and ammunition than those supplied on the *John Grafton*. Although they were not prepared to do quite as much for Ireland, in July 1917 the German High Command allotted arms, ammunition and equipment for an army of 100,000 to be sent to Finland. Cynics pointed out that the Germans were probably waiting for a cut in the Petrograd-Viipuri-Helsinki railway in order to send the arms, and delighted in observing that the Germans had shown little enthusiasm for releasing the Jaegers for duties at home. Mannerheim explained that he did not resign his command when German troops arrived in Finland because it would have meant that von der Goltz would become the commander of the new Finnish Army. The decision to send German troops to Finland was made at a conference of German political and military commands on 13 February 1918. German troops occupied Åland in March 1918, and the Baltic division arrived in April, the German government correctly regarding the small matter of a division as 'a very profitable investment'.

When, on 3 March 1918, the Treaty of Brest-Litovsk was signed, ending war between Russia and Germany, the Finnish civil war entered a new phase. By article 6 of the treaty, Russia agreed to put an end to any agitation or propaganda against the government and public institutions of Finland. Finland and Åland had immediately to be cleared of Russian troops and Russian Red Guards. The Bolsheviks gave the necessary order, and only the icebound Baltic Fleet remained locked in the Helsinki harbour, leaving the civil war to be fought against Reds who were almost without exception wholly indigenous Finns.

The Whites saw the arrival of the Germans as decisive. On 6 April 1918 Mannerheim won his first substantial victory at Tampere, the spiritual home of social democracy, and a week later the capital was taken by Germans who were received by all but the Reds with unambiguous approbation. The White Finns were not only pre-occupied with German relations; many of them also espoused a quasi-religious belief in the creation of a greater Finland. Mannerheim absorbed as volunteers into his new army not only the Jaegers, but also the Civil Guards, whose commander-in-chief spoke unselfconsciously of a Finnish Farmers' Army that would drive Lenin's 'soldiers and hooligans' out of Finland and Karelia.

In May 1918, Svinhufvud was elected regent and appointed J.K. Paasikivi prime minister, whereupon Mannerheim resigned as commander-in-chief, not wishing to be compromised by the pro-German stance of Finnish politics. In Berlin, Svinhufvud had concluded agreements on peace and trade with Germany that had made Finland a constitutional client of Germany almost to the extent that, had Germany won World War I, Finland would have been absorbed into the German state. The trade agreement between White Finland and Germany in 1918 was unpopular even with the enemies of Russia, and the common observation of the time was that the Finns did not think that they needed to sell their independence while their sons were buying it with their hearts' blood. The conclusiveness of Finnish acceptance of German assistance was shown by their invitation to a German prince, Friedrich Karl, Prince of Hessen, to become King of Finland once the civil war was over. There was no point in expecting help from Sweden however, where the government did not believe that Sweden would be strong enough to resist Russia, and where, in any case, the Social Democrats were sympathetic to the revolutionaries in Finland. Moreover, Sweden hoped that as a result of the confusion it would be able to recover the Åland Islands – a just expectation from many points of view, especially as the Åland Islanders wished to be Swedish, and the largest islands were obviously closer to Sweden than Finland. The Swedish Foreign Affairs Department pointed out that to intervene in Finland's affairs would place it on Germany's side and, apart from the success in maintaining neutrality since 1915, it was obvious to the Swedes at least that Germany was likely to lose the war.

When Germany lost the war, the eyes of the Finns turned back nervously to Russia. Russia had supported (not always with discretion) the Reds in the civil war, but the Russians were prepared to let bygones be bygones, at least for the present, and as a result the Finnish left was able to reorganise, under Väinö Tanner, on the lines of the Swedish Social Democrats. A khaki election was held in March 1919, and the exercise of the democratic process took the steam out of the class war. The election of 1919 was a victory for republicanism and a defeat for Mannerheim's policy of enlarging Finland's borders: eighty Social Democrats were elected out of the house of 200. But since many of the Social Democrat members were in prison, or in exile, parliamentary power was shared between the Old Finns, Young Finns, Swedish People's Party, Agrarians and National Liberal Progressives, who drew up the constitution, which was based on the Swedish-Finnish tradition.

On 25 July 1919 the Finnish parliament approved a

republican constitution. Post-war Finns were firmly determined on a parliamentary and democratic course of constitutional development. Political leaders had the task of reconciling the victors and the vanquished in the civil war, and ensuring that weapons were not buried to be used again in the near future. In this way Finland became a republic (in which the president took over the role destined for Prince Friedrich Karl Friedrich of Hessen) and, on 14 October 1920, Finland signed a peace treaty with Russia and the state of war between the two countries was over – for twenty years.

Finland's constitutional parliamentary democracy began life without most of the Social Democrat members who had supported the Red Guards or participated in the civil war on the losing side. Under the constitution, members of parliament were elected for four-year terms by a general secret ballot. The pivot of the system was the president, who was out of phase with the general flux of political life from the beginning, serving a six-year term. The president was elected by a college of 300 voters and had immense power in Finland, which successive presidents did not hesitate to use over the next years. The functions of the state apparatus and the division of power between them had taken shape gradually after the birth of the Swedish-Finnish realm. Thus the president of the Republic of Finland in the 1920s was invested with essentially the same kind of power that the Swedish monarchy wielded towards the end of the eighteenth century. The evolution of Finnish parliamentarianism was influenced by the fact that, except in a few cases, the council never gained the same authority as the monarch in Sweden or Finland. The president was commander-in-chief of the army, had the power to conduct foreign policy on the basis of personal diplomacy, and was able to 'participate in legislation' by exercising his powers to sanction laws, of suspensive veto, to issue decrees, and to appoint minority cabinets without support in the parliament, in defiance of the constitutional requirement that cabinets possess the confidence of parliament.

In the early twentieth century it was dangerous to travel to Finland, but the other Scandinavian countries were open and popular with European tourists. New roads, railways, hotels and steamboat routes brought travellers to Norway to see the trolls at first hand. Luxurious yachts, some of them 4,000 tons, cruised to Norwegian fiords from British ports, and Bergen, Trondheim and North Cape were inspected by the curious. Hardier tourists walked or cycled around the Hardanger Fiord or the Sognefiord. Mountaineers tackled the Jotunheim. In Sweden, tourists fished for salmon and trout and travelled round the Baltic ports and on the canals. The Swedish state railways boasted trains that averaged twenty miles an hour. In Norway rowing boats and horses were more usual, and visitors to Lapland girded themselves against the gnat. In 1900 a Norwegian law provided for a general licence to shoot in the government-owned forests and mountains, with supplementary costs of 200 crowns being levied to hunt reindeer, stag or elk. The 1908 Baedeker for Norway, Sweden and Denmark provided a select bibliography of over thirty books in English for the serious traveller to the area. And there were many of them.

The visitors who strolled through the zoos and museums of Denmark, Sweden and Norway were probably unaware of the great social changes that were ushering in the twentieth century. Electric trams were on the streets of Stockholm and Gothenburg and they were used, not by the grand tourists, but by the hungry workers of the cities.

Finland was the bloodiest region in Scandinavia in 1900–20. Denmark, by comparison, was the nation least wracked by war and conflict. The Danes had done the fighting in the previous century. Indeed, the great constitutional re-arrangements of the Napoleonic era were to have an unexpected benefit for Denmark in the twentieth century, as the Danes, divested of Norway and yoked to no one, were free to pursue a course of democratisation and economic development. The Danes entered the new century with a new spirit of liberalism. Copenhagen, the capital of Denmark, had 480,000 inhabitants in 1901, and was larger than Stockholm, Helsinki or Oslo. It was the centre of trade in Denmark, and exported and imported more than the rest of the kingdom. Steamers connected Copenhagen with London twice a day and there were also services between Newcastle, Harwich and Esberg. By 1901 a Liberal government presided over the beginning of constitutional changes. The 1901 election was the first held by secret ballot. It resulted in a sweeping victory for the left, but as King Christian IX had power to dismiss and appoint administrations, he used what room to manoeuvre he had by calling for not the political leader of the left, J.C. Christensen, who had worked so hard for the victory, but a professor of law, J.H. Deuntzer, who oversaw the establishment of parliamentary democracy and convinced the king that it was necessary for a cabinet to represent the views of the majority in the lower house. Deuntzer constructed a judicious blend of democratic talents and began a programme of educational and tax reform in 1903: such other plans as votes for women and a wider franchise had to wait until the pressure of the 1914–18 war made them irresistible.

The Danes, who had been scorched by war more than any other Scandinavians in the nineteenth century, did not neglect the problem of defence in the twentieth. Deuntzer tried desperately to promote a policy of neutrality, and that was the object of the Danes when war broke out between the Great Powers in 1914. Although Denmark proved to be a lucky country during World War I, the first few days were anything but a portent of what was to follow. On 5 August, Germany requested Denmark to mine the international waters of the Sound to prevent the Baltic passage of warships. But at the beginning of August 1914, Denmark joined Sweden and Norway in declaring neutrality, and the three Scandinavian monarchs and their foreign ministers met in Sweden in Malmö in December 1914 to explain their determination to remain neutral. George V kept in touch with his Danish cousin, Christian X, and the two monarchs were able to reassure their prime ministers and peoples that neither constituted a threat to the other.

Initially, World War I was not disruptive for the Danes. Danish firms manufactured goulash for the Germans, carried on commerce normally with the other Scandinavian neutrals, Sweden and Norway, and were even able to trade with Great Britain, bartering primary produce for coal. The boom conditions of full employment lasted until 1917, when unrestricted German submarine warfare began to take the jam out of the Danish pastry. One of the perils of neutrality was that once a breach in the principle was made, a neutral nation was fair game for both sides. In 1917 the United States entered the war, and in order to strengthen its naval bases and lines of communication the new belligerent expanded its interest in the West Indies. The Danish possessions in the Virgin Islands had a harbour at St Thomas, which was on the shortest route from Europe to the Panama Canal, and so, for strategic reasons, the United States made the Danes an offer they could not refuse. In order to add to Danish goodwill towards the United States, the US government had declared in 1916 that it had no objection to Denmark extending its sovereignty to the whole of Greenland, where the Danes had maintained a foothold since the dissolution of the Dano-Norwegian union in 1814. For the Norwegians, World War I was only the last in a series of crises they faced during the twentieth century, opening for them with the constitutional matter of the Swedish union, which stretched nerves to breaking point. Liberal Norwegians fought Swedish domination and the refusal of the middle class to surrender its privileges in the face of the growing pressure from the left.

Edvard Munch, serving as a touchstone, changed his style during the twentieth century and represented the problems in Norway with his usual striking imagery. *The Rich Man*, in 1902, showed a well-fed, well-dressed burgher doling out money to a group of beggars surrounded by dogs gnawing bones. In a series of works at the University of Oslo in 1915, Munch painted trees growing from heaps of bodies. One fruit tree was subtitled *The Neutrals* and was a protest against the profits that Scandinavians made during the war. Faced with a series of personal problems that his art could not resolve, Munch suffered a nervous breakdown, which turned him to political introspection and concern for the working class. His fellow Norwegian artists, Grieg and Ibsen, were committed (however much they might disclaim it) from the start.

In 1901, Ibsen had his first stroke, and his war with trolls was near its end. Oslo newspapers prepared their obituaries. But Ibsen refused to die, and indeed survived the Swedish-Norwegian Union although he was in a poor condition to celebrate it. In the twentieth century Norwegians repeated their claims for a separate consular service for Norwegian nationals, and the most internationally famous Norwegians began to conduct a campaign in the columns of the world's press. The Arctic explorer Fridtjof Nansen had an international reputation that ensured that his words 'any union in which one people is restrained in exercising its freedom is and will remain in danger' would be widely publicised. The relationship between Norway and Sweden became so strained that the possibility of war could not be ruled out. This unpalatable fact has been largely suppressed in contemporary Scandinavia. But the national military museum in Oslo contains relics of the Norwegian mobilisation movement, and most elderly Norwegians, if not elderly Swedes, can recall family traditions which include oral histories in which relatives were prepared and believed themselves to be on the point of dying for Norway in a war against Sweden.

Christian Michelsen, a Bergen entrepreneur with shipping interests, masterminded the Norwegian political strategy that resulted in independence. The ninety-year union was peacefully severed with a suddenness that surprised observers. On the very eve of independence Grieg, for example, thought gloomily of the probability of mobilisation. He knew that in Norway and Sweden most hoped that the union would be dissolved without bloodshed, as the contrary would be an unparalleled crime. But the Norwegians were ready and faced with such prepared-ness that the Swedes would, he thought, be deterred from attack. Grieg personified the Swedish nation as 'middle-aged', and argued that since Norway was still young some form of conflict was inevitable. He contrasted the antediluvian attitudes of the Swedish aristocracy and king with the democratic temper of Norwegians. Grieg was invited to give a concert in Finland at the peak of the constitutional crisis, but the Swedes would not let him travel to Finland through Sweden. Norwegians living in Sweden were driven across the border, and the audience hissed when Grieg's music was performed. As part of Michelsen's strategy to break the union, the Norwegian delegates to the Stockholm court presented King Oscar II with a bill marking the establishment of a separate Norwegian consular service. In accord with Swedish public opinion, which regarded unilateral action on the consular question as illegal, Oscar II refused the bill, or to accept the Norwegians' resignation in lieu, and the delegates returned to Oslo knowing that a break with Sweden was inevitable. Michelsen published the government's proposals on 7 June 1905. Since Oscar II could not form an alternative min-istry, Michelsen regarded Oscar as having failed in his primary duty as a constitutional monarch, that the monarchy had ceased to function, and that the union, which existed by virtue of a common monarch, had come to an end.

The Norwegian parliament invited Michelsen to continue

to govern and to absorb the royal prerogatives. At Karlstad, in Sweden, the Swedish and Norwegian governments negotiated on the procedure for dismantling the union with the two major problems: the filling of the vacant crown of Norway and the question of Norwegian border fortifications. Oscar II formally abdicated as King of Norway on 26 October 1905, and Prince Charles of Denmark was elected by the Norwegians to succeed him. Charles, who took the name Haakon VII, had the great advantage of being married to Maud, Edward VII's daughter, and the Norwegians knew that such an election would ensure British support for their foreign policy objectives in the dark days ahead. Grieg declined to compose a Coronation Cantata. His natural republicanism was conditioned by unhappy experiences with two monarchs, Edward VII and Wilhelm II. In 1904 Wilhelm II, on a tour of the fiords, dropped anchor at Bergen and imperiously commanded Grieg to breakfast with him. Grieg was forced to discuss music over breakfast and was only slightly mollified when the kaiser called for his forty-player orchestra after the coffee and, with a Germanic 'front stalls please', allowed Grieg the privilege of hearing a programme of his works including *Wedding Day at Trollhaugen*. Wilhelm II was a music lover and an accomplished amateur musician, but Edward VII was not. During a command performance in 1906 Grieg twice stopped the orchestra when Edward VII's conversation could be heard over the music. But he took part in a festival celebration and was summoned by Haakon VII and Maud to the royal box. Whereas Grieg had only two years to live, Haakon VII had fifty, and was to play a crucial role in two world wars.

Haakon VII was the Norwegian spokesman at the meetings of the Scandinavian monarchs in 1914 in Malmö and Oslo in 1917. He had taken as his motto 'All for Norway', and during the war, in which Norway suffered great losses despite its neutrality, he lived up to his promise, as he was to do again. By 1915, German trawlers had entered Norwegian waters to increase German food supplies by purchasing fish from Norwegian fishermen. Great Britain retaliated by threatening to withdraw supplies of coal and oil and, on 3 August 1916, a formal agreement laid down a system under which Britain made pre-emptive purchases of Norwegian fish. Unfortunately, this deprived not only the Germans, but also the Norwegians, of fish. The Norwegian merchant marine stood fourth in the world by 1914: in 1918 it had fallen to sixth, as German submarine warfare, responding to the enforced chartering of Norwegian merchant shipping to Great Britain, sank over 1,000,000 tons of shipping and cost 2,000 Norwegian sailors their lives. The situation would have been grimmer had Nansen not used his international prestige by negotiating during 1917 an agreement for importing essential supplies from America.

Domestic politics in Norway during World War I were in the hands of a government led by Gunnar Knudsen. The left took advantage of the war to pass through parliament legislation that would have been unacceptable in peace-time. To run a neutral economy in time of war required state intervention in areas on which it had not hitherto trespassed. In 1916, for example, in the face of both conservative trade unions and employers, compulsory arbitration legislation was passed. The left had a majority in the Norwegian government until 1920. In 1917 the Norwegian Labour Party called for revolutionary mass action after the Russian Revolution, but the call to bloody violence was unproductive, and Norway entered the 1920s democratised but not radicalised, voting to join the League of Nations on 4 March 1920, in the hope that salvation in the short term lay in such international organisations.

Like the other Scandinavians, Swedes in the twentieth century found that sheltered waters were all behind them. Stockholm was a civilised city by European standards. Visitors to Stockholm were met by an interpreter, wearing a distinctive cap, who gave free advice, you might say a particularly Swedish characteristic. Omnibuses from the principal hotels met taxis, and horse-cabs carried clients to the Grand, the Rydberg or the Continental, where rare combinations of the English language, baths and air-conditioning could be found. The Operakällaren was Stockholm's best restaurant, and cafés played music in the evenings to what was described by Baedeker as 'rather mixed society'. A well-organised system of tramways took Strindberg's audiences to their homes on seven routes, the pre-war Swedes honestly depositing their uniform fare in a small box. The capital had 307,000 inhabitants, all of whom lived, as Baedeker put it with eminent precision, at 59 degrees, 21'34" N. Lat., at the influx of Lake Malaren into the Baltic.

The battle between the followers of the genius who invented dynamite and the supporters of the innovator who popularised naturalistic drama began in the 1990s. The first Nobel prizes, in accord with Nobel's will, were given in 1901, but Sweden's greatest writer was not to receive one. His realism was too repellent. The refusal of the Swedish Academy to honour Strindberg was a touchstone of Swedish dilemmas. In 1910 and 1911, on the eve of his death, Strindberg wrote a series of provocative articles for the Swedish press, in which he espoused the cause of the workers. In 1911, after their hero again failed to receive the Nobel prize, the Stockholm working class collected 45,000 crowns and presented Strindberg with an anti-Nobel prize, the money being subsequently distributed to the city's poor.

One of the poorest of the city's workers was Karl Alfred Gustafsson, a street-sweeper and alcoholic. He lived with his family in a cramped apartment at 32 Blenkingegatan. The Gustafssons slept five to a room; their daughter Greta, born in 1905, dossed down on a camp bed in the middle of the floor. Greta used to escape to the sloping roof of the apartment's outside lavatory and, in the summer, sunbathe and daydream about white sandy beaches.

While Strindberg threw roses on the workers from the safety of his bedroom balcony, four floors above the crowd, and Greta Gustafsson dreamed on her lavatory roof, the democratic politicians who championed working-class causes did not have the luxury of detachment. In the years leading up to World War I there was a bitter struggle by conservatives in Sweden against Norway's fight for self-determination. Parallel to the conflict in international relations was one in which the privileged classes joined forces with the crown to counter working-class pressure for constitutional reform.

There were two areas of conflict in Sweden from 1900 to 1920: the parliamentary arena and the factory floor. In the factories the Swedish working class fought a series of battles with factory owners. Strikes were followed by lockouts and, after the defeat of a general strike in August 1909, involving 300,000 workers of the Swedish Confederation of Trade Unions, the working class began increasingly to put their faith in the ballot box and Karl Staaff's Liberal Party. Staaff's problem was that the constitutional division of powers between two houses of parliament, of different composition and with different interests, was inimical to reform. At the beginning of the twentieth century, the Swedish first chamber was completely dominated by Conservatives preoccupied with the necessity of maintaining the Norwegian union. The next twenty years saw the growing power of the left as the labour movement joined with Liberals to press the Conservatives. In the background, but becoming increasingly evident, the Social Democrats organised themselves. Staaff's Liberals, who held a majority in the second chamber, briefly had office in 1905–6 until Arvid Lindman's Conservatives displaced them. In 1909 Lindman introduced proportional representation and a wider franchise. Lindman, who had been a naval officer until 1892 and later worked in the iron mining industry, remained prime minister until October 1911, when Staaff again took office. For the next three years Staaff sniped at the powers of the monarch, governing with the help of the Social Democrats, who were gradually increasing in self-confidence and strength as a consequence of their growing support in the community, parliamentary experience and party discipline.

Staaff chose to fight the crown and the first chamber on issues that became increasingly controversial: disarmament and conscription. Farmers led a demonstration hostile to the Liberals. The demonstrators wanted more arms not less, and in carrying banners proclaiming, 'With God and the Swedish People for King and Fatherland', not unnaturally received a warm welcome from King Gustav in the royal palace yard. King Gustav walked into controversy with his eyes open. He told Staaff he intended to meet the farmers and ignored Staaff's views on the impropriety of a monarch going against the prime minister's views. It was a heady moment. Amid the snow and slush King Gustav agreed that the Liberal government was not patriotic enough in pursuing a vigorous defence policy. King Gustav said that he believed defence should be more widely discussed, that the question of increasing expenditure on defence should be decided without delay, and conscription accelerated.

The constitutional significance of the king's decision to speak directly to the Swedish people was enormous. The Liberal ministry protested. The king gave the evasive answer that he was speaking as a private individual, but even so he was unwilling to retract his controversial statements in the palace yard and sent the correspondence between himself and the ministry to the newspapers, precipitating the resignation of the Liberal ministry on 10 February 1914, four days after the speech. King Gustav had made the last successful defence of constitutional prerogative. Staaff and the Liberals were naturally aware of the crisis in international relations in 1914 and would have preferred a policy of rearmament had they not made election promises to the contrary but, in the event, government in Sweden until 1917 was carried on by a predominantly Conservative ministry. The Conservatives' instincts were to adopt a friendly policy towards Sweden's powerful southern neighbour across the Baltic, Germany, and to insist on neutrality in the war. In 1917, however, after the Russian Revolution and the United States' entry into the war, elections were held in Sweden.

The most striking aspect of the 1917 elections was the rise to prominence of the Social Democrats. In Sweden the Social Democrats had espoused socialism rather than Marxism. Like their English counterparts, they had done this to reconcile the trade union movement to the socialist cause. Hjalmar Branting was the key to the success of social democracy in Sweden. Branting entered parliament with the support of the Liberals and then turned his back on them, becoming a member of parliament in 1897 with Liberal support, and being a solitary Social Democrat in 1903 when he was joined by three others. Naturally, as the first member of Parliament elected in the social democratic cause, he was leader of the party and controlled its development. He was the editor of the *Social Democrat* newspaper and was firmly opposed to violent social reform. He favoured the nationalisation of the northern iron mines, and based his argument not on socialist grounds but on the Swedish tradition of co-operation that had existed in the mining region of central Sweden. In late 1914, the Social Democratic party had become the largest in the second chamber and therefore the question of eventual participation in government ministry came to the fore. In 1914 the Social Democratic congress approved a motion to co-operate with the Liberal opposition, and to support a neutrality policy.

In October 1917, King Gustav V accepted the idea of a Liberal-Social Democrat coalition, and insisted that Nils Edén should form a ministry with a reliable foreign minister pledged to a policy of neutrality. Edén, prime minister from 1917 to 1920, was a professor of history at Uppsala. Edén gave four of the ten ministry portfolios to Social Democrats. A short crisis occurred when it was suggested that Branting, as a Methodist, was ineligible to serve in the government under regulations that stated that ministers should be members of the true evangelical faith. But, with Swedish pragmatism, it was found that Branting had failed to remove his name from the Lutheran register, and by default was eligible. The new ministry faced a desperate situation. Inflation had risen to such an extent that civil service salaries were eroded. The increased importance of women to the workforce in World War I meant that demands for their suffrage could no longer be resisted, and as crowds of trade unionists sang the *Marseillaise* and the *Internationale*, Sweden seemed to be on the road to revolution.

When a police chief in Stockholm reported that the Horse Guards were on the point of mutiny, bolts were removed from army rifles to forestall a military coup. On 11 November, the War Department received a report in which the grave effect of anti-militarist propaganda on the troops was described. The defence ministry reported that the attitude of the army and navy was 'revolutionary', as for four years the armed forces of Sweden had been mobilised but inactive. And the fear of revolution from 11 to 14 November 1918 followed the same pattern of ferment as in the rest of Europe, where members of the defeated armies were in a state of effervescent tension bordering on irrespons-ibility. The civil war in Finland was too close to be ignored, and Swedish Social Democrats debated whether or not the Finnish Red Guards ought to be supported with military force. Under the threat of revolution, a special committee was set up under Branting as chairman, which after a week recommended the passing of a third Reform Bill which laid out that women would be permitted to vote on equal terms with men, that plural voting and the business premises votes should be abolished and that the franchise should be extended to 3,200,000 people. These bills were passed expeditiously, so ending the period of parliamentary reform in Sweden that had begun in 1866 when the estates had been supplanted by a popularly elected second chamber and a senatorial upper house, and been continued in 1907 when the franchise to the second chamber was widened and various property qualifications abolished.

By 1920 Scandinavian problems were temporarily solved. Harmony seemed to be in sight. Social problems certainly remained, but constitutional reform had made parliament responsive to public opinion, and it seemed only a matter of time before new parties and laws would facilitate the building of northern utopias. Most important, the major boundaries of the region had been stabilised, it was hoped, for the rest of the twentieth century. In order to maintain them, and to continue to enjoy the fruits of modernisation and progress, it was necessary to rewrite history – just a little. So on the eve of the 1920s, the Scandinavians began a conscious policy of reinterpreting their past.

The Finns, who were the most vulnerable and exposed, began their revision early. Gustaf Mannerheim directed a major-general, Hannes Ignatius, to write the history of the war of independence 'to get it as we want it'. History was too serious a matter in Finland to be left to historians, with their scant regard for truth. Early Finnish twentieth-century history was thus defined as a victorious war of independence against Russia in which the Bolsheviks were defeated and Finland aided by Germany's military power. What was a war of independence to the Whites was a civil war to the Social Democrats and a class war, unresolved, and by no means ended, to the Finnish Communists. Thus by 1920, Finland and Norway had become free from their nineteenth-century masters, the Russians and the Swedes, and the Finns proposed to see the twentieth century out with a republican constitution. The three Scandinavian kingdoms of Sweden, Denmark and Norway had faced nothing so serious, but in Oslo, Copenhagen and Stockholm history became a tool of politics, and its precise meaning and definition a prime concern of men in the street as well as in the foreign offices and the parliament. As the jazz age of the 1920s started, Scandinavians began their gloomy long weekend. They were too close to the decadence of Berlin for German cabaret to be funny. The intermezzo between the two great dramas of the first and second wars was brief, but it was not light.

CHAPTER 5

Intermezzo

The 1920s and 1930s were decades of discovery for Sweden. It found a new form of political organisation that served it well for the rest of the century, and its exports and entrepreneurial skills put the country at the forefront of the world economy. Swedes also discovered the unique vitality of their own culture, and caught up with the national chauvinism that had been triggered in Denmark by the Schleswig-Holstein conflict, and in Norway and Finland by the devolution movements against Sweden and Russia. In a symbolic discovery in 1921, the Swedes found the rococo Royal Court Theatre at Drottningholm, built in 1766 but unused for years. Agne Beijer, who was working on a book and looking for illustrative paintings to reinforce his text, decided to fossick in the theatre, which he knew was being used as a storeroom. Beijer found more than his painting. The theatre was exactly as it had been when it fell into disuse after the assassination of King Gustav III in 1792. He found elaborate sets left from eighteenth-century plays and operas, and machinery that produced rolling thunder and allowed devils to spring from trapdoors and goddesses to fly around the stage. With the help of a four-man windlass beneath the stage, whole scenes could be changed in ten seconds. The theatre was quickly recommissioned and one portion of what had been designed to be the Swedish Versailles began production again, periwigged and costumed in the eighteenth-century style. It was appropriate in the new democratic spirit of Sweden in the 1920s that Drottningholm theatre should be revived and used, not as a museum, but as an inspirational setting for the radical artists of the post-war period.

The Swedes knew that another century had intervened. There were no peasants whose labour could be exploited by an imitative monarch. Although the first productions at Drottningholm were period pieces, the social realists soon took over and created a new Swedish identity in the 1920s. The Scandinavians watched as battles were fought between the forces of fascism and communism. They felt defenceless in an increasingly harsh climate. For Scandinavians the jazz age was grim with prohibition, the beginnings of the social democrat state, and flirtation with right-wing radicalism. All these movements were symptoms of the north's failure to deal with the speed of the inter-war era. Internationally, Scandinavia saw threats from communism and fascism as Abyssinia was gobbled up and civil war raged in Spain.

For Sweden the first twenty years of the twentieth century had seen precarious gains in economic and political fields. In the 1920s and 1930s the Swedes were to perfect a system of government that appeared to outsiders to be the nearest thing to an earthly paradise. In the shadow of the Soviet Union, Swedish Social Democrats worked at a furious pace to forestall any thought that social democracy would not work hand in hand with middle-class capitalism. Indeed, in 1928 legislation was passed that made strikes illegal while collective agreements between the Swedish Confederation of Trade Unions and the Swedish Federation of Employers were in force. Although the workers protested against the no-strike clauses, the collective agreement of 1928 remained the basic platform for industrial harmony in Sweden until the 1980s.

The period 1920 to 1932 was one of minority governments,

as the Conservatives fought a desperate campaign to prevent the Social Democrats achieving government. The echoes of King Gustav's palace-yard speech still reverberated. In general terms, the war years, with the establishment of a broad coalition government in 1917, brought the first irresistible pressures of social reform. In March 1919 Nils Edén steered Sweden into the League of Nations and passed the eight-hour day legislation. Sweden then experimented with a bureaucratic rather than a political ministry, left in the hands of administrators rather than party politicians. But this early trial failed. The pressure of unemployment placed such strain on the governing coalitions that they often could not cope with running the ever-expanding Swedish administration. A largely apathetic electorate turned its back on the opportunity to vote, and seldom more than fifty per cent of the electorate went to the polls. The conduct of Swedish parliamentary affairs was described in colloquial Swedish as 'cow bartering', an appropriate term in so far as the Baptist prime minister Ekman had himself worked as a farm hand. In 1932, the Liberal government resigned amid the scandal accompanying the crash of one of Sweden's proudest international and commercial concerns, the Kreuger Match Company, and the Social Democrat Age dawned.

The Kreuger match companies were the creation of Ivar Kreuger. Kreuger was to international finance what Nobel was to explosives. From small beginnings his ingenious business practices created an empire built of matches. By the 1920s, Kreuger controlled half the world's match production, and was in the business of making loans to sovereign states. France borrowed $75 million from Kreuger in 1927, Germany $125 million in 1928, and thereafter, until he blew his brains out in Paris on 12 May 1932, only impeccable clients could tap his vast resources. After the suicide, investigators found that Kreuger's basic technique was to raise loans on non-existent assets and to borrow from Peter to pay Paul. By a colossal confidence trick he had got so deep into debt that death was his only way out.

Ivar Kreuger was the managing director of the Swedish Match Company, one of the large group of Swedish companies that aimed to set up factories outside Sweden and internationalise their enterprise. By 1932 Kreuger's company conducted its accounts in Australian pounds, Argentine pesos, Belgian francs, Chilean pesos, Colombian pesos, Danzig guilders, Yugoslavian dinars, Danish crowns, Egyptian pounds, Estonian crowns, Portugese escudors, French francs, Finnish marks, Dutch florins, Uruguayan gold pesos, Czechoslovakian korunas, Latvian lats, Romanian lei, English pounds sterling, Italian lira, Lithuanian litas, Mexican dollars, Norwegian crowns, Palestinian pounds, Hungarian pengoes, Philippine pesos, Spanish pesetas, German reichsmarks, Indian rupees, Austrian schillings, Swiss francs, Swedish crowns, Peruvian soles, US dollars, Japanese yen and Polish zloty. This richness of currency, besides being a demonstration of the breadth of Kreuger's financial empire, which lasted until 1932, was an accountant's dream. Exchange rates could be juggled, transactions faked, and the books balanced with a commercial inventiveness that defied description and posthumous investigation. The Swedish historian Ulla Wikander has taken Kreuger's enterprises from the field of fiction where Graham Greene firmly established them in the novel *England Made Me*. Wikander's analysis of the global nature of the Swedish match industry shows that Kreuger controlled or had share ownerships in about 200 companies, many of them, like Bryant and May, household names in their own countries. Kreuger's was among the first Swedish firms to become multinational, and he was the most successful. His methods of gaining control of worldwide match production and trade involved the signing of export/import agreements with match industry companies, the acquisition of match factories outside of Sweden by fronts, secret purchase and by leasing match monopolies from foreign states in exchange for loans to the countries in question. Kreuger eventually acquired monopolies in fifteen countries. The idea of a monopoly was nothing new. The English Civil War was caused to some extent by dissatisfaction with royal monopolies, which were farmed out to entrepreneurs. In the late nineteenth century Bismarck tried to start a monopoly in Germany but failed to get the approval of parliament. Kreuger was more successful. In the twentieth century, it was easy to start a match production enterprise. In the 1920s there was no alternative product. In the late nineteenth century there had been a demand for household lighting, an increase in the number of heating and cooking stoves, an increase in cigarette smoking, and the almost exclusive use of solid fuels, so that by the beginning of World War II the annual consumption of matches throughout the world was about 6,500,000 cases, containing 50 gross of match boxes each with 50 match sticks per box. On the eve of World War I Sweden had captured the second largest share of the world's market, selling 389,000 cases. Its competitor at the top of the table was Japan, with an export record of 823,000 cases in 1910–13. Japan, however, hampered by the rising values of the yen and the growth and internationalisation of Kreuger's empire, lost the Chinese market in the 1920s and failed to maintain its share of the world market thereafter. Swedish Match bought aspen from Russia, continuous matchmaking machines from Germany, and took advantage of the lifting of British import restrictions to open negotiations with Bryant and May which, in 1927, culminated in the formation of the British Match Corporation, a holding company designed to unite the interests of Bryant and May and to develop the British and Commonwealth market. The Great Depression, however, increased unemploy-ment dramatically, and the consumption of matches was reduced by a psychological reaction to the crisis (which had several odd effects, including an increase in savings at a time of reduction in income). When the Kreuger empire fell, all his old partners deserted him. In England, after the Economist had outlined the state of Kreuger's books, the chairman of the British Match Corporation, George Paton, assured shareholders that his company was not involved in the terrible financial debacle caused by the 'unscrupulous financier' Ivan Kreuger.

When Kreuger died, the economic base of Sweden was strong, for the Kreuger empire was only one of a series of successful ventures into capitalist economics by Swedes who used their skill and high technology to make Swedish names, even if they were not always recognised as such, household words throughout the world.

Sweden's foreign policy in the intermezzo years was based on faith in the League of Nations and, as the 1930s ended, an understanding that international organisations could be of little use unless the defender was armed with sufficient forces to deter potential invaders. In an inauspicious beginning, Sweden lost its first case before the League of Nations over the Åland question, which no doubt confirmed its resolution to be self-reliant. The islanders sought incorporation with Sweden in 1917, fearing that their cultural independence as Swedish-Finns would disappear once Finland became independent and solved the matter of language. Their pessimism proved unfounded. With the insular bloody-mindedness typical of island sailor-farmers, they opposed the Russians garrisoned on the islands in 1918, and mistrusted the Swedes, Germans and White Guard Finns. A referendum on the islands in 1919 resulted in a ninety-five per cent vote in favour of union with Sweden, and the matter was raised at the Versailles peace conference. But until 1922, when Åland was granted a sort of demilitarised grand duchy status within Finland, the problem was unsolved.

The Swedes were more successful in their fight for

temperance. The consumption of alcohol in the north had long been recognised as being well beyond normal. But it was not until the immediate post-war years that the temperance movement, inspired by the success of similar social reformers in other fields – those working for a reduction in factory hours, or votes for women, or an extension of the suffrage – began to use the techniques of pressure groups in an assault on the demon drink. The Swedes devised 'the Bratt system', named after its originator, Dr Ivan Bratt, which ingeniously avoided the evils of total prohibition (smuggling and a black market) by rationing purchases to individual consumers, preventing the development of beer or spirit barons by granting a monopoly in manufacturing and importing alcohol to a state company, and putting the management of retail liquor in the hands of individuals responsible for temperance in their areas. In 1922 the Swedes rejected by referendum the idea of total prohibition, but the system was not an absolute success as groups pooled their resources for binges, and some individuals felt bound to drink their quota as soon as the date for its permitted purchase fell due.

In the 1920s Sweden gradually developed its economic base and social institutions. But when the Great Depression hit Sweden and intensified the class struggle, the bloody events during May 1931, when strikers were shot dead by troops in northern Sweden, badly affected the Conservatives. Despite rumblings, Sweden had few of the violent clashes that characterised Finnish labour relations in the early twentieth century. But at Ådalen the Swedish class war took such a repugnant form that employers and employees eschewed violence as a means of solving industrial disputes and the electorate put its faith in the Social Democrats as the most likely political party to succeed in bringing Sweden a permanent peace between the classes. At Ådalen, militant communists among striking timberworkers organised demonstrations. The provincial governor, however, called in troops and in a confused riot five died. The last occasion when lives were lost in industrial disputes had been in Sundsvall in 1879.

When the Social Democrats won power in 1932, they were in a similar position to the Labour Party in Britain. They had to govern a country that distrusted them and doubted they had the experience or intelligence for the job. They also had the problem of harnessing the power of the Swedish Confederation of Trade Unions, which was hard-put to restrain its members from using their muscle power on the first government of their own. In 1936 the Swedish Federation of Employers met the Swedish Confederation of Trade Unions and began a series of deliberations designed to establish industrial peace. In 1938 at the seaside town of Saltsjöbaden a basic agreement was made, which continued in revised form throughout the twentieth century. The 1938 agreement allowed for a labour market council to handle disputes with 'third parties' – the government. The agreement laid out negotiation procedures, established guidelines on dismissals and layoffs, dealt with the disputes threatening basic public services, set down limits for economic sanctions and tried to work out how to protect 'third parties' to industrial conflict. The co-operation between capital and labour worked, and the Swedish standard of living rose steadily. By 1939 there were 250,000 motor vehicles registered in Sweden, an index of prosperity envied by Sweden's Scandinavian neighbours.

Ekman was succeeded as prime minister by the Social Democrat of Per Albin Hansson, who remained leader of his party until 1946. Hansson, the son of a bricklayer, was the technocrat who put down the enduring foundations of the Swedish welfare state and urged the adoption of Keynesian principles. He built hospitals, roads, electrified the railways and tried to create an atmosphere where all Swedes benefited by expertise in social engineering, albeit sometimes in a totalitarian spirit. The first signs of these tendencies accompanied the Nazi rise to power in Germany. Sweden had always maintained a close contact with Germany, a natural trading partner and a close cultural neighbour. Prince Gustav Adolf was married to Princess Sibylla of Saxe-Coburg-Gotha. Some Swedes thought that the Third Reich was moving along correct lines, and two Swedish economists, Gunnar and Alva Myrdal, argued in 1934 that the working class ought to be persuaded to abandon its selfish practice of raising its living standards by birth control.

In the 1920s, during Sweden's preoccupation with living standards, the Swedish film industry had become a successful cultural export. Greta Gustaffson was discovered by Mauritz Stiller, a Jewish refugee who moved to Stockholm from his native Helsinki to avoid conscription into the Russian Army. Stiller marketed her under her stage name Greta Garbo, considered a more euphonious surname than Gustaffson in all parts of the western world except Australia, where the word was popularly used to describe the occupation of Greta's father. Greta was whisked off to Hollywood, where she made, besides such classics as *Anna Karenina, Queen Christina*, in which she disguised herself (not very successfully) as a boy. Perhaps John Gilbert's poor eyesight explains her refusal to marry him, and her subsequent personification of the Nordic stereotype of solitariness, immortalised in her oft-quoted wish to be alone. Scenes from *Queen Christina* were described by its Swedish historical adviser as utterly insulting to Swedish royalty. But the impossibility of grapes being served at a Swedish inn in mid-winter could not dim the worldwide enthusiasm for things Swedish.

The possibility of exploiting Swedish know-how was not lost on the outside world. In the world of cinema, the American producer David O. Selznick instructed his office to look for foreign talent. He missed Ingmar Bergman, who completed his tortured adolescence in the 1930s, but in 1936 Selznick's New

York office saw a Swedish film called *Intermezzo*. It featured the wife of a Swedish dentist, Ingrid Lindström who, having built up a small following using the stage name Bergman, refused to change it for Selznick and the non-Nordic market. She did, however, sign a contract and take English lessons and by 1939 Selznick had an English version of *Intermezzo*, modelled on the Swedish original, playing to full houses.

Garbo and the Bergmans were the icing on the cake. The Swedish welfare state was based on a build-up of economic apparatus financed by banks and life insurance companies. Investors' profits were ploughed into companies like ASEA (which was a pioneering electrotechnical industry producing transformers) and Bofors (which made guns, pig iron, rolled steel, forgings, castings and motors). Swedish technology led the way in the 1920s and 1930s, as the number of consumer durables increased and a new technology made life sweeter and easier to manage. AGA built gas accumulators, aeronautical lights, level crossing and traffic signals. Elektrolux (softened for non-Germanic consumers by the alteration of the 'k' to 'c') liberated Swedish women by providing them with a new range of home technology: refrigerators, floor polishers and vacuum cleaners. Husqvarna made not only small arms but bicycles, motor cycles and sewing machines.

One of the most obvious, most spectacular and most lasting successes was the growth of Volvo. In 1924 two Swedes, Assar Gabrielsson and Gustaf Larsson, decided to begin a local car industry and in 1926, with a capital investment of 200,000 crowns, they established the Volvo company. Their first series-produced Volvo rolled off a production line at Hisingen in Gothenburg in the early morning hours of 14 April 1927. Gabrielsson and Larsson nicknamed the first car Jakob. It was a copy of an American design and had a four-cylinder side valve engine that gave a top speed of sixty kilometres an hour. Jakob was built as an open tourer, but its elegant ash and red beech frame soon fell victim to the Swedish winter, and subsequent Volvos were covered sedans. The first Volvo truck, the LV40, developed an impressive twenty-eight horsepower and could manage a payload of 1.5 tons when it began production in 1928. By the outbreak of World War II, Volvo had established an export plant in Finland, built a streamlined model and had manufactured vehicles in numbers and quality that made it a potential force in the world's automobile industry.

During the 1920s and the 1930s the giants of Swedish industry were formidable by any standards: iron works, saw mills, paper pulp producers, mechanical engineering works producing locomotives and railway carriages, ship building slips and dry docks, bridges, cranes, sugar refining technology, diesel engines, hydraulic turbines were all made in Sweden. Many firms exported and brought in foreign exchange, although few covered the range of currency that Kreuger dealt in. By 1929 SKF had established itself throughout the world as the market leader in self-regulating ball bearings. De Laval's separator was indispensable to the world expansion in dairy products before World War II, and the glassworks, Orrefors and Kosta Boda, showed that Swedish high technology could be beautiful.

Although Swedish artists were popular throughout the world in the inter-war years, Norwegians were not. Greta Garbo and Ingrid Bergman were better received than Edvard Munch, and not merely because they were prettier and marketed in Hollywood. Their messages were value-free and without political content. Munch was aware that by 1929 many people in northern countries were against his way of viewing the grey exploited masses who provided everybody else's needs. They were, he complained, against painting on a large scale, and against the treatment of psychological phenomena. Explicit art, with its treatment of details, its sleek execution and its small scale, was accepted everywhere, but Munch believed that this art would have to give way to a new sort. The small picture with its little frame belonged to the living-room and was bour-geois art, if not art for the art dealer's sake. This genre had gained in importance after the middle-class victory in the French Revolution, but Munch predicted the time of the workers had arrived, that art would soon belong to everyone and have its place on the walls of public buildings.

Adolf Hitler believed that the best decorations for the walls of public buildings were slogans supporting his policies. In 1935 Munch's art was included in an exhibition of degenerate art in Munich and, a year before the Germans invaded Norway, the German government held a clearance sale of Munch's paintings and graphics in German collections, allowing many of Munch's early masterpieces to be recovered by the Norwegians. Hitler included the Norwegians in the master race and through painstaking diplomatic activity, an underground net of German sympathisers grew in Norway during the 1920s and 1930s. Their leader was Vidkun Quisling, whose surname has been incorpo-rated as a noun in the dictionaries of most European languages and is a synonym for traitor.

Vidkun Quisling was born on 18 July 1887 into a family of Danish immigrants who settled in Telemark, southern Norway. His father was a village pastor and rural dean. Quisling was distantly related to Ibsen and on the eve of his execution wrote his family history saying that he was brought up among Viking graves, amid scriptural history and the sagas. He belonged to an ancient house and was inculcated with the belief in the value of family pride, family history and the Quisling responsibility to Norway. The name 'Quisling' was no foreign name, he explained, but an ancient Nordic name, meaning a cadet branch of a royal house. 'Q' was not an outlandish Latin letter but an ancient protective rune.

In 1905 Quisling entered the Norwegian military academy at a crucial period in its history. Nationalism was at a peak following the successful end of the Swedish union. Quisling was top of the class that graduated in 1908. At the outbreak of World War I he was fluent in English and German, to which he quickly added Russian and Chinese. He served in a most sensitive posting as an instructor in the Imperial Chinese Army until the Russian Revolution closed China to the outside world. On 5 April 1918 he was ordered to go to Petrograd, which was then the diplomatic capital of Russia. He would normally have travelled through Finland, but because of the civil war he was unable to reach Russia from that direction and so he was given permission to travel through Germany and the Eastern Front. He used the opportunity to see as much as possible of conditions in the war zone, and even managed to visit Trotsky but, when the Norwegian government broke off relations with the Soviet Union, he left Russia with the rest of the diplomatic corps. On 8 October 1920 he was ordered to go to Helsinki to take up the post of military attaché and legation secretary and to help the famous Norwegian scientist and explorer Fridtjof Nansen to repatriate exiled victims of the Russian Revolution. He had to deal with the heart-breaking conditions brought about by the disastrous famine of 1921 and 1922. The scale of famine relief in Russia in 1922 and 1923 was only approached by the famine relief schemes in Ireland in 1846–49, when millions of people were fed by, and many depended on, government aid and relief systems.

Quisling was no salon-fascist. As he said, 'For three months I travelled in the stricken areas among the starving people and lived like a dog plagued by vermin, hunger and disease, cholera, smallpox and fever.' In 1923 he worked in Bulgaria helping to repatriate Russian refugees. He spent eighteen months in the Balkans and went on to be an agent for Nansen and the relief commission once his duties in Bulgaria were finished. In 1925, when massive relief was no longer required, he found himself temporarily unemployed. A friend gave him a job with a Russian-Norwegian wood company in Moscow, which crashed after the discovery of fraud on a large scale. When, in May 1927, diplomatic relations between the United Kingdom and the Soviet Union were broken off, Norway took over responsibility for handling British affairs and Quisling, who had considerable diplomatic experience, spoke English and was resident in Moscow, was offered a position as secretary to the Norwegian legation in Moscow until diplomatic relations between the Soviet Union and Britain were resumed. From October 1929 he spent two and a half years in the Soviet Union, conditioning his outlook on geopolitics and racial identity.

In Norway, and elsewhere in Scandinavia, there was conflict between socialism and fascism. The Norwegian fascists operated under the banner of the Fatherland League, which Quisling joined because he was in sympathy with its political aspirations. His hero and colleague Nansen was also a supporter and, on Nansen's death, he wrote a short article for the journal of the right wing, *Tidens tegn*, where he first addressed the question of freeing Norway from class warfare and party politics and carrying through national revival and unification on the basis of sound political and economic principles. The obituary on Nansen's death was overshadowed by a more important article entitled 'Nasjonal Samling' – the name that Quisling gave to his political party. The national unity party took its ideology from the National Socialists in Germany. In the 1930s, however, there was a relative lack of interest in Hitler's political philosophy in Norway and so Quisling attributed the poor showing of his party at the polls to an implausible conspiracy of Jews, communists, socialists and the other malcontents who were perverting the truth and destroying any chance Norway might have had of joining an Aryan cartel in the north. Quisling's moment of triumph had to wait. His party had little appeal to the Norwegians, preoccupied as they were with unemployment, the League of Nations' failure, the Great Depression and the problems of rebuilding an economy devastated by World War I.

The post-war slump affected Norwegian shipping, the country's main supplier of foreign exchange. By 1921, 1,300,000 tons of Norwegian shipping were rusting at anchor. In 1923 the Norwegian Communist Party was formed. It allied itself to the Third International, and in the late 1920s the Social Democrats began to defeat the extreme left and the extreme right, beginning a series of conflicts with the Farmers' Party that ended with electoral victory in 1935 – which, like the Swedish one, seemed to be the beginning of a new age when only the Social Democrats could be entrusted with the national administration.

Norwegians, like Swedes, had a huge problem with drunkenness. No political party had the answer. In 1917 temperance enthusiasts had managed to lobby to reduce the production of spirits so that Norway's precious wartime grain supplies could be used for food. In 1919 a vote was held on prohibition and, following its overwhelming support, in 1921 Parliament declared Norway dry. Until public opinion changed and prohibition was abandoned in 1932, smugglers joined moonshiners and venal doctors (who could prescribe alcohol for medical purposes) to defeat the aims of the lawmakers.

The 1914–18 war had produced cohesive nationalism in Norway. In 1917 proficiency in the vernacular 'language of the land' was made a university entrance requirement, a turning point but not the end of the long debate in Norway on the matter of language. The campaign to evolve a national language was part of the romantic nationalist attack on Danish hegemony, Danish having been the language of towns, and hinterland dialects being spoken in the countryside. During the 1830s Henrik Wegeland had begun a campaign to modify Danish by slow degrees into 'the state language'. At the same time Ivar Aasen produced a form of written Norwegian 'language of the land' collected from the western districts, and based, to some extent, on old Norse. From 1907 orthographic reforms gradually reduced the differences between 'the language of the land' and 'the language of the state'. Old Norse place names were substituted for those with Danish con-nections. In 1924, the name of Norway's capital was changed from Christiania to Oslo.

Besides solving the language questions, Norwegian politicians turned, like the Swedes, to the creation of a welfare state and to the establishment of neutrality in foreign policy. In 1935, the government, led by Johan Nygaardsvold and supported by the Farmers' Party, passed unemployment insurance legislation and laws to provide pensions for those over seventy. The foreign minister, the historian Halvdan Koht, was the mastermind behind the change in Norwegian foreign policy following the failure of the League of Nations to protect small nations from the predatory attacks of larger ones. In July 1936 Norway joined Sweden, Denmark, Finland, the Netherlands, Spain and Switzerland in a declaration that they would not support League of Nations sanctions. The shield of neutrality that had protected the Scandinavians in 1914 was put aside by the Norwegians who lacked Sweden's strong economic base and the concomitant power to turn from a peace to a war economy and mass-produce machine pistols instead of vacuum cleaners.

Norway's southern approaches were in theory protected by Denmark. But the Danes had not forgotten the failure of pan-Scandinavianism at the time of the Schleswig-Holstein wars, and declined, in the 1920s and 1930s, to be regarded as 'the dog on the chain'. Nor were Dano-Norwegian relations helped by the dispute between the two Scandinavians over Greenland. The World Court decided in favour of Denmark in 1933, but the protracted squabbling between the two neighbours was a sign to Germany that its plans for hegemony in the north would not be affected by the possibility of Danish and

Norwegian co-operation. At the Versailles peace conference and during negotiations in the immediate post-war years, critics said that the Scandinavians had been as rapacious in their attempts at aggrandisement as any nineteenth-century imperialists. They sought tropical colonies to offset their war loans and were successful at snapping up disputed territory. Norway was given sovereignty over Spitzbergen (which was renamed Svalbard in 1925), and took over part of the Antarctic and the Jan Mayan Islands in the North Atlantic. Norway and Denmark continued to fight for over a decade over fishing rights in Greenland. Greenland had been a Danish colony since 1721 and had not been lost to Norway in the post-Napoleonic settlement, so the Danes fought hard to keep Norwegians off their territory and were successful in 1933. Greenland's strategic importance was not exploited until 1951 when the United States was allowed to update World War II meteorological equipment and establish early warning radar networks and airforce bases.

Danish foreign policy was successful on two other issues: Iceland and Schleswig-Holstein. Iceland, like Greenland, was a Danish possession. In response to the demands of Icelandic nationalists in 1904, the Danes granted Iceland home rule on a model similar to that demanded by Irish nationalists. The Danes passed an act of union that gave Icelanders equal rights under the Danish monarchy but kept foreign policy in the hands of the Danish parliament, to which Icelanders sent elected representatives.

The issue of Schleswig-Holstein was less straightforward. The war had placed a strain on German-Danish relations, which neutrality and the goulash trade could not disguise, and nowhere was the strain more difficult to bear than in the border regions of Schleswig-Holstein, where Danish-speaking Germans were conscripted to fight for the kaiser but forbidden to use their mother tongue. Danish sociological research has proved the extent to which Danish cultural ties had been broken in the border area, especially Flensburg. Danish public opinion took the view that whatever the cultural behaviour and political sympathies of Flensburg, Germany had lost the war and the Schleswig-Holstein representatives in the German parliament ought to be encouraged to press for a return to the old border, which they felt sure the British and United States governments would support. Reason prevailed, however, and after voters in a referendum in Flensburg chose overwhelmingly to stay German, only north Schleswig was incorporated into Denmark in June 1920. King Christian X climbed on his horse and rode across the old boundary to the cheers of Danes fortified by aquavit. There had been some difficulty with this project, as historical tradition demanded that the king ride on a white horse, and a horse of such a colour proved so difficult to find that a dark one was painted. When a mount was produced, it was twenty years old, and had to be shot the following year, an ill-omen, and the Germans were to take revenge for Christian's equine bravado on more modern transport within twenty years.

Enthusiasm for Germany was not confined to Flensburg as Denmark faced the inter-war years battle between socialism, communism and fascism. The pressure from the right grew up in response to the behaviour of the workers, faced from the 1920s with growing unemployment. The Danish fascists were encouraged by the right-wing views of the sovereign who did not fail to use the royal prerogative to dismiss governments working against the interests of the bourgeoisie.

At Easter in 1920 there was the first crisis that brought down the government of Carl Theodore Zahle, who had led the left wing since 1905. After the May 1913 elections, he formed an administration that lasted until 1920, kept in office by Social Democrat votes. Christian X, who had glanced east at the victory of the Bolsheviks, backed his judgement that public opinion was against Zahle's policy of self-determination for minorities and precipitated an election by dismissing the government. Crowds outside the royal palace gathered and shouted for a republic. The trade union movement prepared for a general strike. The entrepreneurs and farm and factory owners said that they would respond with an indefinite lockout, and the crisis was only defused by the hasty passage of a bill permitting proportional representation and the issue of writs for a new election.

The right wing in Denmark was heartened by the result, which swept the wartime political leaders from the parliament, and made way for new foreign policy initiatives, such as membership of the League of Nations, and the dismantling of wartime measures, such as rent control and rationing. In the 1920s, production fell, unemployment increased, and speculators moved against the Danish currency. In this crisis in 1924, the Social Democrats, led by Thorvald Stauning, were elected. Apart from a brief interregnum from 1926 to 1929, Stauning's party governed Denmark until 1940 with a programme concentrating on social reform and (inappropriately as it turned out) disarmament.

With parliamentary power firmly in the hands of the Social Democrats, the right wing organised, and in 1930 the Danish Nazi Party was formed. Stauning relied on public opinion and the passage of legislation forbidding any civilians but boy scouts to wear a uniform in public, but there was support for the extreme right, especially from the conservative farmers hit by the depression and largely unaffected by social reform measures that improved the way of life of the urban working class. The Danish version of Hitler Youth dressed informally, but they were effectively drilled by their leader, Fritz Clausen, and represented in the Danish parliament in 1939. Kai Munk, a Danish priest and the most important Danish dramatist in the 1920s and 1930s, believed in 1938 that Mussolini was just about the only man in Europe who could get things done. Munk was shot by the Germans in 1944 as a reprisal against Danish resistance, but before that time he realised the irony of his admiration for totalitarian political methods.

In Finland there was general conflict between the forces of fascism and the forces of communism, even though the Communist Party was for much of the period in exile beyond Finland's borders. Those on the right of politics throughout the 1920s and 1930s continually pressed for further restrictions on working-class political organisations, and a conflict developed that was only to be ended by the threat to national identity posed by the beginning of the Winter War. Although there were a number of major and dramatic incidents in the 1920s and 1930s that gave the impression that Finland was a stronghold of right-wing radicals, beneath the surface the left-wing also flourished, and, forged by shared experiences in the civil war and its aftermath, continued to be a cohesive target for attack both inside and outside parliament.

A crucial factor in intermezzo politics in Finland was the armed forces. In the period following the civil war, the divisions intensified which had existed in the Finnish military forces in 1914 between the Finnish-Russian officer corps and the Jaegers. On their arrival in Finland in 1918 from Germany, the Jaegers had opposed Mannerheim's plan to use them to lead the Civil Guards. In the period after the civil war, many of the Jaegers were set on a military career as soldiers of Finland and resented the hold that the Russian trained officers of high rank, personified by Mannerheim, had on the military machine. In 1924 there was a minor mutiny when 458 officers in the Finnish Army submitted their resignations rather than serve under the older generation. But, despite their testiness, the two cliques within the army continued to support parliamentary democracy, which was threatened only by the Civil Guards, who considered themselves above the law in so far as their patriotic enthusiasm for preventing revolutionary attempts at a communist takeover was in accord with national destiny and the will of the middle class.

Other Scandinavian Social Democrats looked askance at Finland and were critical of the controlling role played in Finnish politics by Svinhufvud. They pointed out that Svinhufvud was Regent of Finland in the pro-German phase 1917–18, that as prime minister in 1930 he had steered through parliament laws that made membership of the Communist Party not merely illegal but an act of treason and, moreover, as president from 1931 to 1937, he had refused to allow Social Democrats into the government. Even from the 1920s, in Finland, there was a debate whether the letter of the law accorded with political realities. According to the Form of Government Act, the annual budget had to be included in the revenue and expenditure estimates for the financial year, and parliament therefore controlled expenditure. This was accepted until 1939, but in other respects the requirements of the constitution were not always observed. Political parties were not included in the constitutional law but in Finland, as elsewhere, the basis of political action was the party bloc where representatives of pressure groups were listened to and unofficial cabinet meetings called 'evening school' were held to test the water.

The role of the Communist Party was only one of the problems faced by inter-war Finns. Alcoholism was another. The Finnish nation, like its Scandinavian neighbours, suffered great social damage from alcoholism and, in response to the staggering number of drunk Finns, parliament passed prohibition laws in June 1919 to put the nation officially, as far as the government was concerned, on the wagon. The prohibition laws failed utterly. In 1921 the agency responsible for the enforcement of the prohibition laws seized millions of litres of alcohol and 11,000 people were charged with violation of the prohibition laws. In 1930, 35,000 people were prosecuted, so after a plebiscite in 1931, the Finns agreed to abandon the prohibition experiment. In its place they set up the Alko system, under which the state regulated the distribution of alcohol. The state had a monopoly on the import and sale of alcohol, and thirty-five per cent of the profits went towards promoting the ideals of temperance and the provision of old-age insurance benefits, thirty-five per cent towards general revenue, and thirty per cent towards public works. Whether in response to the climate, or to political pressures, it seemed to foreign observers to be part of the Finnish character to drink to get drunk. There was no widespread general tradition of wine or even beer drinking in the northern countries and, despite the efforts of Fazer and a few sophisticated restaurants, polite drinking was almost entirely absent from Finland as it existed elsewhere in Europe in Anglo-Saxon pubs or French cafés. Many Finns bought alcohol in spirit form in the maximum permitted legal quantity from the Alko distribution centres, drank it, and got drunk.

In contrast to their cultural precursors, Finnish artists of the period between the wars were, as architectural historian Sir James Richards has observed, sober, sincere and unassuming. The link between Finland and international architectural developments was Alvar Aalto, who was born in 1898, in the vampire era, saw the Russian Revolution as a child, and began to practise after independence and the civil war. Aalto created bent plywood furniture, which had a seminal effect on world furniture design, and his work was as important as Gropius and Le Corbusier in bringing his nation's unique identity before the public eye. Equally eye catching were the glass and porcelain of Wärtsila-Arabia-Notsjö and later the fabrics of Marimekko.

With the exception of the years of the Great Depression, the Finnish economy had no large-scale unemployment.

During the boom years, the class struggle intensified, although not of course at Fazer's where there were few such problems. Fazer air-conditioned his shops, cafés and Konditori. As a model employer, Fazer had appropriate recreations. He was a keen birdbander, imported hares from Russia to shoot and, like any other magnate, entertained such guests as Mannerheim on his country estate. He was regarded as a popular and benign employer, but other Finnish captains of industry were not so popular, and clashes between capital and labour occurred in the Finnish woodworking industry, and during a metal industry lockout in 1927 and a dockstrike in 1929.

Parliament responded to the conflict by increasing the power of the courts to deal with disturbances. The Finnish right wing, made up of ex-servicemen and the sons of the unemployed farmers who comprised most of the blacklegs, began to hold rallies. Suspected communists and sympathisers with the Soviet Union were 'taken for a ride'; they were beaten up and thrown across the Russian border.

The biggest crisis came when Svinhufvud learned on 28 February 1932 that the Lapua movement forces intended to march on Helsinki. Lapua was in southern Ostrobothnia, the heartland of Mannerheim's resistance to the Red Guards during the civil war. In a caucus of cabinet, the commanding general of the army, the commander of the Civil Guards and three other generals, Svinhufvud declared that not even one armed man might come to Helsinki. The generals obeyed their commander-in-chief. The railway and road approaches to Helsinki were sealed, tanks and artillery and regular forces were moved into the city and a state of emergency declared. Svinhufvud used powers that had been created earlier to harass the Communist Party against the Lapua movement. Freedom of the press and assembly was ended, the Lapua movement leaders were arrested and the Civil Guards ordered to return to their homes. Svinhufvud made a personal radio appeal to the Civil Guards, observing that he once marched with them, and the revolt collapsed. The Lapua movement, like the Communist Party, was banned. Although the government of the Soviet Union was pleased to see strong action against Finnish fascists, it was disturbed by the growing anti-communism of Finland in the 1920s and the 1930s. The Russians feared the Finns no less than the Finns feared the Russians. For while the Lapua movement and Finnish fascism were a sociological index of the state of community values, Finland's long-term foreign policy objectives for border peace and security were firmly tied up with its relationship with the Soviet Union. Although the Peace of Dorpat ended the state of war between Finland and Russia, in the 1920s and 1930s the Finns made few moves towards normalisation of the relationship at diplomatic, trade and cultural levels.

Finland's position in northern Europe was crucially important in the event of conflict between Russia and any other great power. The Finnish west coast and the position of the Åland Islands gave Finland control of the Gulf of Bothnia, dominated the sea approaches to Stockholm, and controlled the normal route for the export of Swedish iron ore to Central Europe. In the far north, the Finnish province of Petsamo divided the Soviet Union from Norway and direct access to the Atlantic Ocean, the Finnish border was only sixty miles from Murmansk, the only ice-free Russian port in the Arctic ocean, and Petsamo contained one of Europe's richest deposits of nickel. Along the eastern border of Finland ran the Murmansk railway that linked Murmansk with Leningrad and the interior of Russia. The unique position of Murmansk among Russian ports meant that the railway link was vital. Thus the Russians looked with understandable suspicion at the trend of Finnish foreign policy and public opinion in the 1920s and 1930s. The most important strategic factor was the Finnish south coast where, from Hanko eastward, the shipping channel to Leningrad was dominated by the Finnish coast and archipelago and by islands in the Gulf of

Finland belonging to Finland. This control of the coastline could block the Gulf of Finland and all sea access to Leningrad, the second city in Russia and the only Baltic port of the Soviet Union in the 1920s and 1930s. Moreover, the border fortifications put up by the Russian tsars were intact and in Finnish control. On the Karelian Isthmus, the Finnish frontier at its closest point was only thirty-two kilometres from Leningrad, well within heavy artillery range of the city and the naval base of Kronstadt. The dangers to Leningrad were obvious and perplexed the Russian High Command from 1920 onwards.

Although Finland was one of the smallest independent states in Europe and contained only about four million people, the Russians considered it likely that Finland would allow a third party to use Finland as a landing base for attacks on their country, and whether the enemy was British before 1933 or German afterwards, did not alter the geo-political facts. Russian diplomats noticed that in Finland people welcomed the revival of German military power under Hitler, that Finland was unenthusiastic about the Russian entry into the League of Nations in 1934, that there was no trade between Russia and Finland after 1934, and although in December 1935 the Finnish government announced a policy change under which Finland would be allied with Scandinavian neutrals, the Russians believed this was window dressing and that in reality Scandinavian neutrality had a pro-German bias. The Finnish government was quick to respond to Russian appreciation of the situation, and in the general election in 1937 a new, more progressive government came to power. The foreign minister, R. Holsti, criticised Germany and tried strenuously to improve relations with Russia. He visited Moscow, talked with N. Litvinof and K. Voroshilov, but this was overshadowed by the goodwill visit of a German naval squadron to Helsinki in 1937 and the arrival of a strong German delegation to Finland in 1938 for the twentieth anniversary celebrations of the White victory in the civil war.

In April 1938, B. Jartsev, second secretary of the Russian embassy in Helsinki, warned the Finnish government that the Russians knew that Germany planned to invade Russia through Finland and that Finland could prove its goodwill by allowing Russia access to Finnish territory to repel an inevitable attack. In July 1938 Sweden and Finland agreed in principle on joint plans for the defence of the Åland Islands and, since the Russian government was opposed to the militarisation of Åland because of Germany's approval of it, the Finns were able to offer the Russians access to Finnish territory to defend itself in exchange for the end of Russian opposition to the defence of Åland. The Russians in return suggested that Finland should state its willingness to accept assistance in repelling attacks and that Russia should be allowed observers on the Åland Islands and given naval facilities in the Gulf of Finland in return for trade agreements. The Finns refused to discuss these proposals on the grounds that this would be inconsistent with neutrality and, in March 1939, the Russians offered to exchange territory elsewhere for a string of islands on the Gulf of Finland that covered the sea approaches to Leningrad. Mannerheim suggested that a small power like Finland could not continue to rebuff Russia, that the Russian negotiators should not be sent away empty-handed, but his suggestion was turned down by the government and the Russians concluded that their assessment of the situation had been substantially correct, that the Finns were pro-German and a danger on one of their flanks. Simultaneous negotiations with Germany were more successful and, in August 1939, by a secret protocol to a German-Soviet Treaty, mutual spheres of interest were defined and Russia was given Finland.

When World War II broke out in September in Europe, Finland joined the other Scandinavian countries in declaring neutrality.

On 25 September, Stalin told the German ambassador in Moscow that he was going to 'solve the problem of the Baltic states'. Estonia, Latvia and Lithuania were offered a mutual assistance pact, which they accepted and, on 5 October, Molotov presented a note to the Finnish ambassador asking that the foreign minister, E. Erkko, should come to Moscow to discuss concrete political questions. But neither the Russians nor the Germans realised that the Finns were not likely to yield to the Russian demands and were, as the Finnish foreign minister put it, prepared to let worse come to worst.

CHAPTER 6

Presents from Hitler

The worse eventually did come to the worst. As part of the legend surrounding Mannerheim, the Finnish hero of this period, many Finns believe that in the 1930s Hitler offered Gustaf Mannerheim a Mercedes Benz as a birthday present. Mannerheim rejected it and returned his own gift. He sent Hitler a pistol to blow his brains out with. Thereafter – so the legend goes – Hitler decided that the Finns did not understand normal courtesy and put his faith in an alliance with Russia, Germany's hostility to Finland having been given an edge by the Kallio regime.

In a reversion to Napoleonic diplomacy, the Russians and the Germans made a secret agreement to partition Europe between them. The names were different; it was not Alexander, nor Napoleon, but Stalin and Hitler who agreed to the secret protocol. The real-estate deal was made between the foreign ministers, Molotov and Ribbentrop. But the effects were the same. The Russian and German governments agreed, on 23 August 1939, to 'a territorial rearrangement' in Finland, Latvia, Estonia, Lithuania and Poland.

On 1 September 1939, the Germans invaded Poland. Shortly afterwards, the Russians began to pressure the Baltic States to enter into an agreement with them that amounted to a surrender of sovereignty. From 25 September to 5 October the

Balts filed to Moscow where they naïvely accepted Stalin's guarantees that their constitutions would not be affected by an
agreement to give Russia access to ports, airfields and military
installations. In the summer of 1940 the Baltic states were incorporated into the Soviet Union, a development the Finns foresaw
for their own country.

On 9 October 1939 the Finnish prime minister, A.K. Cajander,
the speaker of the parliament, Väinö Hakkila, and J.K. Paasikivi
(the Russian expert who spoke the Russian language and eventually held the Order of Lenin) put on gloves, heavy coats and
Homburg hats for their journey to Moscow. In the Kremlin,
Stalin offered the Finns a mutual assistance pact. The Russians
also wished to lease the Hanko Peninsula in south-west Finland
and were prepared to exchange some of Karelia for islands in the
Gulf of Finland needed for the defence of Leningrad. The
Russians also asked for adjustment of the border in the Petsamo
region and on the Karelian Isthmus.

Warily the Finns negotiated for a month, while at the same
time preparing for war. On 13 November discussions ended. In
the meantime the Finns had sent President Kyösti Kallio to
join Haakon VII of Norway, Christian X of Denmark and Gustav
V of Sweden to try to repeat the 1914 accord. In 1939 all the
Scandinavian heads of state again pledged themselves to neutrality, but with sinking hearts.

The bloodthirsty Finns attacked the Soviet Union at the end
of November, or so the Russians claimed. The more usually
accepted sequence of the events, which led to the Winter War,
was that the Russians manufactured a *casus belli* on the Karelian
Isthmus. They shelled one of their own posts, killing a few of
their own frontier troops, and then, as Molotov put it, it was time
for the soldiers to negotiate. The Russians expected to defeat
the Finns within weeks; the Finns worried about where they
would find space to bury all the Russians massed on the border.
When the Russians crossed into Finland, Otto Kuusinen became

leader of the Democratic People's Government of the Finnish Republic, established at Terijoki under Russian patronage. Kuusinen was the only Finn the Russians would deal with, which was a diplomatic error, as he had been in exile since 1918. Following Lenin's example, Kuusinen had visited Finland illegally since the Finnish Communist Party's foundation days. The short distance between Leningrad and Helsinki and the long border made crossing easy, but by 1939 Kuusinen was well out of touch with Finnish public opinion. The attempt to legitimise the puppet regime forced any Finns with illusions to realise that they were to be Russified like Latvia, Lithuania and Estonia. Russian troops were instructed not to cross the Swedish border as they made a confident six-pronged attack along the 1,000 kilometre border from Petsamo in the Arctic to Karelia in the south-east Baltic region. Russian aircraft bombed Helsinki. Fazer's café put sandbags around its windows and tried to trade as normal. Sibelius took up his hunting rifle and fired desultory shots at Russian military aircraft overflying his villa and signed letters appealing for help from the western opponents of Stalin's Russia. An attempt was made to mount an Anglo–French expeditionary force to help Finland, but many Scandinavians wisely suspected the motives of what they saw as western capitalism and, as one Finnish historian put it, the appeal to help Finland was never made by the Finns.

Mannerheim, after a rousing rejection by the electorate in the years immediately following World War I, had returned to the service of Finland in 1931 as chairman of the Defence Council. He spent the next eight years preparing Finland's defences for an assault from the east that he believed was inevitable. As part of his plan, the Finns sheltered behind 'the Mannerheim line', and tried to defend Finland in the south by cutting up the enemy in the border regions where swamps made the lines of communication for the much larger Russian forces difficult. Behind the Mannerheim line, seven divisions of Finns held up twice as many Russians, some of whom had never seen snow and many of whom were sent into battle undertrained and ill-equipped. Finns, looting from the bodies, noticed that dead Russians had belts made from harvester webbing.

Not having the luxury of a large population, the Finnish Army fought without reserves and lost one-third of its combatants in the desperate war. In December 1939 and during January 1940, the temperature stayed around forty degrees below zero. During this white-out the Finns used their skill on skis to invent tactics which were at first stunningly successful. They contemptuously described the Russians as bundles of firewood and, by breaking up large Russian formations and isolating the small and diminishing groups, they burnt the bundles one by one. A complete Russian division was slaughtered, to the amazement of the world's press, whose correspondents watched Finland for the lack of a better spectacle during the phoney war. Many foreign journalists and military diplomats watched the Russians' early defeats for signs that the military colossus of the Bolshevik state was weak.

Stalin changed the situation when he threw the veteran General S.K. Timoshenko into the Winter War. Timoshenko found that the serious miscalculation about Finnish determination could be overcome by more planned use of the Soviet Union's greater resources. The severity of conditions in the Winter War began to turn the scales as the Russians and Finns fought to the death. When the ice froze so solid that Russian tanks could travel across the lakes and swamps in the border region, the Finnish ambassador in Stockholm, J.K. Paasikivi, began to talk about peace. Paasikivi had had no less than fifty conferences with Stalin and Molotov and had learned that prestige meant more to them than anything else, that their invariable policy was to obtain what they could for as little as possible and then ask for more, that they never sacrificed immediate gains for considerations of the future, that they paid no attention to what was said but only to what was done, that they endeavoured to be paid a high price for what they realised they must do anyway, and that they were impervious to ethical and humanitarian factors or to those of abstract justice, being influenced exclusively by practical and realistic considerations. On 7 March 1940, a Finnish delegation led by Risto Ryti flew to Moscow on a Swedish aircraft. The plane was identified by its registration number SEAFB, but the passenger list was largely fictitious, as under such assumed names as Sundström and Blomgren the Finns flew to a meeting where they would be the recipients of an unjust settlement in a dictated peace. The Peace of Moscow was signed on 12 March 1940.

For three months the Finns had fought and, when the war ended with a Russian victory and territorial concessions, Finland had managed to stay independent, thus proving that it is sometimes correct to fight despite the inevitable prospect of defeat, a lesson which the Latvians, Lithuanians and Estonians might have ruefully observed. But at the end of the Winter War, there were no prizes for Finland. It lost twelve per cent of its territory, the eastern border being put back to a frontier line that had existed in 1721. In the north the Salla district was surrendered and the Russians leased Hanko as a naval base. Fazer's huge factory complex at Hanko, which contained ten buildings, the largest so big that it was three storeys high and needed twenty windows on its frontage to let the light in, was closed. Fazer's workers formed part of the refugee exodus as 420,000 Finns who had lost their homes and livelihood moved west across the new border to avoid becoming citizens of the Soviet Union. It will never be known why the Russians did not completely crush Finland after the Peace of Moscow. Lack of archival material makes certainty impossible, but it is plausible that the Russians had a plan for dealing with Finland, incorporating it again in a Swedish union, and waited only on co-ordination with German foreign policy decisions before proceeding.

The Germans had other plans and in September 1940 President Ryti, who had succeeded as head of state on Kallio's death, the Russians having blackballed Tanner, agreed with Mannerheim's suggestion that it might be prudent to allow Germans transit rights through Finland. On 25 and 26 May 1941 Mannerheim's chief-of-staff, General E. Heinrichs, visited the German High Command at Salzburg and had talks in Berlin that laid the foundation for the eventuality the Russians had feared throughout the 1930s: an attack on the Soviet Union from Finland. At the end of May, Finnish diplomats spelled out the Finnish situation to the Germans, the implications of which became clear in the next month. The Finns mobilised in early June and two divisions were placed under German command. Although the government officially disapproved, a new generation of Finnish Jaegers dusted off their German dictionaries and prepared to enlist. They served under a surprisingly large number of the earlier Jaeger battalion members.

In June 1941, the Finns received their not wholly unexpected gift from the Germans. Repeating the mistake of Napoleon, the Germans invaded Russia at midsummer and turned on their old ally. The Ribbentrop-Molotov accord was valueless. The English and the French governments and the forces helping them in the battle against Hitler and Mussolini underwent a colossal change of heart, embraced Stalin as the saviour of the ethical standards of western civilisation, and put aside their views on political economy, Marxism, Leninism and even totalitarianism in their joy at finding an unexpected ally. With the opening of an eastern front, the Germans were expected to be so extended that they could not adequately carry on the task of subjugating Great Britain and its empire.

Naturally the Germans did not share this pessimism, and their top priority was to remind the Finns that from the German point of view it was German bayonets that saved Finland from the Red Guards and the establishment of a Communist state in World War I and that they were prepared to do so again. Mannerheim returned for the third time to save his country, pursuing the most consistent foreign policy objectives in Finland and insisting that German troops in Finland not be incorporated with Finns, and that the Finns were fighting only to recapture Karelia and other lands that had been surrendered in the Peace of Moscow.

The conflict lasted three years. Finnish historians call it the Continuation War. The best account of the spirit of it is in Väinö Linna's novel *The Unknown Soldier*. There was little enthusiasm in the Finnish Army for Hitler's manic declaration on 22 June 1941 that German troops stood on the Arctic coast with their Finnish comrades determined to defend Finland's territory in joint action with the Finnish heroes of liberty. Immediately after the German attack on Russia, Finland declared itself neutral and was recognised as such for a few days by the United Kingdom.

But the reality was otherwise. Russian aircraft again bombed Helsinki, and the Finns declared war on Russia, fighting cheek by jowl with the Germans under a system invented for the occasion and called 'co-belligerency'. By December 1941, the Finns were digging fox holes in Karelia. In the next three years of fighting they lost 53,750 soldiers killed and 59,500 wounded. In the Continuation War, Mannerheim deliberately ignored German directives, and refused to advance beyond the old borders, or to take part in the siege of Leningrad or the attack on Murmansk. Even so, Hitler (who had a penchant for anniversaries and was not the type to give up easily) visited Mannerheim's headquarters in June 1942 to congratulate him on his seventy-fifth birthday. Photographs of the birthday group are often reproduced, but guests and host look understandably jaundiced and rather less than festive.

Notwithstanding Hitler's personal efforts, in February 1943 the Finns considered that the Germans looked like losing, and decided to cut the German connection entirely and make a separate peace with the Russians. Diplomatic manoeuvres failed to extricate Finland, however, and on 9 June 1944, the Russians began to break the stable Finnish front line in Karelia. Viipuri fell to the Russians on 20 June. Finnish troops east of Lake Ladoga began to withdraw, leaving behind them the poles the Russians had driven in to mark the 1940 border. In Stockholm on 16 February 1944 the Russian ambassador in Sweden, who, in an echo of more gracious times, styled herself not Comrade but Madame Kollontai, told Finns what to expect. They had to pay for every tree they had cut down in Karelia. Madame Kollontai had begun the final negotiation phase for the armistice on 20 November 1943, when she informed an under-secretary of state at the Swedish Foreign Office that if Finland was willing to negotiate a peace treaty, her representatives would be welcome in Moscow.

By 1944 the Finnish nation was in a desperate state. Many of the children had been evacuated to safety in other Scandinavian states. The adult population was left behind living on fish, berries and mushrooms, and such luxuries as cigars were almost unheard of (although American admirers sent them to Sibelius from abroad). The Russians, however, would not sign a peace treaty until Finland surrendered. Fearing what was in the wind, and knowing that the Finns' first priority was the preservation of the nation rather than a demonstration of fellow-feeling for Germans and the German war aims, Foreign Minister Ribbentrop flew to Helsinki on 23 June 1944 and demanded that the Finns stop negotiating with the Russians. Put up to it by Mannerheim, and knowing that he was acting in an unconstitutional way which would later be repudiated, President Ryti gave Ribbentrop his personal reassurance that Finland was a committed ally of Germany. According to plan,

Ryti resigned as president on 1 August, his successor denounced Ryti's agreement with Ribbentrop, and Mannerheim became President of Finland.

Under Mannerheim, a new administration accepted an autumn armistice with Russia. The conditions were negotiated by Paasikivi and Carl Enckell (a former minister for foreign affairs) in September 1944, and once again the Finns accepted Russian terms. The Russian delegation was led by V.M. Molotov and included General A.A. Zhdanov and Sir Archibald Clark Kerr, His Majesty's ambassador to the Soviet Union. The frontier was put back to its 1721 boundary. The Karelians who had re-established themselves behind the front line in 1941–44 became refugees once more and travelled west to new homes in new subdivisions. The commission overseeing the cease-fire ordered the Finns to drive out the German troops left in Finland. The Germans retreated with typical thoroughness, leaving scorched earth behind them. As their final train crossed the border, it pulled up the last railway sleeper with an ingenious dangling hook designed for that purpose: US$120 million worth of damage was done by Finland's former co-belligerents to military and civilian property, mostly on roads, bridges and the homes of noncombatants. Rovaniemi, the most important Finnish town near the Arctic Circle, was razed. Sibelius's name was struck off the list of composers approved to support the German war effort, as the Finnish Army expelled 200,000 German troops from Finland. The Russians, on the second occasion, wisely chose to remain on Finnish soil and set up camp at Porkkala, a suburb twelve miles west of Helsinki, which they compulsorily leased as part of the 1944 agreement. The Soviet Union now had a military base on the very doorstep of the Finnish capital, and the message of Finnish dependence on Russian goodwill was rubbed in by a regulation that required Finnish train carriages to have their windows blinded as they passed through Porkkala. During the armistice negotiations

Molotov rejected Finnish protests and reminded Enckell that the Finns had destroyed so many Russian towns and villages 'that Porkkala was but a trifle compared to it'. The terms of the 1944 peace treaty were so savage that a lesser nation could not have survived them and this, no doubt, was the aim of the Soviet Union. Finland, however, defied Russian expectations and continued to pay financial reparations until 1952. US $600 million was eventually received by the Soviet Union.

The Finns did not expect the other Scandinavians to fight with the grim defiance they showed from 1939 until 1944. As Max Jakobson, ambassador and permanent representative of Finland in the United Nations, put it, to make a choice between complete submission and heroic sacrifice was seldom required in statecraft. Nor, he argued, should anyone criticise the decision of the Danes in 1940 to submit to occupation by a foreign power without a fight. In May 1939 Hitler gave all the Scandinavian countries the opportunity to join in a non-aggression pact with Germany. Norway, Sweden and Finland refused. But Denmark agreed, and on 31 May 1939 both parties signed a document designed to guarantee that neither country would go to war under any circumstances, or resort to force to solve diplomatic issues. Hitler had not accepted the 1920 border settlement imposed against Germany's interests as binding, and the Danes feared that north Schleswig at the least would be vulnerable if Germany began to fear hostility in Copenhagen towards their foreign policy objectives. So it was paradoxical, but not unexpected, that the only Scandinavian country to sign an agreement with Hitler should be Germany's first victim, ten months later.

The German troops who entered Denmark considered themselves (as at first in the case of Finland) representatives of a friendly state. They exhibited their good nature by leaving the forms of government, King Christian X and his parliament, undisturbed. But fourteen Danes died in the battle for Denmark during the two hours the king and cabinet spent making up their minds on whether or not to surrender. They had already been told on the diplomatic grapevine that Denmark was doomed. The head of German intelligence, Admiral Wilhelm Canaris, leaked the war plans to the Dutch military attaché in Berlin, who passed them on to the Danish ambassador on 4 April 1940. At four o'clock in the dark spring morning of 9 April 1940, the German ambassador in Copenhagen asked for a meeting with the Danish foreign minister in order to explain to him the need for Danish co-operation with Germany, as Germany had decided to move into Denmark to forestall a British coup. The Danish foreign minister learned that German mechanised forces, who were crossing the start line on their way to seize airfields in Jutland, would bomb Copenhagen if the Danes did not surrender; if they co-operated, Denmark would be used only as a base for operations, and the Danes would be left unmolested. The Danes surrendered before breakfast. At six o'clock German soldiers destined for Denmark on the troop transports relaxed. The operation that had been planned for as early as 20 March, but which had been postponed until ice in the southern Baltic melted, was a complete military success.

The Danes were spared a repetition of the bombardment of Copenhagen in 1807. King Christian X was able to ride his horse around Copenhagen and in and out of the city's bicycle traffic throughout the first years of the war. That he did so, in military riding habit and with a forage cap, without any demonstration of disapproval or need for an escort, was evidence of the initial thoroughness of Denmark's incorporation into the Reich as a model protectorate. The prime minister, when Denmark capitulated, was Thorvald Stauning, the bald, bearded, portly elder statesman of the left. Stauning was a pacifist who believed that Germany would win the war against Britain, France and eventually Russia, and that it was necessary for the Danes to prove their acceptability as Germanic rather than

Scandinavian people in order to get a more favoured minority treatment when the surrender terms were eventually signed, and a new Treaty of Versailles enacted.

The Germans overlooked their Nazi protégé Fritz Clausen (who led an unsuccessful coup attempt in November 1940) and were content to supervise a modification of the existing government, which was widened on 10 April 1940 to include members not elected to the parliament, the most suitable of these being Erik Scavenius, who was given the power to direct foreign policy. Scavenius, who had pursued a pro-German line during World War I when he was foreign minister, immediately turned his energies and prestige into a policy of collaboration. He spoke of the government's admiration for German military victories, Denmark's readiness to find its place in the new Europe, and was Germany's best advocate in talks aimed at the circulation of German currency in Denmark, equal rights for citizens of both countries and normalisation of customs and tariffs. The Germans, using what has become known in Scandinavian historiography as 'the Danish salami technique', not only placed their own unequivocal supporters into positions of power, but also sliced off their opponents one by one. Denmark, however, was not an occupied country under the control of the SS: it was guided by the German foreign ministry under Ribbentrop. And thus the Danes were free to express a certain amount of individuality by not being compelled to inform on communists after the Germans invaded Russia and by not having to join the German Army. The attempt to form a few battalions of Danish Jaegers, *Frikorps Danmark*, was successful, however, and some Danes fought with the Germans on the eastern front.

On May 1942 Stauning died, being spared the embarrassment of seeing his war-time forecast of a German victory proved wrong. The Social Democrats continued to govern under Vilhelm Buhl until, during November 1942, the basis of government in Denmark was altered after Christian X mismanaged his answer to a birthday telegram from Hitler. Christian X merely replied 'Thank you' to Hitler's 'Happy birthday', and as a result, the German leader (who was sensitive on such issues) interpreted Christian X's lack of appreciation and warmth as symptomatic of a general cooling off in Dano-German relations, which had deteriorated in a couple of important respects. Danish soldiers fighting for Germany had not been welcome when they took rest and recreation in Copenhagen's Nyhavn; on the contrary, they had been abused as traitors. And Christmas Möller, leader of the Danish Conservative Party, successfully fled to England where he became the centre of resistance to what was described, even in Denmark, as occupation. Möller made propaganda broadcasts on the overseas service of the BBC, stiffened the resolve of the Danish underground, and sponsored the illegal press.

It appears that both Hitler and Christian X were too hasty. Christian X assured Hitler that he meant no disrespect, and that 'Thank you' was his normal response to birthday telegrams, but the Danish minister in Berlin was given his passport and told to leave, his German counterpart in Copenhagen was recalled, and the Social Democrat government of Vilhelm Buhl resigned and Erik Scavenius was installed in his place. The Germans sent a new minister to Denmark, Werner Best, and under his auspices a new parliament was elected with the totalitarian proviso that the election results could make no difference to Scavenius. In March 1943 elections were held, and the results variously interpreted. By the normal standards of Nordic apathy, the poll showed a huge turnout: ninety per cent of the electorate voted, the Danish Nazis receiving two per cent of the votes, being most cast for the traditional Liberal, Social Democrat, Farmer and Conservative party blocs. The Germans hailed the election as a triumph that showed how free elections were possible under the new model Europe. But in the summer of 1943, despite reprimands from Christian X and Scavenius, Danish saboteurs began an effective series of clandestine operations, and on the factory floor a series of paralysing strikes in Esbjerg and Odense ended with Best being forced to declare a state of emergency.

At around four o'clock in the morning on 29 August 1943, at what seemed to be the normal hour for policy changes to be announced by German civil servants, Best took over the administration of Denmark. A curfew was proclaimed, assemblies of more than five persons forbidden. The Danish Army was disarmed, and radio broadcasting and the press were put under direct German censorship. Martial law was proclaimed. It was announced that henceforth the death penalty was to be given for sabotage. Even Scavenius's government was sacked. By an oversight the apologetic trotting king was not, and in the long tradition of Scandinavian monarchs, Christian X stalled the German constitutional takeover and insisted pedantically that he was unable to find an alternative government leader. Best put an end to his belated obstructionism by provisional internment. The government of Denmark was placed in the hands of bureaucrats under the permanent head of the Danish Foreign Office. To complete the takeover, the Germans sailed away with what was left of the Danish Navy, much of it having been scuttled by its crews, or sailed to Sweden at the last moment when sloppy security allowed the Danish underground word of the impending confiscation.

The first victims of the new regime were the Danish Jews. Scavenius had scrupulously avoided giving prominence to Jews in public life when he was in power, but the fact remained, and was irksome to Heinrich Himmler, that in Denmark Jewish descent was no bar to success in commerce, administration or even local politics. Once the Ribbentrop lines of government were severed, Himmler was able to issue a directive that Danish Jews should be arrested and deported to concentration camps. Best, however, was a machiavellian humanitarian, and leaked the news to Swedish politicians. When the knock on the door came, there was scarcely a Jew to be found – most of them had fled to Stockholm. Espionage and counter-espionage became fierce. Terror groups were formed of pro-German Danes and the German Secret Service. They blew up the Copenhagen Students Union and the Conservative head office and burnt buildings in the Tivoli. The Germans shot so many Danes branded as anti-German that in June 1944 there was a general strike in Copenhagen. As more Danes were shot for sabotage the population became radicalised in the British cause. In London a Danish Freedom Council was set up to co-ordinate operations when Denmark was liberated.

It was one of the set pieces in the establishment of a totalitarian regime that the police force had to be under the control of the Führer. Accordingly, as the Danish police were increasingly failing to support the martial law regime, from September 1944 Danish policemen vanished from the streets: 2,000 were arrested, disarmed and deported. The rest went underground and joined the resistance. As part of the protest movement, huge crowds massed to sing Grundtvig's nationalist hymns. Students wore red, white and blue knitted skull caps. Fishermen advertised for sale 'mackerel as fat as Göring'. The sabotage of rail traffic through Denmark increased, and in March 1945 the headquarters of the Gestapo in Copenhagen was destroyed.

By the end of the war in Denmark, the Danes had salvaged their reputation and were once again treated kindly by the victors in the post-war reconstruction phase. There was little fighting on Danish soil once Germany capitulated. In Bornholm the German garrison wisely refused to surrender to the Russians, the Germans reasoning that while the Finns might be forgiven by the Russians, some Germans were so compromised that they could never be spared. While the German commander begged to be allowed to surrender to the British, Russian aircraft bombed Rønne, and for the Germans the occupation of Denmark was over. Vilhelm Buhl was recalled as prime minister and oversaw the return to a civilian economy and the settling of scores. Under pressure from the resistance, 34,000 collaborators were arrested, interrogated, released or tried. Forty-six were executed and 10,000 imprisoned for a minimum period of four years.

The Danes also suffered from the influx of refugees from the areas of Germany occupied by the Russians after 5 May 1945, and there were anxious moments in Copenhagen while the Russians decided whether or not to leave Bornholm. The Russians withdrew, but the Americans decided to remain in Greenland, and Denmark's foreign policy problems in the 1950s were irritated by the Faeroes inhabitants' reaction to a taste of independence under British patronage during the war years, although Danish diplomats did not have to worry about Iceland: Iceland had become independent in 1944. The final return to normality was signalled when Danish historians began to write the revisionist account of the war years, playing down the early days of collaboration and stressing the importance of what was to become known in Denmark as the period of 'Norwegian conditions'.

Although Denmark and Norway were both included in the same battle plan, there was never any pretence that Norway would be other than conquered. During the Winter War, Quisling travelled to Germany where he pointed out to Alfred Rosenberg, the Nazi specialist on racial matters, that the Norwegian parliament was led by C.J. Hambro, a pro-British Jew. If this was not bad enough, in December Quisling met Admiral Erich Raeder and both agreed that Britain would not respect Norwegian neutrality and that a plan should be drawn up to occupy Norway. Within the German hierarchy a temporary dispute arose over the role the navy would have after the conquest in patrolling the North Atlantic. The chief of submarine warfare, Admiral Doenitz, urged the early establishment of bases in Trondheim and Narvik.

Confirmation of the correctness of Quisling's views was not long in coming. On 16 February 1940 a German supply ship, the *Altmark*, was attacked by a British destroyer in Norwegian waters. Both Germany and Britain claimed to have international law on its side, and each accused the other of violating Norwegian neutrality. In the action almost three hundred pirated victims of the *Graf Spee*, who were being taken on the *Altmark* to prisoner-of-war camps in Germany, were lifted to safety in an operation described by its admirers in Fleet Street as worthy of Sir Francis Drake. More prosaically, the *Altmark* incident showed that the British had the capacity to invade Norway themselves and both they and the Germans had early notice of the ripeness of the Norwegian prize – access to Swedish iron-ore fields, an essential component in the total war about to come. In Britain, enthusiasts for such a coup pointed to the Finnish Winter War as the ideal *casus belli*: on the pretence of aiding defenceless Finland against the Russian bear, Britain could move an expeditionary force through the Norwegian port of Narvik (ice-free in winter) and seize Swedish iron-ore mines before the deposits could be exported from the ice-bound Swedish port in the Gulf of Bothnia. This plan would have had the benefit of forcing the issue on both Norway and Sweden, so that Sweden would be in the war whether it liked it or not, and would be either conquered or incorporated as an ally, depending on its response. Churchill favoured this plan. Groups of volunteers trained to fight in Finland. From as far away as Australia small contingents of pro-Finnish youths prepared to die for a just cause, in much the same way as their elders had fallen in the Spanish Civil War. They planned to travel to Finland across Norway and Sweden as crusaders against Russia, but the Finns cannily refused to be implicated as an instrument of Anglo-French aggrandisement and the Peace of Moscow was signed before the British cabinet had made up its mind on Churchill's side. The Chamberlain government contented itself with a holding operation of mine-laying in the Narvik leads, to the angry protests of Halvdan Koht at the Norwegian foreign ministry. General Alfred Jodl, the chief of operations against Denmark and Norway, gloomily noted in his diary that the peace between Finland and Russia had deprived not only Britain, but also Germany, of the political basis for action in Norway.

Niceties had to be left aside. Hitler was convinced that British action was imminent in Scandinavia and the Baltic, and he moved to protect a potential Swedish iron-ore supply and to establish naval bases in Norway to give his navy and air force the best conditions for war against Britain. On 5 April the German embassy in Oslo invited the diplomatic corps to a film evening during which they showed movies of the invasion of Poland. It was rather like the effect of *A Doll's House* on the happily married Germans who squirmed through the pioneer performances of Ibsen's work. The Norwegian audience was softened up by the film evening for what was to come and left the theatre variously frightened, forewarned, determined to resist, or ready for capitulation.

There was a new moon on 7 April and the Germans used that period to cross the start line, not because of Wagnerian Valkyrie associations, but to make the most of natural light in the high northern latitudes. The whole of the German Navy was involved in the operation, which was so audacious and successful that Anglo–French intelligence could not believe the evidence of the German victory as it grew and grew. Amid snowstorms and gales, the coast from Oslo to Narvik was attacked and the ports of Trondheim, Bergen and Stavanger taken. Paratroops took Norwegian airfields. At Kristiansand, the German battle fleet flew British and French naval ensigns, and at Narvik the German troops wore Norwegian uniforms. Edvard Munch, who lived alone in his old wooden house on the Oslo fiord, saw the German battleships steaming in. Surrounded by debris (in sixty years he never used a waste-paper basket), he complained about tanks parked on his neighbour's farm and was disturbed by the anti-aircraft batteries placed on a nearby hill. The Germans confiscated his property, but relented on their initial order that Munch was to move, and he stayed by his fiord, muttering about degenerate German philistinism, until his death in 1944.

Neither Munch nor the Norwegian masses capitulated as did the Danes in 1940. The German heavy cruiser *Blucher* was sunk by gunfire from a Norwegian fort as it ran up the Oslo fiord. Norwegian troops took alive the admiral and general in command of operations and also captured a Gestapo task force entrusted with arresting King Haakon VII. The king himself had wisely left the capital Oslo for Hamar, where his seizure was more difficult. C.J. Hambro urged the Parliament to give the government emergency power, and thus in constitutional terms the Norwegian state was on an immediate war footing. Curt Brauer, the German minister in Oslo, gave foreign minister Halvdan Koht an ultimatum of nineteen typewritten pages in which he demanded that Quisling should lead a new government. The error was parallel to the mistake the Russians made in supporting Otto Kuusinen. Quisling had less than two per cent of Norwegian votes, admittedly more than Kuusinen, but his party was unrepresented in the Parliament, being even less credible than Clausen's Danish Nazis.

The crown was as important to the German tactics in Norway as it was in Denmark because it was the royal prerogative to appoint ministries. But Haakon VII made a different choice from Christian X. He replied to the German ultimatum with a brief history lesson. Haakon VII recalled that he had been king of Norway for thirty-five years and, as a constitutional monarch (who had been elected by the people in 1905 when the Swedish-Norwegian union was dissolved), he worked in the Norwegian tradition and therefore could not appoint Quisling, whom he knew enjoyed no confidence either with the people or with their representatives, the parliament, or the ministers of state. Haakon

VII concluded that despite the fact that so many young Norwegians would have to give their lives in the war, he would oppose the demand of the German minister. Hambro left for Stockholm where he thought he could better pursue Norwegian diplomatic objectives.

A token force of French, Polish and British came to the king's aid with landings in northern Norway, but gained little more than a toehold. The Poles got drunk on the wharf and were terrified by the Luftwaffe's machine-guns. British troops, largely undertrained territorials, were routed and demoralised. The French forgot their snow shoes. The only positive result of the debacle was the fall of the Chamberlain government and the late arrival of Churchill at the head of the British war effort. The Norwegians were abandoned in late May by their allies, and the one possibility left for continuing the struggle was for the king to escape and government to be set up in exile.

German troops had been told to use force, if necessary, to capture the king. As the Swedes refused his safe conduct through central Sweden, he withdrew north, pursued by German para-troops. At Nybergsund he was attacked with machine-guns and picked up a spent bullet from the snow, remarking that it was a personal gift to him from Hitler. Ruling out flight by ski and rein-deer because of his age, Haakon VII left for England somewhat less romantically aboard the cruiser *Glasgow*. By the light of the burning town the crew loaded the king's heavy baggage which contained Norway's gold reserves. When the *Glasgow* docked it was found to contain also the cabinet members of the legal government of Norway led by Johan Nygaardsvold.

The illegal government remained behind. When the king refused to appoint Quisling prime minister, the Norwegian High Court created an administrative department responsible for the government of occupied Norway in an attempt to keep the machinery of government in Norwegian hands. The attempt failed when, in April 1940, a civil Reich commissioner, Josef

Terboven, was given the essential powers of crown and government: Terboven was personally responsible to Hitler. Like his colleague in the Netherlands, who had a similar function, Terboven could legislate by decree and review existing laws. Since many of the administrators who were to run Norway after its conquest were dead in the Oslo fiord among the wreckage of the *Blucher*, an unplanned power vacuum existed. Quisling tried to step into it and the German war effort in Norway was weakened by the long struggle between the supporters of Terboven and the patrons of Quisling. When Terboven abolished the Norwegian Administrative Council and banned all political parties in Norway except the Nasjonal Samling Nazis, he was augmenting Quisling's power within the state to a degree he disliked. The eight Norwegian commissariat ministers under Terboven's control were put in a difficult position: they were charged with the Norwegian administration and responsible to Hitler for it. But in the early stages of the takeover, Quisling, as head of the Norwegian Nazis, was determined to exercise power wherever he could exert his influence. This dualism made Norwegian resistance to the occupation easier than it would otherwise have been.

The government became official on 1 February 1942, when Quisling presided over a cabinet composed of Nasjonal Samling members. By then opposition to the Norwegian collaborators was more bitter than hostility to the Germans. In a systematic flouting of the occupying forces, the major organs of representative democracy in Norway turned their backs on the German-Norwegian regime. In Oslo the rector of the university, the bishop of Oslo, and the chief justice were among the first to speak out and face imprisonment in a concentration camp at Grini, an Oslo suburb. Viggo Hansteen was the first but not the last martyr of the trade union movement.

Quisling's supporters, textbook fascists, established an organisation called 'the Hird' – an old Viking term – and complemented it by a system of informers, torture and courts. From March 1942 Norwegian churches were almost empty because the pastors refused to operate under Nasjonal Samling auspices. Under Quisling's plan all boys and girls between ten and eighteen were required to join the Nasjonal Samling and their teachers an equivalent organisation. When the teachers demurred, 1,300 of them were arrested. Norwegian workers were also drafted into a compulsory labour force. By 1943 it was clear to the Germans that the Norwegians were not merely erring, but hostile. As a result 700 university students and 271 'unreliable' policemen were rounded up and deported to concentration camps. But pirate broadcasts from the troublesome radio persisted in beaming out the opinions of Haakon VII.

Military activity against the Germans in occupied Norway was limited but obvious. The British launched commando raids, destroyed industrial plants and took back Norwegian volunteers to be trained to fight for the liberation of their country. The raids on the heavy water plant at Rjukan were the most spectacular of these operations but another group attached limpet mines to enemy shipping in Oslo. The collection of military intelligence continued throughout the war. News of German military and naval dispositions was sent by secret transmitters in the mountains. Resistance work was co-ordinated by the Milorg organisation and its supply of arms, instructors, radios, and couriers was in constant jeopardy from Gestapo infiltration as the war continued. When, in autumn 1944, retreating Germans devastated the Finnmark area, the Norwegians began to worry that they might suffer a scorched earth policy on their own territory. Few harboured illusions about the damage 350,000 German troops could do in an ugly mood if they were pulled out of Norway and directed home through Denmark.

On 7 May 1945 the Germans unconditionally surrendered, and within a month the Nygaardsvold government was back in Oslo with Haakon VII. The purge of collaborators began. Quisling was among the twenty-five Norwegians executed for war crimes.

The Swedish people were as helpless in 1939 as they had been in the Napoleonic era and their failure to aid the Finns, whose people they had governed as late as the early nineteenth century, or the Norwegians, from whom they were only constitutionally separated in the early twentieth, reflected not so much a renunciation of pan-Scandinavianist ideals as a response to the grim realities of power in their section of the north. In few places was gloom and despondency more marked than in the Swedish foreign ministry in 1939. Letters went out in the diplomatic bags instructing Swedish ambassadors to remember, when carrying out their conversations, that the situation in 1939 was very different from that which had existed in 1914. The secretary-general of the Ministry of Foreign Affairs pointed out that the idea of neutrality in the event of another conflict would differ from the neutrality that had existed between 1914 and 1918. If war broke out between the great powers the rules of international law could be regarded as non-existent. The military and political situation had changed to such an extent that the Baltic Sea could be expected to be dominated by German naval forces, and, with the development of air power, Sweden was more vulnerable than it had earlier been. It was in the interest of both groups involved – the Germans and the Italians and the British and the French – that Sweden should not be dragged into the war. Moreover, the Swedish military establishment was of a size sufficient to command respect and in Sweden internal unity was so great that there was little chance of a coup being organised and orchestrated by a fifth column. There was no Quisling, Clausen or Kuusinen in Stockholm.

The diplomatic instructions dealt with the German interests first. It was clear that Germany dreaded the prospect of encirclement and would require that Sweden be neutral at the very least. Germany had an important interest in obtaining raw materials from Sweden, particularly iron ore. But the Swedes thought that Germany could not reasonably expect Sweden to deprive itself of its own goods.

The Swedish understanding of the allied powers was also well founded. The Swedish foreign ministry considered that it would be tempting for them to try to compel Sweden to join the encircling chain, but by doing so the Anglo–French alliance would run the risk that Sweden would be subjugated by the Germans and that Swedish raw materials, especially iron ore, would be lost forever. There was no possibility that the allies would be able to get their navies into the Baltic, and therefore it was easy to persuade them that it would be better for Sweden to remain neutral and to continue to maintain its trading ties with Germany than for Sweden to be dragged into the war.

When war began, the Swedish foreign minister, Rickard Sandler, began immediate negotiations in London with a view to establishing a war-time trade policy. Sandler was an experienced and respected diplomat, having been a minister since the Social Democrats gained office in 1932. Swedish exports of iron-ore to Germany were one of the main stumbling blocks to an agreement with Britain, but the success of the negotiations was of fundamental importance in establishing Swedish neutrality over the next six years. The agreement allowed for continued trade to the allies and for the import of goods that were important to Sweden's survival. And this agreement, which was styled the '1939 War Trade Agreement', had an added attraction for the British because the Swedish government allowed the British to gain control of the Swedish merchant navy, except for those ships that Sweden needed for its own import/export trade.

At the same time it was clearly necessary for Sweden to establish a trade agreement with Germany. The Polish export market in coal and coke had disappeared and it was also going to become more difficult to obtain chemical fertiliser and agricultural and industrial machinery not made in Sweden. The Germans decided that they wanted to extend the mining of waters to deny the Baltic to British submarines, a strategy resisted by Sweden because it meant losing control of territorial waters that it had maintained for a century and a half. Swedish ships were being sunk on their way to England, and those on their way to Holland, Belgium and the United States were being stopped by the German Navy and searched for contraband as both Britain and Germany operated a blockade with equal success. In order to obtain the War Trade Agreement with Germany, the Swedes offered the Germans seven million tons of iron-ore in 1940, and the Germans laid mines in what had hitherto been Swedish territorial waters.

By Christmas 1939 the negotiations with the British and the Germans were concluded. Short announcements were issued and the press was asked to abstain from comment for the obvious reason that statements could prompt both the British and the Germans to investigate Sweden's undertakings with the other party. Although nobody in Stockholm was able to predict how long the war would last, agreements entered into in December 1939 with Britain and Germany could be assumed to guarantee the viability of the Swedish economy for the foreseeable future. Although both the belligerents acknowledged Sweden's policy of neutrality and were willing to permit Swedish trade with the outside world, neither of them was happy. Germany, for example, refused to accept the four-mile limit of Swedish territorial waters and Britain was disappointed with Sweden's exaggerated regard for Germany and its interest in short-term gains.

It would be wrong to suggest that Swedish-German relations during the early months of World War II were happy. The German minister in Stockholm, Prince Victor zu Wied, was called back to Berlin to report, a measure intended to express Berlin's displeasure with Stockholm, and Hitler and Göring were annoyed at the attitude of the Swedish government and the criticism in Swedish newspapers. Göring was the Germans' highest-ranking expert on Sweden. He could speak Swedish and was married to a Swede, Karin Fock. After Karin's death, the Germans tried to exaggerate her role as a symbol of Swedish-German co-operation and built a Wagnerian opera-style mausoleum to her memory in the hope that it would become a shrine. While the Swedes were less enthusiastic about this link than the Germans, they kept the avenues of communication open between Sweden and Germany through Göring and a Swedish industrialist working in Berlin, Birger Dahlerus.

As part of an even-handed approach the Swedish government put pressure on the British not to extend its naval operations into Norwegian waters, and the British *chargé d'affaires* in Stockholm, William Montagu-Pollock, was told bluntly at an early stage that if the British extended naval operations in Norwegian waters this would lead to the German occupation of Denmark and probably to the loss of independence for all Scandinavian countries. The Swedish diplomat, Erik Boheman, secretary-general of the foreign ministry 1938–45, added, 'I should have thought the British government had the fate of a sufficient number of small states on their conscience as it is.'

While diplomats prepared for a briefcase war, the first casualty was the foreign minister, Rickard Sandler, whose pro-Finnish stance during the Winter War was unacceptable to Prime Minister Hansson. Sandler left the government because he knew that the Swedes could not afford to antagonise both powers in their region, Russia and Germany, and that the Swedes had their hands full mollifying the Germans. Sandler was a focus for the friends of Finland; he collected money and arranged training and equipment for the few Swedish volunteers who went to Finland and fought in the Winter War. The cultural ties between Sweden and the Ostrobothnian, Åland and Turku areas of Finland were very close, but the Finnophiles were largely confined to the Conservatives, some of the university teachers and those Swedes with family ties in Finland. In December 1939, Hansson pledged that Sweden would give its northern neighbours the utmost material and humanitarian assistance, but many Finns remembered the Swedish failure to do more to help them against the oppressor from the east, a failure seized upon by the extreme Fennomen as yet another reason for bludgeoning the Swedish-speaking minority.

Hansson appointed Christian Günther as foreign minister in Sandler's place, and Günther disowned the slogan 'Finland's cause is ours', being content to act as a go-between in the negotiations between Finland and Russia that ended in the Peace of Moscow. As late as 1 February 1940, some Finns still expected military aid. Prime Minister Ryti asked Hansson for 20,000 Swedish volunteers in self-contained units, as the Finns, while sceptical of Anglo-French intentions, were confident that Sweden had never been an aggressor. Günther, who remained foreign minister until 1945, closed his ears to the request for military help and, in a neat piece of diplomatic duplicity, told Madame Kollontai that the Finns had come to Stockholm to seek peace in exchange for territorial concessions. The Russians appreciated Günther's efforts, and Molotov hinted that a quick resolution of the Winter War by diplomatic means would result in Russian support for Sweden's resumption of possession of the Åland Islands. This bribe was as unnecessary as it was counter-productive. On 17 February 1940 the king made a stirring speech on Finland's behalf, but Russian tanks in Karelia made the question of Swedish military assistance an academic one.

Within a month of the ending of the Winter War, the Swedes were faced with threats nearer home, as Denmark and Norway fell into German hands and the precarious aim of neutrality and prosperity was again threatened. After the end of the war the Swedish Army was gradually demobilised, and the government was caught napping by the intervention of the British and the Germans in Nordic affairs in April 1940. On 6 April Günther was asked whether the German naval and troop concentrations were new and disturbing. He replied to the parliamentary foreign policy committee that although they were new he could not yet say whether they were disturbing. On 8 April Sweden received news that the British had mined Norwegian territorial waters and later in the day it was reported that German warships and transports were sailing north through the Sound and the Kattegat and that a long column of German troops was on its way north through Schleswig towards the southern frontier of Denmark. The Swedish commander-in-chief asked for mobilisation in the south, but because the Swedish government underestimated the efficiency of the German thrust, mobilisation was incomplete when Germany occupied Denmark and took control of the biggest towns in Norway.

In April 1940 the Swedish government was convinced that Sweden did not have the strategic importance of Denmark, Norway and Finland and therefore would be able to remain outside the conflict. It was obvious that Russia had attacked Finland in order to seize Karelia and thereby defend the approach to Leningrad from overland assault. For the same reason, to prevent attack from the north, it was necessary for the Germans to capture Norway and Denmark and equally important for the British to take the four major harbours at Narvik, Trondheim, Bergen and Stavanger in Norway to protect their sea trade in the North Atlantic.

Sweden was left aside because the territory did not have the same strategic importance as its neighbours. Even so, the Swedish defence staff mobilised 320,000 men by mid-April and was clearly prepared to defend Sweden against a German attack if necessary. On 11 April 1940 Ribbentrop had assured the Swedish ambassador that Sweden would be left out of the action undertaken against its neighbours, and that Germany's main aim was to keep Sweden neutral. As recounted, an early test of Sweden's bona fides as a neutral power came over the proposed flight of the Norwegian monarch. When the Norwegian foreign minister, Halvdan Koht, asked if King Haakon and Crown Prince Olaf (who were planning to flee from the Germans across the Swedish frontier) could be given guarantees that they would be allowed to return to Norway, the Swedish government replied that although they were welcome in Sweden no such guarantees could be given. At the same time the British were told that should they cross the Norwegian-Swedish border their action would be resisted violently as indeed would be the case if the Germans did so.

In reality during the early years of the war Swedish neutrality was slanted in Germany's favour. From the beginning of the war with Norway, the Germans put pressure on Sweden to allow the passage of military supplies to their troops in Norway, and they said that in return they would give German weapons to the Swedish Army. The Swedish government agreed that from the end of April civilian goods, on a scale consistent with normal peace-time requirements, could be sent through Sweden. The Germans replied by threatening to restrict imports of vital supplies to Sweden and to prevent Swedish access to the Baltic. In the beginning of May, when the Netherlands were occupied and Belgium fell, the Swedish government did not underestimate the possibility that the Germans (in their mood of success) would also turn against Sweden. The first test of Swedish stomach came on 16 May when Ribbentrop asked in vain for the transit of a hundred railway cars with military equipment and clothing for the German troops in north Norway. The refusal was accepted for the time being. And the tricky question of how far the Swedes should help the Germans in the conquest of Norway was shelved when the Norwegian government capitulated.

No sooner had the Winter War ended than the Norwegian War commenced; no sooner had the Norwegian War ended than the Germans attacked Russia with Finland's help. There was no respite at the Swedish foreign ministry and no time for the usual niceties of parliamentary debate and consultation: the prime minister and foreign minister made all decisions on their own (as the constitution permitted in time of war). Parliament was rarely even summoned for the next five years, although the government did call some secret sessions to reassure itself that crucial decisions had been taken correctly. In the next years individual members of parliament had little chance to discuss with the prime minister or foreign minister the questions of foreign policy which, in any event, they were told little about. Not that there was anything surprising about that. In Finland, policy discussions were taken by an inner ring consisting of Mannerheim, Ryti, General K.R. Walden, Foreign Minister R.J. Witting and Prime Minister J.W. Rangell, and they too were unresponsive to public opinion and at times forced to act unconstitutionally.

The Swedish government thought that unless Sweden bent it would find itself a German state. The strength of Swedish neutrality was based on its expertise in the intelligence field and its capacity to anticipate developments in the Baltic area. In mid-April 1941, the Swedish military attaché in Helsinki reported that the Finnish and German general staffs were collaborating on a technical level and that the expectation in Helsinki was that if Germany attacked the Soviet Union the Finns could regain the territory lost by the Peace of Moscow without serious fighting, and would therefore be given a chance of establishing a more satisfactory frontier. At the same time, senior officers on the active list had recruited a Finnish volunteer battalion to fight for Germany. The Finnish government did nothing to oppose this force, which they considered was more of political than military value. The German military attaché in Helsinki told his Swedish counterpart that the Germans intended to attack Russia in June, and that in return for transit rights through Sweden, with the approval of the Finns, the Swedes could expect to gain the Åland Islands.

Before the beginning of the Continuation War, the Swedes had cracked the German diplomatic code and were able to read telegrams sent from Stockholm to Berlin. They knew that Finland had become a deployment area for the German troops and that 40,000 men were stationed in north Finland, east of Rovaniemi. The Germans also wanted to have permission to fly over Sweden and undertakings that airmen who made emergency landings would not find themselves and their aircraft impounded. The Swedes agreed and laid down a few conditions that they expected to be observed by Germans using Swedish railway tracks. Soldiers on leave were to travel without their weapons. Single travellers had to give notice. Leave traffic was to be a pendulum traffic and not used to reinforce German troops in Norway, although a limited number of troops were permitted to use Swedish railways to travel between Trondheim and Narvik.

When war broke out between Germany and Russia the Swedes re-affirmed their neutrality. But 106 trains transported the Englebrecht division across Swedish territory. Swedish troops armed with machine guns watched and oversaw the unarmed Germans entrain. No one was deceived. King Gustav had threatened to resign unless the Englebrecht division was allowed to move, and both he and the prime minister considered refusal of this request would have led to immediate seizure of Stockholm by the Germans. The Swedes also completed a minefield south of Åland that met a German field stretching from Lithuania and introduced further censorship to avoid displays of provocative public opinion. In London, Washington and Moscow, Sweden's concessions to Germany were regarded as the price to be paid for neutrality within the German sphere of influence and there was little attempt to try to change the direction of Swedish foreign policy.

By March 1942 the British Foreign Office's understanding of the situation in Sweden was expressed in this way: that the British government wanted the Swedes to be as united as possible, for that was the only hope of effectively resisting German demands for a German invasion. The British wanted to get as much as possible out of the Swedes in the war and get the Swedes to give Germany as little as possible. In World War II there were no neutral parties, there were only belligerents and non-belligerents and the latter trimmed their sails according to the strength of the winds blowing from the former. Accordingly, the British government was urged by the Foreign Office to press the Swedes relentlessly for what they wanted out of them, so that when the Swedes took the line of least resistance it would be in Britain's favour rather than in Germany's.

With the American entry into the war the Swedish diplomatic problems increased, and in 1942 and 1943 the Swedes faced a bewildering variety of decisions. As the British Foreign Office observed, it was in the nature of belligerents never to be satisfied, and once the Germans were on the run the Swedes were put under more and more pressure by the British and the Americans. Every act that was pro-British was used as a lever to obtain a further concession and so, from the end of German transit traffic in 1943 until May 1945, the Swedes bent their neutrality in a new direction, encouraged by the German defeat at El Alamein, the British and American landings in French North Africa, Russian offensives at Stalingrad, the invasion of Sicily and the fall of Mussolini.

The new direction was popular not merely on account of Swedish expediency. Jews flooding across from Denmark had told the Swedes what they might expect if Germany won the war. In 1944 the United States let the Swedes know that SKF ball-bearing plants (to take one example) would be bombed if they continued to prolong the war by making up production shortfalls for German factories that had been destroyed in mainland Europe.

As the Russians moved through the Baltic states during the spring of 1945 in pursuit of the Germans, the Swedes felt a new effect of the Soviet Union's war effort against Germany: 30,000 refugees from the Baltic states fled to Sweden to try to escape the consequences of their support for Hitler. In 1945, 149 Latvians, 7 Estonians and 11 Lithuanians compromised their putative refugee status by arriving in Sweden still wearing German military uniforms. The Russians immediately demanded that they be handed back. The Swedish king asked Stalin for mercy and was refused, and the terrified Balts were handed over in January 1946. Still in their German uniforms, they were dragged on to a Russian ship at Trelleborg, amid the first of many humanitarian demonstrations that have become a feature of Swedish life in this century. Rarely, however, has the violent drama of the Trelleborg deportations been matched. One of the Balts stabbed himself in the neck and bled to death on the wharf, the first casualty of the Cold War.

CHAPTER 7

The Social Democratic Harvest

The Cold War was particularly chilly in Scandinavia where the climate and latitude had a singular appropriateness. The Swedes were better off than their neighbours in Denmark and Norway and Finland, but World War II and its aftermath were to set back economic development and social reforms for a generation.

To greater or lesser degrees, all the Scandinavian states were at the mercy of the great powers in much the same way they had been in the Napoleonic era. When Russia emerged from the war as the master of an Eastern European network, the United States tried to counter the new strategic imbalance by beginning a fresh series of diplomatic relations. At their boldest, the United States initiatives took the form of Marshall Aid (the European Recovery Plan), and the inauguration of the North Atlantic Treaty Organisation.

Each of the Scandinavian states responded differently to the situation: Denmark and Norway, for example, were among the original signatories of NATO (along with Belgium, Canada, France, Iceland, Italy, Luxembourg, the Netherlands, Portugal, the United Kingdom and the United States), but Sweden and Finland remained aloof. Finland had little choice, but Sweden deliberately set out to enter the 1950s and the 1960s with its neutrality inviolate, believing that consistency at least was a virtue that might mitigate the psychological remorse that some Swedes suffered for their war role, characterised so often by their unsympathetic neighbours as marked by profiteering and self-interest.

Despite the shadow of the atomic bomb and, later, the development of new and more devastating nuclear weapons, it was during the period 1945–68 that Scandinavian capitalism reached its highest stage so far. The apparatus of the welfare state was improved to an extent undreamed of. Social engineering seemed to be on the brink of a breakthrough that the Scandinavians had hitherto only learned to expect from high technology in the electro-mechanical field. Enthusiasts, supporters and harsh critics of Scandinavia gathered in Stockholm, Oslo, Copenhagen and Helsinki to discuss the merits of the Scandinavian response to both internal problems, and to the great international crises: the Cold War, the Korean War, the Berlin airlift and the Middle East situation, the moves for an economic community in Europe and the unacceptable face of American imperialism in Vietnam. This was a mixed bag, and naturally the Scandinavians did not deal with all their problems coherently or successfully, but for every critic who claimed that Sweden, for example, was the home of the new totalitarianism of the welfare state, another supporter rose to praise the labour relations in the Volvo plant at Gothenburg or the Kockums shipyard at Malmö.

The Swedish economy was one of the wonders of the world, but it was based on protection and defence of the excellent local product at the expense of cheaper imports. Thus while L.M. Ericsson communications equipment was as first class as ASEA's electrical engineering products, and in many respects led the world, the two Swedish firms had a monopoly on the domestic market. The post-war development of the welfare state was carried on as Sweden's economy strengthened. Contributory old age pensions for all were granted from 1946, irrespective of income. In 1947 children's allowances were added, and ten years later a national referendum was held over the Social Democrats proposal to expand the state pension system by charging national superannuation to employers. The new pension would have guaranteed Swedish workers sixty-five per cent of their average wage calculated on the most productive fifteen years of their life. Such a comprehensive scheme took ten years to gain the necessary parliamentary majority. Educational reform began after the war ended.

The 1960s saw the gradual conformity of Swedish society to social democratic values. Most doctors preferred to leave private practice, and it began to seem as though soon only septuagenarians would charge fees, as the young medical practitioners conformed to community expectations that they take salaried posts in the expanding hospital system. By 1968 in Sweden mental illness was accepted as normal, in much the same way as the Californians at that time regarded divorce.

Just as technicians joined the workers to support the social democratic state, so cultural craftsmen joined the May Day procession for the first time in 1962, and a Department of Cultural Affairs was created to direct their labours in the vineyards of art, music, drama, cinema and the dance. Jan Troell, Bo Widerberg, Birgit Nilsson and Berit Lindholm were launched but, unlike Greta Garbo and Ingrid Bergman, they flew with a state subsidy in a country rapidly developing into a sheltered workshop.

Others, less kindly, have described it as totalitarian, and indeed the totalitarian model had a superficial appeal in describing Swedish development as the Cold War years stretched to the Vietnam era. Ronald Huntford in *The New Totalitarians* is the best representative of this group of critics of Sweden. Huntford argued that Sweden became the apotheosis of the ideas expressed in George Orwell's novel *1984* of a state where economic security led to totalitarianism. In this provocative assessment, Huntford claimed that Sweden was always the basic supplier of material for the wars of Europe. From the time of sail Sweden provided maritime nations with pine and spruce. When copper prices rose, Sweden obliged with supply. Cultural opportunism followed trade. During the Napoleonic era French culture was aped, to be followed by German and Prussian models when Bismarck's Germany was predominant. German was Sweden's second language until the collapse of Germany and the emergence of the United States as a super power swept German culture from Sweden, substituting Americana instead. In a long catalogue Huntford attributed to the Swedes only such virtues as skill in engineering innovation and bureaucratic expertise. The fault with Swedish society, according to Huntford, was not only that it was totalitarian: it was also medieval. The film *The Seventh Seal* was a typical example of modern Swedish cinema, in so far as individual values and spontaneity were overshadowed by a dark, oppressive sense of destiny, in a land, Huntford concluded, untouched by Shakespeare, Boccaccio, Cervantes or Pushkin.

In the period 1945–68 Swedes built up standards of ostentatious consumption and per capita incomes which rivalled those of the United States. Those few who wished to drop out immediately after the war, however, were denied the pleasures of existentialism. The heirs and followers of Kierkegaard met not in the cold cafés of Stockholm but at boulevard bistros in the sunshine of Paris. Nevertheless, if the Swedes lacked a Jean-Paul Sartre, they did at least possess an Ingmar Bergman and a Per Olav Enquist. In 1968 Enquist summed up the problems of the period by publishing *The Legionaires*, a novel about the deportation of the Balts at the end of World War II. In *The Legionaires*, Enquist observed that the Swedes possessed the world's only portable consciences, travelling the globe as professional moralists.

The most influential professional moralist of them all was Ingmar Bergman, whose work was obsessed with exploring the Swedish psyche. In 1946, he was utterly indifferent to politics or social matters. He worked in Gothenburg at the Municipal Theatre with a group who included, as only Sweden could, old ex-Nazis, Jews and anti-Nazis. Bergman turned from conventional theatre to writing screenplays and directing films. As he later described it, while he was making *This Can't Happen Here* in 1950, a film about the war, he bumped into, as he put it, 'the real thing'—Baltic refugees. He realised that what he was playing at, to them was grim reality. It took some years, however, before his new social conscience was expressed overwhelmingly in his films. The moment of awakening coincided with a protest stoppage of the Swedish film industry. Bergman then had three families to support and six children. His 'spotty-faced period' (his phrase) came to an end with the first of a series of films that turned him into a cult figure: *Summer with Monica* (1952), *Sawdust* and *Tinsel* (1953), *A Lesson in Love* (1954), *Journey into Autumn* (1955), *Smiles of a Summer Night* (1955), *The Last Couple Out* (1956), *The Seventh Seal* (1956), *Wild Strawberries* (1957), *So Close to Life* (1957), *The Face* (1958), *The Virgin Spring* (1959), *The Devil's Eye* (1959), *Through the Glass Darkly* (1961), *The Pleasure Garden* (1961), *Winter Light* (1962), *The Silence* (1963), *Now About These Women* (1964), *Hour of the Wolf* (1966), and *The Shame* (1967).

The amazing output of Ingmar Bergman was produced by the juxtaposition of social democracy's cinematographic arm, Svensk Filmindustri, and Bergman's own band of technicians and artists: Sven Nykvist, Bibi Andersson, Max von Sydow and, last and most literate, as the author of an autobiography in her own right, Liv Ullmann, with whom Bergman shared his paradise island of Fårö for a time. With so many films, and an innovative technique that recalled the French new wave, Bergman was profitable, if not always understood, at the box office. With *The Shame* Bergman, Nykvist, Liv Ullmann, Max von Sydow and the Swedish film industry broke new sociological ground. *The Shame* was explicitly concerned with what would have happened in Sweden if the Nazis had occupied it. Bergman's chief preoccupation was, as always, personal, but he was triggered into making that particular film on the eve of one of the most momentous years in the twentieth century – 1968 – by seeing a documentary film from Vietnam. It did not show war scenes, but rather the third parties to the war. Bergman was taken by one horrible shot that showed two peasants, an old woman and an old man, holding a half-starved cow. Meanwhile, in the background, an American military helicopter was starting. Bergman saw the cow pass water and try to gallop away. The tough old woman clung to the cow and disappeared with it in a cloud of dust. The old man was left in tears staring at the roaring helicopter and the disappearing pair. Bergman wrote the script of *The Shame* in 1967, before the escalation of the Vietnam war or the occupation of Czechoslovakia. In it he asked an unpopular question in Sweden: what sort of situation was needed to turn Swedes from good Social Democrats into active Nazis? *The Shame's* pessimistic answer, with its characters lacking an ideology that would serve as an antidote to conformity under a totalitarian regime, was heavily criticised.

The collective weight of Swedish shame built up slowly – shame for not helping the Finns was replaced by shame for turning their backs on the Norwegians, for not standing up against the Germans, for sending some Balts to certain death – until shame and guilt seemed to be the natural state of the Swedish conscience. As the problem increased and sin became the national preoccupation, the social democratic state chose to expunge it by declaring old sins no longer sinful, and permissiveness blossomed into a form of pornographic expressiveness that achieved its apotheosis in Stockholm and Copenhagen, but not in Oslo and Helsinki, where the peasant puritanism of the Norwegians and the alcoholic athleticism of the Finns sublimated the guilty fixations of their neutral and collaborating neighbours.

Guilt at their war role was not the only problem faced by Swedes in the immediate post-war years. In July 1945 the coalition government, which had been responsible for the conduct of the war, was dissolved by Hansson, and the Social Democrats governed in their own right. But Hansson led Sweden for only a year before his death, in October 1946, precipitated a constitutional crisis when King Gustav V refused to accept Ernst Wigforss as prime minister. In Wigforss's place the Social Democrats chose Tage Erlander: Erlander was a mathematical physicist who had broadened his outlook with a social science degree. When he became prime minister he had one year's experience as a minister, but his grasp of sociological change was sufficient for him to guide the Swedish Social Democrats until the accession in 1969 of Olof Palme, when a new era demanded a new broom.

There was outstanding growth in post-war Sweden, which can be attributed in part to the economic strategy of Gunnar Myrdal. He set about organising the harvest due to the labour movement, which had for thirty years sunk its interest in class warfare for the greater good of the progress of Sweden. Myrdal moved from the Swedish trade ministry in 1947 to become secretary-general of the United Nations Economic Commission for Europe, a recognition of Sweden's pre-eminence among economic planners. Myrdal had the good fortune to work with an economy unscathed by war. No Swedish factories were bombed, moved with their workers to an entirely different region, or sabotaged. On the contrary, the war years were boom years for entrepreneurs and blue-collar Swedes. The only setback to the Swedish takeoff was that Sweden's trading partners were in a parlous state in 1945, and until the other Scandinavian, German, British and general European markets improved, the productive capacity of the Swedish economy was under-exploited.

'The Swedish economic miracle' was based on an institutionalised response to problems. The chief means of controlling the economy was the Labor Market Board, which used its investment funds to encourage investment at the approach of recession and to restrict investment when the economy was buoyant. The investment fund legislation was set up in 1938 and amended in 1947, 1955 and 1963, so that every Swedish company was permitted to set aside forty per cent of its profits before tax to an investment fund. Forty-six per cent of the money was kept in a blocked account in the Bank of Sweden, and the funds could generally be spent only after government authorisation or that of the Labor Market Board. The funds grew from 414 million crowns in 1955 to 3,345 million crowns in 1965, and the Labor Market Board used its money during the recessions of 1958, 1962 and 1967, and on such worthy projects as training the handicapped and promoting regional development.

It was little use planning to redistribute wealth in the interest of workers in Sweden, if the state lacked a coherent foreign policy in the era of the atom. So Sweden adapted quickly, joined the United Nations, where its nationals, with their indigenous bureaucratic expertise, soon filled key positions. Typical of the model Swedish bureaucrat was Dag Hammarskjöld, who had an impeccable pedigree for the high world office he was to hold. Dag Hammarskjöld spent his early teenage years as son of the Swedish prime minister, and between 1914 and 1917 the Hammarskjöld family was privy to the deepest agonies and benefits of being a neutral. Dag Hammarskjöld studied law and economics at Uppsala and Stockholm universities, and in 1936, after a period as professor of political economy, joined the civil service as permanent secretary to the ministry of finance and later president of the board of the Bank of Sweden. The Social

Democrats appointed Hammarskjöld to oversee international financial and economic questions. After a short apprenticeship as permanent secretary-general of the ministry of foreign affairs, Hammarskjöld was elected to the Swedish cabinet in 1951, and as deputy foreign minister directed Swedish policy in the United Nations. His talents stood out in the 1950s and, in 1953, he was elected secretary-general of the United Nations. Hammarskjöld's experiences had taught him that Swedish neutrality could best be guaranteed in the years ahead if Sweden took a responsible role in world affairs, and it was not surprising that Swedish troops were sent to Korea as peacekeepers.

Hammarskjöld was the most important neutral diplomat in the bitter fighting between UN members during the Suez Canal crisis in 1956, and for the success of his good offices he was rewarded by re-election to the secretary-generalship of the United Nations. He was tragically killed in an air crash on a peace mission to the Congo on 18 September 1961. Many Swedes were distressed but not surprised to read accounts of Hammarskjöld's internal life bared in a work entitled *Markings*, which was published three years after his death and gave details of what Hammarskjöld described (in a typically Swedish metaphor) as his 'negotiations' with God.

Negotiation was to be a key skill of the new internationalist Swedish diplomatic cadres; Gunnar Jarring, for example, was given the task of trying to stem the growing breakdown of relations between Israel and the Arab nations.

When the Cold War began, Sweden was in as good a position as any nation to anticipate the coming clash between the forces of east and west. Two Swedish Catalina air force planes that strayed into the wrong airspace were shot at by the Russians. Swedish diplomats knew that to counterbalance the new power and menace of a victorious Russia it was necessary to bolster a divided Germany and to build up the capacity of German industry to mobilise if necessary to counter a blitzkrieg from the east. The Swedes also understood that the Americans would remain in Europe for the foreseeable future. But, since their own military strength was considerable, they preferred not to compromise their neutrality and stood aloof from NATO.

As part of the Social Democrat peacetime policy of encouraging freedom of expression, a lively extra-parliamentary debate raged about the issue of joining NATO. The *Dagens Nyheter* newspaper urged Sweden to follow Denmark and Norway into NATO, but others pointed out that such a decision would possibly provoke Russia into conquest of Finland to protect its eastern flank. The realities of Sweden's geopolitical position made neutrality inevitable. Although the Swedes coyly described themselves as a hedgehog with spines pointed in all directions, the homely metaphor was out of place. With squadrons of SAAB and Viggen jet fighters hidden in the woods, a highly trained army with sophisticated weapons and a twice-demonstrated capacity to mobilise the economy on a war footing, the cost of attacking Sweden was soon recognised as not likely to be worth the benefit.

Like the hedgehog, the Swedes were remarkably successful in their early post-war adaptation. Their foreign and domestic policy-makers evolved quick and appropriate responses to the United Nations, the question of Scandinavian defence, NATO, and at the same time perfected social institutions that approximated to the ideals striven for in the 1930s. By the normal criteria Sweden was next to the United States in affluence in the western world, and the economic miracle seemed to be assured of continuation, as Social Democrats influenced policy and administration from the boards of banks, shipyards, engineering works and all the important instruments of Swedish economic development. The situation was summed up as follows: capitalism provided and the state distributed.

Rudolf Meidner was one of the architects of the new philosophy which saw ownership of enterprises as immaterial.

Meidner was the leading social democrat ideologue, and a director of the Stockholm Enskilda Bank: he reassured his shareholders that although they were unable to exercise power in the day-to-day decision-making of their institution, the dividends were safely entrusted to the expert managers who were their employees and could be entrusted with control. By then Sweden had gained a reputation as one of the most socialised states in the west. By the criterion of ownership of the means of production, capitalism had a stranglehold. By 1968 only six per cent of Swedish industry was in government hands, and 200,000 employees on the government payroll, amounting to seven per cent of gross national product. Co-operatives (a feature of Scandinavian economic organisation) accounted for a mere five per cent, the rest of Swedish industry being in the hands of private shareholders.

There were clouds on the horizon in the 1960s, however, although few Swedes looked up and in that direction. In the 1960s the Swedes established their first nuclear energy plant at Agesta, near Stockholm, and began to produce electricity through a technology that was to become more controversial in the next decade as concern for the environment developed into a political issue. In a typically Swedish manner, one of the most powerful families in Sweden, the Wallenbergs, entered into a joint venture with the Social Democrat government to develop nuclear energy. ASEA-ATOM was designed to run as a 50:50 joint operation between the state and an industrial giant, which together pooled their resources to manufacture nuclear reactors. In Sweden, until 1968, many things were 50:50. The new left, however, was gradually becoming disenchanted with the way in which a large percentage of the private sector's wealth was in the hands of a few families, of which the Wallenbergs were the best, or perhaps the worst, example.

In the 1960s the Wallenbergs owned a large interest in

seventy corporations with over 180,000 employees, (almost a fifth of those employed in private industry) and had a majority interest in Svenska Maskinverken (heavy industrial equipment). They also had dominating interests in Atlas Copco, L.M. Ericsson, SKF, Alfa Laval, Elektrolux, Scania-Vabis trucks, SAAB jet planes and automobiles, and had diversified into matches, tramways, investment funds, steel mills, iron works, light industrial equipment, disposable nappies and department stores, and they controlled one of the largest banks in Sweden, the Enskilda. While the Wallenbergs and their fellow directors were prosperous, and divided the spoils equitably, the critics' cries of 'monopoly owns Sweden' fell largely on deaf ears. But when external pressures on the Swedish economy contracted the room to manoeuvre and the profitability of Swedish private enterprise began to fade, the disillusion with big business became more general, and spilled over to implicate the great political party, the Social Democrats, who had fostered the relationship. The collaborators who designed the 50:50 state went down fighting. In the early 1960s they had tried to form an economic trading group to rival the Common Market and Swedish neutrality was abandoned, in at least one area, when Sweden joined the European Free Trade Association, EFTA, in 1960 and tried to enter the European Economic Community as an associate member in 1961.

Denmark was no more successful than Sweden in cushioning the pressures of the 1950s and the 1960s, and began the post-war years in an unsound position. The war ended with Denmark deprived of the luxury of factories in full production, and facing the problems of a combatant nation: how to deal with the solid citizens who had become re-defined as war criminals, how to cope with the war criminals who had been re-defined as solid citizens, and how to reconstruct society to face the problems of the Cold War era and the 1960s. It is ironic that Denmark, which suffered less than Norway in the occupation, dealt out the death penalty with much more severity than the Norwegians. Perhaps the Danes felt that severity in sentencing would deflect attention from their earlier supine acceptance of model protectorate status.

On 5 May 1945 Buhl was reinstalled as prime minister, not according to constitutional procedures, but in the spirit of necessity that governed when Denmark faced post-war uncertainty with a large war debt of 8,000 million crowns and economic pressure heightened by the need to repeal all the German legislation of the occupation period. Elections were held in October 1945, and the Danish Social Democrats were still the largest single party represented. But with only one-third of the members, and lacking the necessary aura of moral probity (their self-righteousness having been dented by the swift acceptance of German hegemony in 1940), the left wing drifted towards communism and the Agrarian Liberals formed the government led by Knud Kristensen.

Denmark moved towards the Cold War era with eighteen communists in Parliament, the party members basking in Stalin's liberation of Danish soil and Stalin's prompt propriety in leaving immediately the work of cleaning up fascists had been finished. But Kristensen no sooner moved into the prime minister's office than he was faced with another round of Schleswig–Holstein problems. His personal prestige was high, having demonstrated good sense and patriotism by turning a blind eye to Scavenius's administration and standing out against draconian punishments for Denmark's war criminals, but the Schleswig-Holstein issue brought him down. History repeated itself, as although some Danes argued that the border boundary ought to be left at its 1945 point, chauvinistic Danes tried to move the border south and incorporate Schleswig into Denmark. Knud Kristensen, Christmas Möller and the Danish Union Party brought the crisis to the point where the British government, which had an occupation army in German Schleswig, demanded an unequivocal policy statement on the matter, and Kristensen's administration, being unable to give one, fell on the issue.

On 28 October 1947, the Social Democrats formed a minority government under Hans Hedtoft and, given a huge shot in the arm by Marshall Aid, began to copy Swedish patterns of social organisation. Marshall Aid began to trickle in 1948, but by 1953, as the Cold War intensified, US$278 million had been given to Denmark to bolster American influence. Hedtoft was a resistance hero to his party and had the three major tasks of reviving the Danish economy with the Marshall Aid bonanza, working out a foreign policy and defence programme to meet the realities of power as Russia increased its strength in the Baltic region, and trying to continue with the reforming spirit of social democracy. In 1949 Hedtoft steered through parliament a Small Holdings Act in the tradition of those passed in the 1890s and after World War I. Like its two predecessors in 1899 and 1919, the new legislation continued the process of subdivision of large estates and the increase in freehold farms. Unlike Norway, the Danes could farm ninety per cent of their countryside, and by the 1960s seventy-five per cent was used for agriculture. But Hedtoft worked to increase industrial production and reduce Denmark's reliance on agriculture. This policy was successful. Chemical and metal industry exports took their place alongside Danish farm products, and the country became recognised as more than a producer of beer, butter and bacon.

Hedtoft, who was thrown out by the voters over the issue in 1950, had the problem of drawing up new guidelines for Danish defence. This involved cutting the links with the Soviet Union. Public opinion in Denmark was in favour of a western alliance, especially after the communist coup in February 1948 in Czechoslovakia, which resulted in the virtual ostracism of Danish party members. When Hedtoft's attempt to form a defence alliance with Sweden broke down, there was little alternative but to face the fact that, for Denmark, neutrality was impossible and that the best hope of survival came from joining

NATO, which Denmark did in April 1949.

Hedtoft was defeated on the technical matter of butter rationing but was pleased to leave the helm at a time of increased buffeting, when the fruits of social democracy were becoming more difficult to pluck. It fell to the Conservatives, led by Erik Eriksen, to carry out the non-socialist necessities of rearmament, increasing direct and indirect taxation and assaulting imports and inflation by tariffs and restrictive banking procedures. Compulsory savings were introduced, and by 1953 the economy had improved to such an extent that the electorate considered it sociologically appropriate for the Social Democrats to govern again. Hedtoft became prime minister at a time when the last vestige of the aristocratic constitution, which had been under pressure since the days of the enlightenment and the French Revolution, was swept away, and Denmark's parliamentary system was reformed to comprise a single chamber house containing one hundred and seventy-nine seats: one hundred and seventy-five for Denmark, two for the Faeroes and two for Greenland. Female succession to the crown was permitted and, in a more important change, the voting age for parliamentary elections reduced from twenty-five to twenty-three years.

In the 1960s Denmark began to reassess its traditional alliances in trade and defence. A temporary thaw in the Cold War allowed a Scandinavian visit by N.S. Khrushchev, prime minister of the Soviet Union, after the Danish prime minister Jens Otto Krag had visited to try to work out a Dano-Russian trade agreement. The Russians tactfully avoided complaint about Denmark's membership of NATO and realised that the Danes were hedging their bets because their agricultural trade was likely to be damaged in the unsettled *mêlée* that characterised national rivalry inside EFTA. Krag again visited Russia in October 1965, and was able to get contracts for the Danish shipping construction firm of Burmeister and Wain to build four refrigerated cargo vessels for the Russian trade.

Goulash diplomacy had its price, and while the Danes received 100 million crowns for their export efforts, Krag joined Aleksei Kosygin in a communiqué that led American intelligence officers in Washington to doubt the resolve of their northern NATO ally: Krag declared that the Danish government did not intend to allow nuclear weapons to be stationed on its territory and called for a quick solution of the Vietnam crisis on the principles laid down in the Geneva agreement of 1954.

In many respects, Denmark's economy was the most vulnerable to international crises and when the Arab-Israeli war began in June 1967, the Danes were uneasy. They realised that their membership of NATO, despite their disclaimers, would inevitably result in their participation in the wider war that threatened if the super powers became involved. The devaluation of sterling threw the Danish economy into a state of shock. The Danes followed suit with an eight per cent devaluation, hoping that their farming industry would survive. The balance of trade worsened to such an extent that the Danish parliament considered only membership of the EEC could save them. On 11 May 1967, the parliament voted one hundred and fifty to twenty to apply, with Great Britain and the other EFTA members, for membership.

By then, disillusionment with social democracy was beginning to become established not only in the enemy camp but among the supporters of Danish state socialism. When the Social Democrat Party supported increased defence expenditure concomitant with Denmark's membership of NATO, pacifist radicals began to defect from the party. Moreover, the Social Democrat bureaucrats were unable to come up with an answer to inflation. During 1961 wages and salaries rose by fifteen per cent, pensions by nine per cent and production by seven per cent and the government's only response was to increase taxes. A thinktank of economics professors, employee and employer representatives, bankers, businessmen and farmers met as the

Economic Council, but their best counsel was an ineffectual incomes policy which indexed wages and profits to economic development. Even so, the Danes pressed on with social reform legislation, creating and improving the benefits paid by the state to the unemployed in 1960, the disabled in 1964 and invalids in 1968–69. Public health insurance was in the hands of state-recognised health insurance societies, and unemployment schemes were state financed. In 1964 the old age pension was reviewed and changes made to the law that allowed for phasing out of reductions in the pensions on the basis of other income, and a more Swedish-style system was planned to be phased in by 1970 for all people over sixty-seven.

Nevertheless, until the Arab-Israeli war and the first sterling devaluation, the 1960s were, generally speaking, years of relative prosperity in Denmark. Danes basked in the luxury of imitating their Swedish neighbour. They played a greater part in international affairs and sent peace-keeping troops to Cyprus for the United Nations. At Carlsberg brewery the riches overflowed. The Danish workers were given a free allowance of three and a half litres of beer a day. The next generation, with its concern for preventative medicine, was to discover the damage to the human constitution from such generosity. At this time, however, many young Danes began to feel almost physical revulsion against capitalism. Their protests were to take bizarre forms in later years but, in the early 1960s, they manifested their non-conformity by voting for the Danish Communist Party. The SF, as it was called, was formed in 1959 by Axel Larsen, and it began its drive for votes with the popular slogan 'out of NATO', regarding itself as Marxist–Leninist but not Stalinist, and appealing so much to the voter that by 1966 it held twenty seats in the Danish parliament.

By the mid-1960s one of the last but not the least of the casualties of World War II was becoming obvious. Social democracy was under attack and at the other end of the spectrum the monarch was tolerated rather than venerated. Christian X died in 1947 and was succeeded by Frederick IX, who made a virtue of necessity by travelling around Copenhagen on public transport. Christian X died after a period of public ill health, but his prospects for recovering were not improved by the growing realisation that people were comparing him unflatteringly to his brother, Haakon VII.

Haakon VII himself exhibited no trace of sibling rivalry when he returned in triumph to Norway after the German surrender. He did not need to. Although his talks on the BBC had sometimes bored and often irritated his fellow Norwegians, he had fought a heroic war, being bombed, machine-gunned and rescued. The contrast between the two kings' roles was to be echoed in their nations' response to the problems of the next twenty years.

Haakon VII returned to a Norway in which the ground had been taken by the Germans, but the spirit of the people had not been conquered. In 1945 the Norwegian Labour Party secured a clear parliamentary majority for the first time. The new prime minister, Einar Gerhardsen, had spent most of the war in prison, having been captured while working in the resistance. Gerhardsen was a true son of labour (his father had worked on the roads in Oslo) and in 1945 the stage seemed set for a massive redistribution of national wealth and resources to the working class. Unfortunately, the nation was poor, disorganised and its leaders easily diverted (like characters in an Ibsen play) by peripheral issues. Typical of the problems that bogged down reforms in other areas was that of the rivalry between various forms of orthography, spelling and pronunciation. When Norway was liberated, the Labour Party set about dismantling the German veneer, and in 1949 set up a language commission to plan future strategy. British and Swedish practices were preferred to German–Danish ones. The partisans in the language debate were as fierce as the members of the resistance, and by 1959 the battle was so serious that the makers of official policy were outraged to be told, by the Norwegian translator of *My Fair Lady*, that it was Eliza Doolittle and not Henry Higgins who set linguistic norms in Norway.

Despite the tension between the need to govern a war-ravaged economy and the need to keep parochial issues to the fore, the Norwegian government made firm decisions in the immediate post-war years. On 8 May 1945, the state took over many of the functions hitherto left to market forces and private enterprise. Although the Labour Party had seventy-six seats of the one hundred and fifty in the parliament, Prime Minister Einar Gerhardsen did not hesitate to use his slender margin to direct all the major areas of economic policy: manpower, materials, imports and exports, investment and prices. New currency was issued to replace that hoarded by profiteers. The Gerhardsen measures were originally intended to be temporary, but the series of international crises that led Norway into NATO also made it necessary to keep a tight rein on the management of the economy.

Gerhardsen's Labour Party governed Norway until 1951 when he stood aside, saying that he was inclined to entrust the administration of Norway to fresh hands. He rested until 1955 when his stand-in, Oscar Torp, resigned, leaving it to Gerhardsen to introduce a deflationary budget in the world-wide recession that followed the boom years of the Korean War. It was Gerhardsen who began to introduce measures that were out of step with Norwegian Labour ideology. The bank rate was increased with dramatically adverse effects on the working class, and general disillusionment began to mount about the Labour Party's handling of the economy, especially as its failures were reflected in unemployment and inflation. Despite the setback caused by the invasion of Hungary in 1956, the new left began to prepare for the time when it could fill the power vacuum developing in Norwegian politics from the lack of a credible socialist alternative. A crucial stage was reached in 1957, when a Labour Party conference voted to disallow the stationing of nuclear weapons on Norwegian soil and the party bureaucracy refused to take the necessary steps. The example of the Danish Marxists was followed in Norway and on 16 April 1961 the Socialist People's Party, which contested the elections and held the balance of power in the Norwegian Parliament, was formed. The SPP drew its main support from the radical disenchanted young, and the attack on nuclear weapons was coupled with pressure for a change in public opinion on Norway's NATO role.

The 1960s saw a continued dilution of the influence of the Labour Party. Gerhardsen was thrown out of office in 1963 when the SPP withdrew its support from the Labour Party after the exposure of bureaucratic ineptitude and corruption and a series of mining accidents. In 1962 an explosion at the King's Bay coal mine in Spitzbergen cost twenty-one lives and although the official inquiry did not produce evidence of culpable negligence, the head of the Ministry's Bureau of Mining was proceeded against.

When the SPP withdrew its support from the Labour Party, the Gerhardsen ministry fell. The constitution did not allow for elections to be held immediately, so a fracas developed in which the non-socialist parties attempted to form a coalition, only to find that the best practical course was for the Labour Party to govern as a caretaker regime until the next elections. The defeat of the Norwegian Labour Party in the parliamentary elections of 1965 was the first significant reverse for Scandinavian Social Democrats, but it was not to be the last. The Labour Party was unaccustomed to opposition. It had governed Norway from 1935 until the Quisling-Terboven regime and, except for a period of four weeks in 1963, the Labour Party held office continuously since 1945. Per Borten formed a coalition of anti-labour forces and was to have the task of government reassigned to him by the electorate in 1968.

In 1965 the Social Democrats in Denmark, Sweden and Finland looked warily in Norway's direction, as well they might. Deep community changes had occurred in Scandinavia since the end of World War II and it was clear that social democracy was no longer sociologically appropriate. Just as an earlier generation in the nineteenth century had rejected the idea that efficient foreign government was better than national government, the voters in 1965 declared that they were not convinced that Social Democrat government was necessarily good. Neither the Conservatives nor the Labour Party could deal with the economic problems facing Norway. Nor were the reforms of the Borten era anything like as comprehensive as those in Sweden. In Norway credit restriction was the order of the day. A balance of payments problem proved menacing. Norway depended extensively on its merchant shipping for foreign exchange. Huge tanker fleets that were being commissioned at Norwegian dockyards were one of the important strategic weapons in Borten's private-enterprise solution. Norway had the world's fourth largest merchant tonnage in 1966: eighteen million tons. The Norwegian flag flew on super oil tankers that filled the commercial gap created by the Arab-Israeli war and the closing of the Suez Canal.

The next generation were to find over-expansion in oil tankers a liability when world demand slowed as a result of decisions taken in the Middle East but, in the mid-1960s, the merchant navy was as important as EFTA in keeping Norway prosperous. From 1967 as part of the Social Democrat pay-off, Borten's government introduced Gerhardsen's 'people's pension scheme', which was based on earnings and modelled on the Swedish one. In 1968, the working week was cut from forty-five to forty-two and a half hours, so the gathering of the harvest had room for increased momentum.

The Norwegians were not only concerned with extra-Scandinavian relations but also tried to develop closer links with their neighbours by helping with the creation of a new airline, Scandinavian Airlines System. SAS was a company floated by Sweden, Norway and Denmark and, by a shrewd marketing policy, it developed as one of the world's leading airlines, with a network of lucrative routes based on Copenhagen and self-conscious promotion stressing Viking navigation feats, polar routes, open sandwiches and blonde air hostesses. SAS found it extremely difficult to get rights to overfly the Soviet Union, and indeed relations with Russia were a matter of extreme delicacy for the Norwegians as they tried to tread a path between the great powers. The extent of NATO installations in Norway was of great concern to Russia because Norway, like Finland, shared a common boundary. Immediately after World War II the Russians tried to conclude a defence treaty with Norway over the Spitzbergen Islands. The Russians felt threatened not only by the Norwegian military fortifications of Spitzbergen, but also by the Norwegian foreign office which was, for historical reasons, moving westwards in its search for alliances.

The NATO commitment in Norway had a front line air to it. The northern European command of NATO was near Oslo. Confirmation of the danger in Norway's role was given to the new left of the SPP when Gary Powers' U.2 spyplane was shot down over the Urals by a Russian missile on 1 May 1960. Powers was captured alive, and revealed on interrogation that after his high-altitude intelligence-gathering flight he was sched-uled to land in northern Norway. The Russians made it clear that in the event of nuclear war Powers' proposed landing airbase would be a prime target and neither they nor Norwegian public opinion was convinced by Norwegian officials' denials that they knew nothing about U.2 flights. While the Norwegian foreign ministry dressed down the American ambassador in Oslo, the Russians pointed out that the Norwegians were 'collaborators with the US imperialists' – a style of abuse that was to gain a wider acceptance as the 1960s ended.

In October 1967, King Olaf V (who had succeeded Haakon VII when he died, aged eighty-five, ten years earlier) delivered an official attack on the United States' bombing of North Vietnam, demanding on the government's behalf that it should stop, and anti-American demonstrations began in the streets of Oslo, just as they were beginning in Stockholm, Copenhagen and Helsinki. Per Borten was prepared to sit on the doorstep of his own home and discuss the Vietnam War with young demonstrators, explaining as he went along the delicate nature of Norway's foreign policy, the implications of the souring of the American dream and what weight Russian views held in his government.

Informality was one of the keynotes of relationships between the government and the people in post-war Scandinavia. One president of the republic of Finland was happy to discuss foreign policy with any joggers who could match his pace. The Red Army Choir opened post-war cultural relations with Finland and, although by 1980 the proximity of Russia was more usually announced to the soft strains of the Borodin Quartet, the Finns never doubted the precariousness of their independence. From 1945 to 1968, the relaxing grasp of the Russian fist was the most important factor in Finnish domestic and international affairs, however much Finns and Finnophiles might have wished it otherwise. For in 1944 the Finnish Reds gained the position they had lost in the civil war. The Communist Party of Finland, outlawed in 1930, was re-established, and its 1,200 members reorganised to form a more popularly acceptable front: the Finnish Peoples' Democratic Association (SKDL), which took up the ground left by the Social Democrats. At the same time the Patriotic People's Movement (IKL), which had been the corresponding quasi-fascist front in the 1930s, and held fourteen seats in the 1933 parliament, vanished as an outlawed organisation along with the Civil Guards and the women's auxiliaries.

Parliamentary government was conducted by seventeen minority ministries in as many years, but whereas such veering would have caused chaos elsewhere in Scandinavia, the firm hand of successive presidents, Mannerheim, Paasikivi and Kekkonen, and the administrative expertise of their government departments, usually resulted in relatively small changes of policy, all tending in one direction: the growth of Finnish autonomy out of the shadow of Russia. When the Allied Control Commission was set up in Helsinki to supervise the armistice conditions, it was under the control of a Russian, A.A. Zhdanov. Zhdanov worked hand in glove with Paasikivi, who directed Finnish foreign policy in the crucial years, first as prime minister (November 1944) and later as president. On 19 October 1944, the punishment of war criminals began. The Finnish military high command was purged and, on 23 August 1945, the government introduced retroactive legislation that sent President Ryti and a distinguished group to prison. Ryti was imprisoned, as were J.W. Rangell, Edwin Linkomies, Henrik Ramsay and Väinö Tanner, but all were released with their status enhanced by martyrdom in the national interest once the thaw in Finnish-Russian relations began.

In 1945 there were important elections and important publications. That year Tove Jansson produced her first Moomin book. The allegory was direct and striking. A typical drawing from Tove Jansson's initial period showed a group of Moomins tossed about in a storm. Their dinghy sailed towards a trough, while waves twice as high as the mast curved and rippled. On the scum bubbles of the crest were demonic figures. Lightning forked, the sky was dark, and only two gorgeous mermaids swimming in the water suggested that the Moomins might survive. They not only weathered the storm, but flourished. Moomintroll, Sniff and Snufkin braved poisonous bushes, followed comets, survived great thunderstorms, and had terrible experiences. Their courage was rewarded. After midsummer madness in 1954, a trollwinter in 1957, the Moomins sailed into the 1960s, still in their same old boat, wet, buffeted and wearing oilskins, determined to hold the rudder hard and not to be sick. As it was for Tove Jansson, so was it for all Finns.

In elections in March 1945, the SKDL gained fifty-one seats and controlled key areas of government, including the state police and the broadcasting network. Members of the SKDL reached high office in the cabinet, Mauno Pekkala being premier and Y. Leino minister of the interior. With Communists firmly entrenched in the administration, Russia felt confident enough to sign a peace treaty with Finland in Paris on 10 February 1947: three years after armistice. Mauno Pekkala led the Finnish delegation. The map appended to the treaty was drawn up with Russian place names. Although there were other signatories to this document – Britain, Australia, Canada, India, South Africa, New Zealand, Byelorussian SSR, Czechoslovakia, Ukrainian SSR – the Cold War had reached such a stage that the reality was that the Treaty of Paris allowed for a continued Russian occupation of Finland, with the sanction of the Allied Control Commission, which remained until 1952. Most important, the Paris Treaty continued the fifty years rental lease of Porkkala as a Soviet base and the right of Russia to transport troops to Porkkala on Finnish railways, waterways, roads and through Finnish airspace. The 1947 treaty also limited the Finnish Army to 34,400, the navy to 4,500 (with a total tonnage of 10,000 tons) and the air force to 3,000 men. Nor was Finland to possess, construct or experiment with any atomic weapon or missile. No bombers were permitted. The Russians were taking no chances.

While the Finns were compelled to visit Paris to sign that treaty, they were discouraged, one might almost say prevented, from returning later in the year to participate in discussions about the Marshall Plan. The Parliamentary Foreign Relations Committee discussed the question of Marshall Aid during the summer of 1947 and turned down 'the crumbs from Truman's table' (as the Communists described the offer), preferring to remain outside the areas of conflict in power politics.

Finnish aloofness in the Cold War era was a little like Swedish neutrality in World War II. Some international agreements were more favoured than others. Paasikivi could not oppose the pressure within the cabinet and the dictates on foreign policy of the Russians. He therefore determined a strategy, called 'the Paasikivi line', which neatly turned Finland's geopolitical vulnerability into a strength, beginning with agreement to an unpromising treaty of friendship, co-operation and mutual assistance. Some Finns regarded this idea as a ghost of the Ribbentrop-Molotov agreement, a vestige even of Tilsit; others anticipated an attempted left-wing coup on the lines of the Bolshevik seizure of power in neighbouring Leningrad in 1917, or the internal crisis in Czechoslovakia, where communists had seized power only one week before the Russian offer to Finland was made public in 1948. Paasikivi joined the pessimists. He brought the full weight of the Finnish Navy (one gunboat) into harbour and was prepared to shell insurgents out of the capital if the left-wing tried to stage a coup. At the same time he reassured public opinion that signing such a treaty with Russia was not the end of Finnish autonomy. As early as 1943, Urho Kekkonen had argued that Finland, as a member of an anti-Soviet alliance, would always be in a position of a forward base, which in the event of conflict, would be the first to be overrun, and yet would not be able to affect the decisions made concerning war and peace. Events until 1948 proved Kekkonen correct.

Paasikivi developed the idea that the security of Finland could only be ensured in concord with that of the Soviet Union and replaced the previous orthodoxy of irreconcilable conflict with a concept of Russia's legitimate interests. In Paasikivi's view, the Soviet Union had, vis-á-vis Finland, primarily a military and defensive interest, which aimed to ensure the security of Leningrad in the event of an offensive through Finnish territory. On the basis of this understanding, the security aims of Finland and the Soviet Union no longer seemed irreconcilable, as by satisfying the legitimate security interests of the Soviet Union, Finland could ensure its own in relation to the east. This was expected to remove the conflict between Finland and the Soviet Union, which had persisted ever since the establishment of the city of St Petersburg and which had been one of the ultimate causes of the Winter War. To achieve this, Finland was not required to compromise its own sovereignty, or its traditional way of life. The points of disagreement, outside the legitimate interests of the Soviet Union, would then be no impediment to good neighbourly relations between an independent Finland and the Soviet Union. This Paasikivi-line fitted poorly into the prevailing view of Soviet aspirations during the Cold War, and its chances of success were regarded as limited. The Finnish-Soviet Treaty of Friendship, Co-operation and Mutual Assistance, however, confirmed completely Paasikivi's conception of the realities of Soviet-Finnish relations. The Soviet Union was satisfied with just those limited arrangements required to ensure its legitimate interests as defined by Paasikivi, and agreed to frame a treaty designed to take into account Finland's desire to remain outside the conflicting interests of the big powers.

The Treaty of Friendship, Co-operation and Mutual Assistance was initialled in Moscow on 6 April 1948. Molotov signed for Russia, while Stalin stood behind him in uniform, hands behind his back and Urho Kekkonen looked on. The treaty specifically referred to a German danger, and forestalled Finnish military commitments with the west. It was renewed for twenty years in 1955, when the Finnish parliament signed it. Crowds gathered around parliament house hoping that they were witnesses to a new Diet of Porvoo at the very least. The treaty, on terms acceptable to Finland, was one of the important achievements of Finnish diplomacy. Once relations with Russia were secured, the popularity of the SKDL mysteriously diminished, and a Social Democrat minority government took office in 1948 which gradually brought Finland into line with the social democratic policies of the other Scandinavian states. Karl Fagerholm added long-term housing loan schemes to child endowment and passed a series of laws designed to restore civil liberties and re-start the redistribution of resources in the interests of Finland's working class.

During the period of reparations in 1944–52, all economic effort was bent towards repaying the war debts, but the economic tide gradually turned and by 1960 the United Kingdom had displaced Russia as Finland's most important market. The duality of the Finnish approach began to work to such an extent that there was a modest surplus to redistribute. In 1961 Finland both became an associate member of EFTA and signed a trade pact with Russia, which gave it most favoured nation status. The economic achievements of the Finns were not in the same class as those of their Scandinavian neighbours, but Swedes, Danes and Norwegians who came to the Olympic Games in Helsinki in 1952 were impressed by the stage that post-war reconstruction in Finland had reached. Finnish athletes watched one of their heroes, Paavo Nurmi, light the Olympic flame; Nurmi represented the marathon approach to problems that allowed the Finns to pay off their war reparations debt to Russia in the same year as the Games.

Nurmi's feats were repeated in another sphere in 1954 when Väinö Linna published *The Unknown Soldier* after a marathon of creativity left him drained and his readers exhausted. *The Unknown Soldier* was put on sale on 3 December, and its first publication was followed by a storm of criticism. The book was reprinted, translated, and in 1955 the Finnish film director Edvin Laine produced a film of the book, that included 300 metres of authentic documentary footage shot during the Continuation

War. *The Unknown Soldier* was filmed without government support, which was thought essential for a war epic if authenticity were to be achieved in the use of weapons, soldiers and battle-grounds. When the ministry of foreign affairs declared that *The Unknown Soldier* might harm Finland's relations with foreign powers and stir up damaging controversy at home and abroad, Edvin Laine choreographed the battles in the woods around his summer house with a volunteer cast of extras (including Tampere factory workers and University of Helsinki students), many of whom played both Russians and Finns, changing their uniforms and characters as appropriate. Kekkonen eventually used his influence to borrow a few old weapons from museums and border guards, but the Finnish military high command joined the stiffnecked resistance to the project, which never-theless ended up as one of Finland's most successful cinema export ventures. President Paasikivi attended the first night and with such patronage *The Unknown Soldier* was launched with a bang.

In 1956 the regular Finnish Army won another battle without firing a shot when it re-occupied the Russian enclave at Porkkala, which had become by that time an area shunned by Finns. A few Finns stood on the roadside, some of them on skis, to watch a long file of fur-hatted Finnish troops, two abreast with machine guns slung over their shoulders, goosestep through the snow into Porkkala. Russia voluntarily gave up its right to Porkkala, which everyone knew it had obtained for fifty years. All Finns felt the psychological effects of complete territorial integrity. The Finnish Post Office (which had been a barometer of national mood since Finnish postmarks were changed during the Russification period) produced a first day cover that showed a symbolic Porkkala lighthouse beaming out a message to the world that Finland was whole. The stamp was cancelled by a design that showed the lighthouse tower not shining but crossed with a barrier.

A second milestone was the decision of the electoral college, by one vote, to put Kekkonen into Paasikivi's office as president of the republic. A one vote margin is enough in politics, and Urho Kekkonen governed the new Finland firmly. When a general strike lasted three weeks in 1956, police on horseback and with riot sticks bashed demonstrators who complained that nationalism was not enough. But the 1956 strike saw the temporary end of the push for Scandinavian-style social services, although the left-wing industrial movement was reassured by Russian pressure on the Finnish government to force political parties to work more in the interests of the working class. Indeed, a deep cleavage continued between the supporters of President Kekkonen and the supporters of social democracy. Väinö Tanner was elected chairman of the Social Democrats in 1957 and immediately began a campaign to prevent Kekkonen's re-election. At the end of the Continuation War, Tanner had been imprisoned as a traitor responsible for waging war on Russia, and the Russians would have preferred him to remain in political obscurity. But the democratic institutions of Finland allowed Tanner to rise from his sackcloth and ashes, and as a result a breakaway group of Social Democrats who wished to co-operate with Kekkonen and the Agrarians and who had sponsors in Russia was formed. In July 1958 the Communists were the largest single group returned to parliament, having fifty out of the two hundred. But the anti-left forces rallied and by combining their talents formed a majority which demanded that President Kekkonen appoint their leader, K.A. Fagerholm, prime minister. Kekkonen bowed to constitutional necessity, being aware of the diplomatic crisis about to unfold when Fagerholm refused to have in his cabinet representatives of the new-left Social Democrats or the Communists. And the Russian ambassador in Helsinki was withdrawn and not replaced. In the crisis that followed, Fagerholm was sacrificed to relations with the Soviet Union, and the anti-Kekkonen faction gained another weapon in its armory, for it was the president who persuaded the political forces involved that the circumstances were not right for such a flagrant disregard of neighbourly opinion.

In these difficult times, Kekkonen began his presidency, trying desperately, and on the whole successfully, to ride a middle course between a western and an eastern orientation of his foreign policy. It was symbolically appropriate that during the greatest crisis Finland faced in the post-war era, involving the near collapse of Russian and United States relations over the Berlin question, President Kekkonen was in a hut in Hawaii, relaxing after a tour of the United States. In Honolulu Kekkonen learned that Khrushchev had plans to use Finland in his campaign to 'eradicate the splinter from the heart of Europe'. Khrushchev and the leaders of the Warsaw Pact set a timetable for a solution of the Berlin question by August 1961, and on 13 August the Berlin wall was begun. On 30 October 1961, the Finnish ambassador was handed a note which proposed consultations, in accordance with the Finnish-Soviet Treaty of Friendship, Co-operation and Mutual Assistance, on the measures for the defence of the borders of the two countries against the threat of aggression on the part of West Germany and its allied states. Khrushchev believed that it was naive to expect that West German ambition would be kept under control in NATO. When Kekkonen heard the contents of the Soviet note on a telephone line taken to a neighbouring hut (as the president's did not have one), he went for a swim.

Although Foreign Minister Ahti Karjalainen left for Finland immediately, Kekkonen continued with the rest of his visit to the United States and tried by his example to reassure those who saw October 1961 as a repeat of the days on the eve of the Winter War. Kekkonen could not think of a reply to the Russian note, so it was left unanswered. Karjalainen went to Moscow where the Russian foreign minister, Andrei Gromyko, explained that the Russian military high command wanted to consult on the basis of the 1948 treaty, and added that the Russians feared political instability in Finland. Karjalainen replied that although there certainly were different political groups in Finland, they were all bent on continuing Paasikivi's foreign policy, and tried to convince the Russians that the Finnish people wanted to remain on friendly terms. In order to reassure the Russians, who feared there was a right-winger in the woodpile, Kekkonen used his presidential prerogative to dissolve parliament and call elections. On 16 November, when the Finnish ambassador in Moscow was asked why the Finns had not answered the note, he was told that the security of Finland and Russia was threatened and asked when the Russians might expect to receive a delegation.

Kekkonen then decided to go to see Khrushchev, and eventually the two friends (for such they were, having often shot and hunted together, in the manner of Mannerheim and Nicholas II) met in Novosibirsk, where Khrushchev was touring Siberia. Kekkonen pointed out that holding military conversations between Finland and the Soviet Union was likely to cause concern and fear of war in other Scandinavian countries. But if Russia were to withdraw its proposal, there would be less need for military preparations, not only in Finland and Sweden, but also in the two Scandinavian members of NATO, Denmark and Norway.

Khrushchev agreed. There were no military conversations. The presidential elections were held, and a greater proportion of electors than ever before voted Kekkonen president. As a final paradox, Kekkonen was established as indispensable to both the Russians and the Finns, the Finnish Communists lost their position as Finland's biggest parliamentary party in the elections, and Kekkonen presided, until 1966, over largely middle-class governments.

In 1966, however, the socialists formed a government. The long-dominant Agrarians (Kekkonen's own former party), who had changed their name to the Centre Party, lost ground as did the Communists and Conservatives. The Social Democrat leader, Rafael Paasio, followed tradition and members of the opposition, including three communists and one radical socialist, sat in his cabinet. Paasio drafted progressive social legislation, involving a reduction in the hours of the working week, while Finland had strikes and protests by nurses, midwives and the printing industry. As a result, Finland, which Khrushchev had decided to keep viable as a 'capitalist museum', was firmly on its feet by 1968 and as much a member of the Scandinavian bloc as any other northern country, having all the problems and most of the compensations of its neighbours. The Cold War had thawed, but the boundless optimism of a new generation, critical of past solutions and determined to build, if not a new Jerusalem, at least a new Stockholm, Oslo, Copenhagen or Helsinki, was providing problems of adjustment to all members of the Scandinavian world, which, more and more, was becoming part of the global village.

CHAPTER 8

Unromantic Nationalism

For a little over twenty years after World War II, most Scandinavians assumed that history had determined that social democratic regimes in the north would be able to preside over a spirit of new nationalism in which national values could be improved and consolidated. Social Democrats expected that social engineering based on economic progress would allow orderly development of Swedes, Finns, Norwegians and Danes, not at each other's expense, but in a complementary and reassuring upward spiral of living standards and stability in foreign policy. They turned out to be wrong. Much Scandinavian economic and foreign policy forward planning was made obsolete by the dramatic changes in the Soviet Union under Mikhail Gorbachev. The nuclear energy disasters at Three Mile Island and Chernobyl were as far away as Tilsit and as little known but, as surely as the Napoleonic wars changed the face of Scandinavia, they made it clear that membership of the global village carried penalties as well as benefits. Equally important for Scandinavia was the loss of continuity with the past caused by the deaths of two national leaders, Olof Palme and Urho Kekkonen. At the beginning of the period, life in Sweden and Finland seemed unthinkable without the presence of those dynamic statesmen: by the end of it, Kekkonen was a memory, Palme unmentioned when his Social Democratic successor won the 1988 Swedish general election, and the Swedish Social Democrats defeated by a Conservative Coalition in 1991.

The period 1968–93 began inauspiciously. The failure of social democracy to provide all, not just some, of the benefits of economic development was first signalled by university students in 1968. On 26 November, President Kekkonen went to the Helsinki Students Union to mark the centenary of an organisation that had been an essential part of Finnish national history. Kekkonen was among the first heads of state to recognise that the student world was in turmoil everywhere. He told his seething audience that the unrest among student youth during 1968 raised the problem of the restlessness of the new generation as a whole. Kekkonen faced the fact that manifestations of student dissent implied a social protest that would grow general and more widespread. He knew that the rebellious group were not going to be content with minor concessions and small improvements but demanded a far-reaching change of systems and a transformation of the Finnish way of life. Kekkonen did not regard the savage criticism of Finland and its institutions as a negative and destructive force that had to be met and crushed. On the contrary he wisely recognised that the rebellion of university students, who occupied campus buildings and terrorised the university administrators with savage lampoons of their middle-class values, had a deep vein of idealism. He briefly analysed the change that had given the students the self-confidence to risk their professional futures by anti-social behaviour and attributed it to the strengthening of Finland's external position. In 1968, Finland had for the first time a young student generation that had not experienced war and oppression and did not realise how recent was the bloody history of those who had engaged in polemical turmoil; the students were not afraid to show their passions. For his part, Kekkonen understood the expansive self-criticism inherent in the questioning of old orthodoxies, and he tried to devise a way to harness the waterfall of dissent by programming Finland's culture to meet the new critical idealists.

In Sweden, Olof Palme felt much the same as Kekkonen. He was part of what popular culture termed the Age of Aquarius, an age that opened in 1968 with a great groundswell of reformist suggestions and optimism. The liberal critics of the community values that had developed in Scandinavia since 1945 believed that in 1968 the time was right to tackle problems that had been submerged and neglected for generations. They studied events in the United States and Europe, where the politics of protest had supplanted the existentialism of the beat generation. In 1945 Kierkegaard had been regarded as a saint by those who sought a meaning in individual existence. But in 1968 the times demanded commitment not introspection. And there were causes aplenty for Scandinavians to espouse.

The Scandinavians took their lead from the university students in Berkeley and Paris, who campaigned against the Vietnam war and the treatment of minorities such as blacks and homosexuals. Students in Stockholm, Helsinki, Oslo and Copenhagen supported the protesters in America and Europe, although there were severe problems in adapting non-Scandinavian protests to the Scandinavian area. It was all very well to sing 'We shall overcome', but the real question was 'Who shall overcome?' The cold climate and short summer were not so conducive to flower-power and what Americans called 'love-ins'. The social revolution of the 1960s had given Scandinavians little that was new, apart from marijuana and an underground drug culture, as they tried to adapt Martin Luther King's black ghetto policies to their own minority equivalents, the Lapps and the Finnish gypsies. While Scandinavians deplored the invasion of Czechoslovakia by the Warsaw Pact nations and the arrest of Alexander Dubcek, they reserved their bitterest criticism for the crimes of the US in Vietnam, which were pilloried by the pale-faced pundits of the northern capitals.

Students occupied their universities and demanded a greater say in the running of the institutions. Power and consultation was demanded and received. Not since the 1890s had the aim of the young been so strong and so decisive. Young Danes sang not the hymns of Grundtvig but the protest songs of Peter, Paul and Mary.

Before the onslaught, the ripples of change turned into a tidal wave. Many of those in power gave way. It was no accident that the Swedish film director Bo Widerberg made *Ådalen 31* in 1969. *Ådalen 31*, recalling the industrial martyrdom that ushered in social democracy, was based on Birger Norman's novel, and exactly touched the exposed nerve ends as much of the world was convulsed by demonstrations. It was effective cinema. The realism with which the demonstrators were described in their domestic and earth-centred activities before they marched beneath the red banner on behalf of the working class, only to be murdered by what were described as the agents of the capitalist state, was terrifyingly moving.

Demonstrations were not confined to those without power. In Sweden in 1968 Olof Palme, then minister of education in Erlander's Social Democrat government, led a torchlight parade through the streets of Stockholm supporting North Vietnam in the war against the south. GIs were welcomed in Sweden not as soldiers, but as deserters. The strain on Swedish-US relations was as great as it had been in World War II. After the march, the US ambassador was recalled to Washington and it was more than the government sulking: the US State Department considered breaking off diplomatic relations and, to make matters worse between the two countries, the National Liberation Front opened an information bureau in Stockholm.

The anti-Americanism in the north was exacerbated when a US B-52 bomber crashed in Greenland while attempting a forced landing at Thule, where there was a US air force base. Four unprimed nuclear bombs were on the aircraft, and the crash brought home the danger of radioactivity to the Danes who had been unaware that their territory was being overflown. A fortuitous change of government was followed by an affirmation by the new Danish prime minister, Helmer Baunsgaard, that such flights were forbidden.

For Finland, 1968 saw the continuation of its drive for better relations with the Soviet Union. The Finns protested against the Warsaw Pact intervention in Czechoslovakia, but Kekkonen's personal diplomacy continued to smooth Finno-Russian relations. The Soviet premier, Aleksei N. Kosygin, and President Kekkonen met over sauna, sausage and beer at Hanko. On 5 August 1968 the Saimaa canal was re-opened. The canal, originally built in 1856, wended its way through territory surrendered in 1944 by Finland at the end of the Continuation War, linking the south-west lakes of Finland with the Gulf of Finland. In 1968 Kekkonen was elected to his third term as president of Finland and, as the Soviet as well as the Finnish people's choice, continued with undiminished prestige to further the economic development and political stability of the area. From 1968 until 1981, Kekkonen was a symbol of national identity, having a vast number of personal qualities that appealed to the Finnish collective subconscious. There were by then many Kekkonen jokes, some said to have been minted by the president. His diplomatic encounters with foreign heads of state in the coffee tent on the harbour front quay of Helsinki and his daily jog were irresistibly charming and deeply reassuring. Born in 1900, his extraordinarily vigorous longevity provided a problem for political scientists trying to foresee Finland after Kekkonen, although some were reassured after searching the constitution to find that the president of Finland need not be alive. Kekkonen did not try to unravel the mystery; on the contrary, he bought a turtle and, having been told that turtles live for two hundred years, remarked, 'To a Finn, to see is to believe.'

After 1968 Kekkonen provided the foundation on which the Finns could ride out the protest years. They accepted from him what would otherwise have been unacceptable: deference to the Russians at the expense of some Finnish citizens. Caspar Wrede, a Finnish film director, for example, had no home market for some of his work. In 1971 one entrepreneur tried to import Wrede's brilliant film *One Day in the Life of Ivan Denisovitch*, but the state board of film censorship banned the picture for political reasons. Criticism of Russia was naturally usually oblique (*Fiddler on the Roof* was allowed in), as the political leaders of both countries exchanged holiday visits in the summer, with a scale of hospitality and a concern for their mutual sensibilities scarcely mooted since the halcyon days when tsars, kaisers and most of the crowned heads of Europe cruised in their yachts in the Finnish archipelago.

Kosygin ought to have realised that there was no such thing as a free sauna. The price Kekkonen extracted for his beer and sausages was a guarantee from the Soviet Union that it would supply Finland with uranium in the mid 1970s, when it was expected that nuclear power could be needed to maintain Finland's rate of growth. Finland's first nuclear power station was to be erected at Loviisa, east of Helsinki, by 1966. There was no comfort for the Finnish Communist Party when, after the Czechoslovakian invasion, the Communist Party split into Stalinists and genuine democratic socialists, much to the chagrin of those who hoped the communists would improve their sound showing at the next general election. At the same time, Helsinki's prestige as an international capital was enhanced by the initiative of Finnish diplomats in securing their metropolis as the site for the all-important Strategic Arms Limitation Talks (SALT) between the United States and the Soviet Union.

Stockholm was obviously ruled out, as Olof Palme became Swedish prime minister in 1969, replacing Tage Erlander, who retired after holding the office since 1946. Palme was only forty-two years old when he succeeded Erlander who had presided over the Social Democrats for an uninterrupted twenty-three years, and there was every expectation that Palme would be at the helm for such a period also. Erlander was the leader of the only western European nation that recognised North Vietnam when he retired in 1969, but even more radical departures were expected from Palme who, despite his patrician background, was feared by the conservatives in banking and private enterprise.

For most of 1969 there was no US ambassador in Stockholm. If ever a country was a target for the attention of the CIA it was Palme's Sweden: over 300 deserters lived there, and 200 million crowns were promised in Swedish aid to North Vietnam once the war ended. Erlander could not have chosen a better time to retire to his country cottage. Swedish industrial relations, held up to the world as a model, began to worsen and an optimistic fifty-four per cent of Swedes agreed to forgo a rise in their living standards in order to protect their environment. Palme's Social Democrats had to face strikes which had been almost unheard of since the 1930s, and which threatened to destroy social democracy. In the ore mines of Kiruna 5,000 miners went on two months' illegal strike. The Swedish Confederation of Trade Unions refused to support it, sticking to the implicit principles of the 1938 agreement, but the strikers won and, significantly, the main purpose of their struggle was to keep the ratio of their earnings to the average national wage at 172:100. The wealthy members of the working class were the first to rebel against inflation in Sweden, which reached eleven per cent in 1970, forcing the government to bring in an ideologically unexpected price freeze. Palme thought that the problem was bound to get worse as income differentials widened rather than narrowed. Even university graduates had to struggle to negotiate for better conditions in their work places in the knowledge that there would shortly be too many people for too few jobs and that their negotiating power would soon be diminished forever.

Until spring 1970 it was hoped that the Scandinavian states might agree to a customs union, Nordök, which went as far as a first draft, but the Finns refused to sign, feeling it was inconsistent with their vision of neutrality. When Danes chose to try to enter the European Economic Community, as long as their largest trading partner Great Britain could enter also, another dream of the pan-Scandinavians was sunk.

It was ironical that Denmark's dismemberment in the nineteenth century had been largely at the hands of the same nation that rescued it from economic disaster in the twentieth. By 1971 the British parliament agreed to join the EEC. This obstacle having been surmounted, the Danish parliament was clear to surrender Danish sovereignty through a referendum in 1972 on the issue. The new Danish Prime Minister, Jens Otto Krag, announced that if thirty per cent of the Danes opposed entry to the EEC he would abort the project.

Across the Baltic the Swedes decided that full membership of the EEC was not a realistic possibility, a decision they would have to reverse in 1991. Palme's Social Democrats regarded EEC membership as incompatible with Swedish neutrality. Sweden tried to develop some looser relationship with the EEC that would have conferred upon it the benefit of having a say in community decision-making, but this idea was tossed out of court by the EEC economists, and Sweden was forced to watch its markets decline because of the trade barriers erected by the community. After some hard bargaining, the EEC agreed to allow free trade (except in agricultural produce) between Sweden and the community, phased in stages to be completed by 1977. The two important exceptions were that special steels were not to be duty free until 1979, and paper until 1983.

Finland faced the new situation by coming to a special agreement with COMECON, the Council for Mutual Economic Assistance, to replace the trade it expected to lose from EFTA or the EEC in the 1970s. COMECON was established in January

1949 by East European countries: Russia, Albania, Bulgaria, Czechoslovakia, Hungary, Poland, Romania, and the German Democratic Republic, to provide a counter-economic structure to that set up by western Europeans in 1948. The Russians sweetened the agreement by supplying Finland with natural gas and helping negotiations with Germany about reparations for the destruction caused by the Germans' retreat through Finnish Lapland after the Continuation War. Finland's relations with COMECON provided for technical co-operation, including the exchange of statistics and information on monetary policy.

In 1972 the Norwegian referendum on membership of the EEC was held, and most voted against membership. As a result, among Scandinavians only Denmark was part of the EEC. Denmark joined the EEC on 1 January 1973 after overwhelming support for the move at a referendum, illustrating once again that the Danes' relative affinity with continental Europe was based on more than geographical considerations. The Danes felt a national surge of optimism after the new relationship. From a nation chiefly regarded as the site of the celebrated 1969 'Porn Fair', Denmark expected to reverse its seedy quaint image and base an economic recovery on a greatly expanded opportunity for its agriculture as the community members became the world's new rich. Krag quit while he was ahead. He thanked the electorate for its overwhelming vote for the EEC and stunned them by announcing that he intended to retire to private life and to leave the country and the Social Democrats to a new leader, Anker Jorgensen. Jorgensen's accession coincided with the beginnings of the world energy crisis.

On 6 October 1973, Egypt and Syria launched a surprise attack on Israel during Yom Kippur, the most sacred day of the Jewish religious calendar. The Arabs had set out to challenge the boundaries established as a result of the 1967 six-day Arab-Israeli war. Egyptian President Anwar as-Sadat and Syria's President Hafez al-Assad tried to restore Arab self-esteem by a limited war against Israel. Russia helped the Arabs with an airlift during the fighting. The US supported the Jews. When the smoke in the Middle East cleared and the UN peace-keepers moved in, Israel had again demonstrated its military superiority. The world had nervously avoided a confrontation between the super powers. Then, on 17 October 1973, the move was made that changed Scandinavian history as much as Napoleon's meeting with Alexander at Tilsit, and the Scandinavians had about as much say in it. The organisation of Arab petroleum exporting countries met in Kuwait and agreed to cut the flow of oil by five per cent each month in order to force the United States to change its Middle East policy, the six largest oil producers in the Persian Gulf having agreed the day before to raise the price of crude oil by seventeen per cent and oil company taxes by seventy per cent. Some of the Arab leaders were on their way with their shopping lists to London and Paris, and the Scandinavians were headed for a collective nervous and economic collapse.

When Jorgensen made his opening speech in parliament, the extent of the damage was still largely unknown. In October 1973 he faced congratulations on the country's improved performance since it had joined the EEC and a taxpayers' revolt led by Mogens Glistrup. Glistrup's field of expertise was tax avoidance. He practised what he preached to such an extent that he was able to boast on television that, although a millionaire, he had never paid a crown in tax. Glistrup's appealing message was that income tax was a form of highway robbery, and although his party suffered a setback when police raided his office and took files on tax avoidance schemes, such was the new movement's appeal that Glistrup commanded twenty-six per cent support in the electorate. His programme was to abolish personal income tax, cut the public service to a minimum, transfer civil servants to productive labour and disband the armed forces, substituting an automatic telephone answering service programmed to say in Russian 'We surrender.' Jorgensen was thrown out by the electorate on 19 December 1973. Poul Hartling, an experienced former Danish foreign minister and leader of the minority Liberal government became prime minister.

In 1973 a general election was held in Sweden which illustrated the equipoise of the new age. Both the socialist and non-socialist blocs in parliament gained seventy-five seats. But Prime Minister Palme, realising that politics was the art of the possible, basked in his majority of 0.07 per cent of the electorate, refused to resign and established a new system of gasoline rationing forced upon Sweden by fuel shortages caused by the Arab oil cutbacks.

In Finland there was a crisis to match the others in Scandinavia after the Middle East war. Late in 1972 the Scandinavian press published the text of a secret meeting between Kekkonen and President Leonid I. Brezhnev held at Zavidovo near Moscow in early 1972. According to the text, Kekkonen personally guaranteed that any agreement between Finland and the EEC would not have a negative effect on Finno-Russian relations. There is no doubt the report was authentic. The grand old man of Finnish politics certainly had the stature to have his way with the Finnish parliament. His constitutional status ensured the making or breaking of ministries. But the Russians replied that whatever the benefits to Finland, it was, from the Russian point of view, politically incorrect, and Finland should wait. Finland waited. Meanwhile, heads rolled and the authors of the supposed leak resigned after being reported to have passed secret information to unauthorised persons.

The oil crisis led to an attempt to modify the Finnish constitution for the first time since 1917. The object was to reduce and limit the powers of the president, who was not subject to parliament as was the prime minister. Although a committee of parliament investigated the issues, the president was able to use his authority to block attempts at reform. Thus

Finland faced the 1980s the way it meant to see out the twentieth century, with a constitution well adapted to the possibility of total war, balanced on the fence, and with a supply of ammunition primed against a potential enemy who, history showed, came only from one point of the compass: the east. The world energy crisis, on the other hand, forced Finland to rely more and more on the economic strength of its Russian neighbour. For Finland, the Soviet Union became an even more crucial trading partner. Finland received sixty-five per cent of its oil from Russia, and the massive price increase turned Russia into Finland's largest creditor. After the oil crisis, the Soviet Union supplied twenty per cent of Finnish imports compared with ten per cent before 1973.

As it turned out, Denmark joined the EEC just in time. Denmark was almost entirely dependent upon imports to meet its energy requirements, although the Danish sector of the North Sea oil fields was able to provide 1.5 per cent of the country's needs. In October 1974 Mogens Glistrup was put on trial for tax evasion, but by then his Progress Party was second only to the Social Democrats in terms of parliamentary support, a reflection of the way that Denmark had suffered one of the highest inflation rates in Europe, as well as being at the top level of interest and taxation rates. Half Denmark's gross national product went to fuel the public sector. Poul Hartling's control of Denmark's administration was short lived. He resigned as prime minister in January 1975 and was replaced by Anker Jorgensen after a general election. Glistrup's Progress Party belied its title. The Danes' applecart was upset and the spectre of high unemployment led to demonstrations. The unemployed demonstrated outside Queen Margrethe II's Amalienborg Palace in Copenhagen, crying, 'We will have work *now.*'

The employed were no less vociferous. Fifteen thousand Danes demonstrated outside parliament to protest against a law designed to abolish free negotiation in the labour market as part of a package to help combat the economic ills that forced Denmark to borrow US$292 million from foreign banks to underpin Denmark's balance of payments deficit. The other parts of the package involved an austerity pack that cut government spending, tried to control prices, profits and dividends, limited wage increases to six per cent per annum, and raised taxes on gasoline, cars, coffee, sugar, tobacco and alcoholic drinks.

One of the most significant symptoms of ice-age politics in Scandinavia was the Cod War, where all the ingredients of post-1968 tension and discord were jumbled together as two NATO partners, Iceland and Great Britain, fought over a scarce resource in a conflict that brought to a head matters of national sovereignty, Scandinavian solidarity and ecology. Iceland was a part of Scandinavia often ignored because of its isolated position in the North Atlantic Ocean and its small population of a little more than 200,000, most of whom lived in the capital, Reykjavik. Iceland was not considered to be sufficiently significant in the Napoleonic era to be detached from Denmark. In the nineteenth century it was a favourite haunt for eccentric romantics like William Morris and Sir Richard Burton and in the twentieth century the bachelor Prince Charles, who were among the many who saw in Iceland a pure form of life not much changed since the sagas. The more critical of the Scandinavians tended to look down on Iceland as a desolate volcanic country where excitement was to be gained by predicting when and where the next volcano would erupt and what would be swept away by the lava. Icelandic home rulers were not able or willing to detach themselves from the security of the metropolitan power, which granted them a consultative assembly in 1843, a constitution in 1874, and gave legislative power to the Althing parliament and provided for Icelandic control of finance. Iceland was granted complete home rule by Denmark in 1904, and in the 1918 rearrangement the Danes and Icelanders agreed to be sovereign states under a common king. Although the 1918 Act specified that foreign policy was to be controlled by Denmark, when the Danes were incorporated as a German protectorate the Althing vested power in the cabinet, which voted to end its allegiance to the Danish crown.

During World War II British troops landed in Iceland and in June 1941 they withdrew in favour of the Americans. On 24 May 1944 the Icelanders solved the head of state problem in the Finnish manner by declaring themselves a republic. Throughout the war Americans stayed in occupation as Iceland's strategic importance as a stepping stone in the North Atlantic enhanced its prestige and importance. When the Cod War began, Icelandic communists demanded the withdrawal of the Americans, but as early as October 1945 the Americans had obtained an agreement to establish military bases in Iceland, which, on 30 March 1949, joined NATO and was in the same network as Norway and Denmark.

The Icelanders were, as they had been since the Viking colonisation of the region, largely concerned with fishing. They tried several times in the post-war era to enlarge their sovereignty over fishing grounds in order to try to build up their economic power. In 1948 Iceland extended its fishing limits unilaterally from three to four miles. In 1958, when the limit was set at twelve miles, the Cod War broke out. The technique of warfare was simple. Icelandic gunboats sailed across the warps holding the nets of foreign trawlers cutting the catch and sending the net to the bottom. Great Britain retaliated by sending naval frigates to protect the trawlers, ramming the smaller gunboats if necessary. Since sailors and fisherman usually died if they fell overboard in those latitudes, the bitterness and hostility were enormous. The British Trawlers Association hired a public relations firm which sent fifty journalists on Royal Navy vessels to report the war. With novelists like Michael Frayn covering the story for the *Guardian*, there was no chance that it would slip from public consciousness. The Cod War turned into a new

Icelandic saga, and 'Cod Warriors' were described with style and feeling from both sides. After 1968, however, Iceland suffered an enormous drop in its standard of living. Real per capita income, largely derived from fish, dropped by sixteen per cent, and the overfishing by Icelanders and Norwegians of the cod, and the disappearance of the herring, made Iceland particularly vulnerable to change brought about by the energy crisis. On 1 September 1972 Prime Minister Olafur Johanneson announced the extension of the Icelandic fisheries limit from ten to fifty miles off the coast. Iceland refused to acknowledge the jurisdiction of the International Court at The Hague and as the Cod War worsened it seemed possible that diplomatic relations between Iceland and Britain would be severed. Iceland called in United States diplomats and suggested to them that their NATO base might have to be moved to Scotland or Greenland if Britain did not stop its resistance to the claims of a small nation whose existence was threatened by the depletion of its main economic resource. During the Cod War the Iceland Navy at first fired blanks, but in March 1973 the *Odinn* fired two rounds across the bows of a British tug (ironically named the *Statesman*). The reality was that while Scandinavians were enraged at Britain's bullying tactics, which were described as genocide, the British were in an economic position as perilous as the Icelanders. Following the oil crisis, Britain ran second to Iceland as the country which had the most inflationary economy in the OECD. While the Icelanders had a 1974–75 inflation rate of fifty-five per cent, the British (in 1973) had to contend with twenty-seven per cent.

What exacerbated the problem from the Icelandic point of view was that before the crisis Iceland was a Scandinavian model social democracy. It had a very high standard of living, an egalitarian community, and apart from the appalling severity of the almost lunar landscape and the recurrence of such national disasters as earthquakes and volcanic eruptions, Icelanders were rightly regarded in material terms as the most privileged Scandinavians after the Swedes.

In their desperate situation the Icelanders continued with their appraisal of economic priorities. The Icelandic Marine Research Institute provided the basis for a new approach to fishing, which limited the catches allowed to Icelanders, the government stopped guaranteeing loans for fishing vessels built at foreign shipyards, and on 14 October 1976 Prime Minister Geir Hallgrimsson announced a two hundred mile fishing limit. But most important was the Icelanders' decision to use their abundant resources of geothermal hot water to supply energy. By 1976 geothermal hot water heated half the homes in Iceland. As the cost of oil rose and nuclear power became a more debatable alternative, the Icelanders hoped that they might be able to develop the technology to become a net exporter of electric energy to Scotland five hundred miles south-east, by underwater cable. They also thought of exporting the geothermal hot water to Swedish coastal cities in insulated 200,000 ton tankers, available since the downturn in the world shipping caused by the oil crisis.

The Norwegians were not forced to rely on utopian schemes or aggressive foreign policy to protect their national survival after the 1973 crisis. Norway was cushioned from the worst effects of the Arab oil crisis by the discoveries of Ekofisk oil. The multi-national Phillips Oil Company helped to develop Norway's oil industry and the old 'White foreigners' became the new 'White Arabs'. Moreover, the Norwegians did not have to face the social disruption of frequent elections, which were the rule in Denmark in the mid 1970s. Norway's Labour government emphasised the need to use Norway's windfall wealth as a buffer against recession. The anti-recessionist policies of the Norwegians included public works and a strong overseas borrowing program underwritten by the future oil revenues, which made Norway seem a good risk to the international money lenders. In Norway unemployment was low by world standards, but the social implications of the problems of being out of work were not neglected. The recession in world shipping meant that the Norwegian shipbuilding industry, which had specialised in oil tankers, was hit by a wave of cancelled orders. Norway's own fleet was largely mothballed: one-fifth of all Norwegian shipping and one-third of the tanker fleet began to rust at anchor in the fiords.

Saving Norwegians from unemployment was the Norwegian government's priority in the 1970s, and it was successful. Self-sufficiency in oil supplies gave the Norwegians flexibility in their foreign policy, which enabled them to support President Carter's attack on Iran without fear of the economic results. On the other hand, despite the unexpected windfall prosperity, conservationists and conservatives warned of the danger of precipitate industrialisation due to the quick development of the offshore oil industry, and argued that the Norwegian society could be destroyed by new affluence in much the same way that alcohol eroded it in the previous century. But the development of a petrochemical industry and the start of feasibility studies on piping oil to Teesside in the UK and natural gas to Emden in Germany indicated that Norway was likely to be Europe's first major exporter of oil products.

The new wealth and capacity to begin a second industrial revolution based on oil rather than water was accompanied by a growth in concern for the environment. In summer 1974 a new petrochemical complex was started at Rafnes in the Telemark district. But by autumn the risk of cancer from vinyl chloride gas pollution caused Norsk Hydro, a state-controlled industrial group, to pull out of the scheme to protect the lives of its workers. Simultaneously, the anti-nuclear lobby began to take off, spearheaded by the young.

It was in Sweden, however, that the clearest clash came over the threat to the standard of living caused by the oil crisis. The Norwegians had their own supply, the Danes were cushioned by EEC membership and its concomitant economic growth, the Finns could buy oil from the Russians, at a price, but in 1974 the Swedes were faced with a winter of discontent. President Richard Nixon summed up the problem with admirable conciseness in a letter he wrote to the heads of governments of eight large oil-consuming countries. The letter, released on 10 January 1974, described how developments in international energy use had brought consumer and producer nations to an historic crossroads. The question of energy threatened, Nixon thought, to unleash political and economic forces that could cause severe and irreparable damage to the prosperity and stability of the world.

The turning point in their nation's history was brought home to the Swedes by Ingmar Bergman who captured the audience of half the homes in Sweden with a series of television programs called *Scenes From a Marriage*. In the series two characters dominated: Johan and Marianne Palm (Erland Josephson and Liv Ullmann). In the screenplay 'the monstrosity of cosiness' that characterised the Swedish welfare state (of which Bergman was one of the most celebrated beneficiaries and, later, victims) was shaken by an energy crisis personified by the two protagonists, Marianne and Johan Palm, who were arranging their divorce. Marianne declared that she was fond of a cosy old sofa and an oil lamp that gave an illusion of security, and asked Johan whether or not the two of them were living in utter confusion, secretly realising they were slipping down hill, but not knowing what to do about it. Marianne wrote an obituary for her marriage, which was intended to represent in a symbolic way the Swedish welfare state: 'I don't know who I am ... I have always done what people told me ... In the snug little world where Johan and I have lived so unconsciously, taking everything for granted, there is more cruelty and brutality implied which frightens me more and more when I think back on it. Outward security demands a high price: the acceptance of a continuous destruction of the personality.'

Marianne Palm explained it to Johan; Olof Palme explained it to the electorate. The Swedes, who had sacrificed so much for living standards, had to make a complete reappraisal of their social values and aspirations in the new steady state economy. In January 1974, Palme rationed gasoline for three weeks and heating oil until March. On a per capita basis the Swedes were the world's largest oil consumers, and Palme took the occasion of the Arab nations' cutback to launch an attack on the accepted values of what he described as a gadget society. He argued that good would come out of change associated with economic cut-backs, if the prime minister and the Social Democrats could convince society that human needs should be given priority. Palme explained that his aim was to redirect Swedish resources into such labour-intensive areas as the provision of home help for people shut in their flats, the ill or the elderly. In an interview with a correspondent of the *Washington Star* in 1974, Palme admitted that it was difficult to change Swedish society, and quoted an example to illustrate the comparative defects he saw. In Sweden, Palme said, hospitals were the best in the world as far as hardware was concerned, but in many nursing homes patients were bedded down in the afternoon because of staff shortages and difficulties in mounting an evening shift. In Paris (he had heard) the hospitals were shabby, but patients could take their pet parrots into the ancient wards with them. Palme wished to see a parrot in every Swedish hospital, as an antidote to impersonal bureaucracy.

As an idea, the parrot solution was original, but it was not enough to save the Social Democrats. Palme was not on the same wavelength as his electorate. He set out to shake up a smooth, satisfied society at a time when it was being rocked by the Arabs and by guilt derived from a failure to live up to its expectations as a pacesetter in social reform. In 1969 Palme felt there was much that was wrong in Sweden. Complacency, he taunted, was a terrible danger. 'A politician shouldn't say everything's fine. He should talk about what is wrong. We in Sweden can be happy about not having the excitement of Northern Ireland or the race problem. But there is a real risk for us. You have to try to activate people.' On the eve of the 1973 election, Palme went on air with Swedish radio to answer questions, as was the vogue, in a talkback radio programme conducted for his electors. By then he did not have to stir people: 7,500 Swedes tried to telephone to complain about their taxes, unemployment, inflation and 'the queue society' syndrome that had developed whereby welfare state services and non-emergency medical care, provision of housing and child care were never immediately available. The Swedish constitution fell a victim to the oil crisis. A deadlocked parliament was unthinkable in times of power cuts, petrol rationing, increasing unemployment, high inflation, nuclear energy controversy, and a scandal about Sweden's security service – not to mention the enhancement of normal Nordic winter angst. Nor was the role of the monarch acceptable as a crisis breaker. So, from 1 January 1975, the King of Sweden was declared a figurehead, whose formal assent to legislation was no longer required. The number of seats in parliament was reduced from 350 to 349, thus avoiding the need to draw lots after a tie. The Social Democrats fought to the end. They ploughed state resources into a scheme to give security in the labour market, as well as concentrating on their traditional areas of interest: child allowances, old age pensions, help for the handicapped, housing and food subsidies, improvement of the work environment and energy conservation.

The pressures that Scandinavia suffered after 1968 had a side effect in the way in which Scandinavia was regarded by the rest of the world. Prurient sociologists had always been attracted to

Sweden and Denmark, where their questionnaires elicited exciting information on Scandinavian sex lives, a perennial source of outside interest in the north. On 1 January 1969, the *Dagens Nyheter* published the results of a survey that found that 98 per cent of the married population had had premarital intercourse. Surveys were carried out by vast teams of diligent investigators who fleshed out the statistics and also provided evidence (much to the satisfaction of non-Scandinavians) that in Sweden and Denmark, at least, suicide rates were as abnormally high as pre-marital sexual intercourse. And when the much vaunted Swedish standard of living began to fall after 1968, there was only one word that adequately described the non-Scandinavian response: the critics of Sweden and Denmark gloated at the way the mighty had been brought low. Finland and Norway were spared this unkind response, largely because Norway and Finland were thought to be purer than Sweden and Denmark. Most of the anti-Scandinavian glee was reserved for the fall of Sweden's Social Democrats, and the defeat of Olof Palme was particularly gratifying to those who saw him as getting his just deserts for his insensitive support of North Vietnamese guerillas.

CHAPTER 9

The Ice Age

From the mid-1970s until 1993 Scandinavia was in a political ice age. The optimistic warm feeling which followed on the heels of the almost hedonistic social engineering of the post war years 'economic miracles' in Finland, Norway, Denmark and Sweden, was frozen away by new chill blasts from both expected and unexpected quarters. The ideals of sustainable growth, perpetual augmentation of living standards, and the continual improvement in the services of the Scandinavian welfare states were glacified by a new ice age, as economic rationalists took the helm in the face of economic collapse. Many of the world-renowned household names and flag carriers of Scandinavian superiority were stressed to breaking points, and many broke. Bankruptcy, insolvency, and uncompetitiveness reached the point where the Scandinavians themselves needed to be rescued by the outside capitalists whose products they had hitherto undercut and whose industries they had decimated. Shot gun marriages became more and more common as Scandinavians rugged up for an uncertain future.

The beginning of the new ice age was signalled by the fall of Olof Palme's Social Democrats in September 1976, the mid-point of the ice age was marked by Palme's murder, and the final phase of glaciation was symbolised by the September 1991 return of a conservative Swedish government.

The fall of Olof Palme showed how unromantic nationalism could be. Palme's defeat was the end of the forty-four-year reign of Swedish social democracy, and the importance of this watershed is difficult to exaggerate, although perhaps it was comparable to the end of the Kekkonen era in Finland. Palme's government fell over the nuclear power issue. Technological expertise and industrial need in the 1950s had led Sweden to begin an ambitious program of nuclear power generation: Sweden had large deposits of shale uranium ore. At the time of the 1976 election, Sweden, with a population of 8,000,000, was the world's sixth largest producer of electricity through nuclear energy: 12,000,000 megawatts were generated by Swedish nuclear power stations, the gross output being only exceeded by the United States, Great Britain, West Germany, France, Japan and Canada. Swedish technology was clean. Natural, not enriched, uranium was used as a fuel and after the shock of the oil crisis nuclear power was boosted so that, in the first six months of 1976, Swedish nuclear power produced more electrical energy than Canada and nudged France and West Germany. In the three years of 'equilibrium government', however, the political implications of the nuclear power industry had not been grasped by the Social Democrats. Palme lacked a mandate to push nuclear power as the major solution to Sweden's energy problems in the twentieth century and beyond. His regime was more unpopular than it had ever been and the hand that fed the pets of the social democratic society was bitten to the bone. History was to repeat itself, so far as the Social Democrats were concerned, in 1991. Some of Palme's most important supporters deserted him, many of them famous creative artists. Astrid Lindgren left after she was misinformed by the income tax authorities that she would have to pay 102 per cent tax on her income. The author of one of the world's most celebrated children's book series, the stories of Pippi Longstocking (a character who had the significance of

Asterix the Gaul or Charlie Brown), Lindgren was, along with Abba, among the most highly paid in Sweden. Her satirical response to the situation rallied Palme's opponents. Ingmar Bergman left Sweden for voluntary exile, complaining that social democracy had created a rigidly conformist society administered by heavy-handed tax collectors. Bergman should have known. He was roughly interrogated by tax inspectors investigating his fiscal affairs. Bergman's star artist, Max von Sydow, also left to settle in Rome, and in the late 1980s finally settled a $200,000 dispute with Swedish tax authorities by taking the matter to the International Court in The Hague. The Swedish and world tennis champion Björn Borg – Ice Borg, as the pun ran – joined the exodus. Borg settled in Monaco to prevent the loss of seventy-five per cent of his income in tax. The famous went regretfully. They did not wish to see the ice of the welfare state melt. Bergman doubted that his creativity would stand severance from his mother tongue, and Borg protested (significantly to *Paris Match* not the *Dagens Nyheter*) that he was, even in Monaco, one hundred per cent Swedish, a comment echoed sporadically by Greta Garbo, also living as a tax exile. There was much to be said for being one hundred per cent Swedish. For all its faults, Sweden had model forms of organisation at almost every level. To take one example, tourists who visited the IKEA 'incredible furniture store' in Stockholm did so to see the Swedish way of life. IKEA stores had become another successful world-wide export, largely because of their innovative, unconventional organisation as giant self-service furnishing supermarkets. There were no pushy sales people, customers were free to browse at their leisure, the price was fixed, parking was free, children were welcome, coffee and snacks were available, and IKEA could arrange to truck purchases home. By 1990 IKEA had stores in Australia, France, Belgium, the Netherlands, West Germany, Switzerland, the United Kingdom, Denmark, Norway, Hungary, Canada, the United States, Singapore, the Canary Islands, Hong

Kong, Iceland, Kuwait, Saudi Arabia and plans on the drawing board to open in the Soviet Union.

The Swedes who stayed with the sinking ship shopped at IKEA and voted for a change of captain. They chose Thorbjörn Fälldin. Fälldin led the Centre Party. He projected the image of sincere rural character, wedded to a life of Tolstoyan pastoralism with his sheep and potatoes on the hilltops of his northern farm. Fälldin had been awakened to the dangers of the nuclear industry by the Swedish Nobel prize winner Hannes Alfven. Alfven, a plasma physicist, convinced Fälldin that there was no safe way of disposing of radioactive nuclear waste and that such technology could not be developed, whatever future the optimists and the self-interested projected. Fälldin's policy speech promised a government that would, if elected, stop all current and future nuclear plant construction, and decommission the five plants on line as soon as possible. His party workers saturated Sweden with campaign posters saying 'No to nuclear energy – Yes to safe, secure energy sources', and he repeated the slogan that mankind had intruded into an area where it did not belong, and had to retreat.

Palme's election campaign was unsuccessful in its attempt to woo the voters away from the environmental issues and into a projected system of gambling casinos. The biggest gambler in the country was Fälldin, and his pluck was rewarded with the victory of 19 September 1976, which ended generations of single-party government. But the inevitable retreat from nuclear energy in Sweden was paved not by the Swedish voters against Olof Palme but by two disasters: the first at Three Mile Island, USA, and the second at Chernobyl in the USSR.

Palme had chosen a good election to lose. Fälldin was to share the experience of almost all western heads of government in the new ice age. He saw ruin and despair where once there was optimism and prosperity. Cherished institutions were undermined, and society seemed to be careering out of control, without any recognised set of values. Key Swedish export industries seemed to be on the point of collapse. Shipbuilding was no longer profitable. No one wanted giant oil tankers, and oil costs made most companies preach if not practise conservation rather than expansion. The Swedish State Mining Company began mass layoffs. The production and profitability of Volvo and SAAB-SCANIA dipped. The Swedish currency began a series of devaluations. In the immediate post-war years Sweden had led the world in technological innovation in areas where its wartime neutrality had allowed it to develop research programs, unhampered by the need to start from scratch like Finland, or to spend its resources on the war effort like Norway and to a lesser extent Denmark. By the mid 1970s, such economic supremacy as Sweden possessed had gone as surely as Queen Christina. Sweden began to reap what it had sown. The luxury of boycotting the South African market became more difficult to justify in economic terms. Trade with the USA had been damaged by anti-Americanism during the Vietnam War. Most importantly, the great economic takeoff of the European Economic Community had been made largely at the expense of other trading nations, and Sweden suffered like the rest of the western world. Economic self-sufficiency and economic neutrality were as impossible as military and diplomatic neutrality had been successful.

Nor would the Swedish electorate allow Fälldin to dodge the problems of nuclear power. Evening study groups kept up the level of public debate, which centred on the questions of reactor safety, the fuel cycle, nuclear proliferation and social and environmental costs. Almost unthinkably in Sweden, the opinions of the technocrats were challenged, and the traditional high esteem of bureaucracy further undermined. Fälldin coped with the problem honestly. In 1978 he proposed a nuclear energy referendum, but the Liberals and Moderates in his coalition refused to support him and on 5 October 1978 the

Fälldin government fell and Olla Ullsten became prime minister. Ullsten found that the only area where consensus could be found in Sweden was women's rights, so he began a policy of positive discrimination in favour of women. One-third of Ullsten's cabinet was female, but Ullsten was a mere caretaker. In September 1979 elections were held and the election went narrowly against the centre coalition, which was even more unstable than it had been in 1976. Fälldin was again found to be the best choice for prime minister, and he presided over the nuclear referendum, held on 23 March 1980.

The referendum had three alternative proposals. The first, drafted by the Moderate Party, suggested that no more than the twelve nuclear power reactors in operation should be used and that no further nuclear power development should take place. The second referendum proposal (that of the Social Democrats and Liberals) called for environmental and safety improvements to be carried out at nuclear power stations and demanded energy conservation, asserting that society should have the main responsibility for the production and distribution of electric power. The Centre Party joined with the Communists to support proposal three, which called for an end to nuclear power, for no uranium mining in Sweden and for work against nuclear weapon proliferation. The result of the referendum was that 18.9 per cent voted for the first proposal, 39.3 per cent for the second, and 38.5 per cent for the third. Most Swedes regarded the result as a mandate for the government to proceed with its twelve nuclear reactors program. Thus the Swedish nuclear energy debate showed how in one crucial area, that of energy production, the problems of society could not be solved or shelved, but remained as preoccupations and dilemmas.

An eye to the future combined with a concern for the past. Nostalgia about the world that was lost became a motif of Scandinavian culture after 1968. History achieved a new importance. The greatest cinema success in Sweden in the 1970s was Jan Troell's adaptation of Wilhelm Moberg's epic novel about the Swedes who sailed to America. Moberg was born in southern Sweden in 1898. He worked as a pictorial journalist, published an anti-German novel called *Ride the Night* in 1941, and on his death in 1973 was Sweden's best known author. His trilogy, *The Emigrants, Unto a Good Land* and *The Last Letter Home*, was shown and admired throughout the world in Jan Troell's cinema masterpiece. The twin stars of Scandinavian cinema, Liv Ullmann and Max von Sydow, injected their skill into their portraits of the Swedish emigrants. Emigration was a tearful business. Many Swedes identified with the economic and spiritual problems of the reluctant pioneer Kristina and the existential anti-hero Karl Oscar. Equally significant was the belated discovery, largely through the cinema, of Karen Blixen, who, after studying art in Copenhagen, Rome and Paris, married her cousin, Baron Bror Blixen-Finecke in 1914. As newly married adventurers Karen and Bror travelled to Kenya to manage a coffee plantation. The film *Out of Africa* brought the romance and trauma of Karen Blixen's life from obscurity. Her autobiography was published in 1937, but it was not until 1985 when *Out of Africa* won Oscars for best screenplay, best picture and best director that Blixen became internationally famous. *Babette's Feast*, which followed in 1987, had a Danish setting but was nonetheless successful. Directed by Gabriel Axel, the film was based on a Blixen short story originally published in the *Ladies' Home Journal* and showed the liberating effect of a Parisian refugee, Babette, thrown into a small Danish village during the nineteenth century. Babette transformed the self-denying puritanism of the small closed peasant community by an incandescent generosity expressed through the provision of a spectacularly self-indulgent feast.

In Finland, the government reacted to the changing world with concrete rather than cinematic displays of self-confidence. The people of Helsinki once more became proud that their city was a beautiful example of Russian empire architecture. It was fine to be Russian, bad to be Soviet, and such was the aplomb of the city fathers that in Helsinki some of the old imperial symbols reappeared. The doubleheaded eagle, removed from the crown on the head of the statue of the Russian head of state because of its scary associations, was put back, and Finns strolled by the statue without a shudder at the memories of their moments of precarious national existence. A portrait of a tsar hung in a place of honour in Helsinki university. The commercial centre of Helsinki remained Alexander Street: the most significant square, bounded by the cathedral, the ministry of foreign affairs and the university, had as its centrepiece a statue of Alexander II. The main street of Helsinki, Aleksanterinkatu, begins at a statue of three blacksmiths, the pedestal of which has been left marked by Russian bombs which fell in 1944. The symbolism of the inter-section of Aleksanterinkatu and Mannerheimintie is not lost on the Finns. In October 1974 President Kekkonen rewrote history at the thirtieth anniversary celebration of the armistice between Finland and Russia. In the presence of the Russian president, Nikolai Podgorny, Kekkonen told his audience who were stunned to hear it, that the Finns had attacked the Russians. The accepted account before 1974 was that Finland declared war on Russia only after the Russians had bombed Finnish cities. Finland nevertheless remained free, independent and self-confident, with the term 'Finlandisation' largely meaningless. In October 1981, however, the Kekkonen era ended. The Finns, like their Scandinavian neighbours, were on their own. Kekkonen resigned at the age of eighty-one through ill-health, and the Finns were faced with the problem of establishing a new head of state in a role traditionally given more than ordinary scope for directing the nation's development.

The 1980s and the 1990s were to see a major change in direction for all the Scandinavian nations, some looking backward to the golden age before the nineteenth-century struggle for independence and domestic reform. A new spirit of national chauvinism permeated the north, expressed in both progressive and retrogressive attitudes to the problems of the region. The most symbolic indications of the new directions that society was taking were often small but nonetheless portentous. By 1981 the Swedes were self-confident enough to detain for a week an ageing Russian submarine which ran aground about twelve miles south of a Swedish naval base at Karlskrona. A year earlier, in April and May 1980, Sweden had been shattered by the worst strikes in its history. Forty-two years of industrial peace were broken by a strike in which a quarter of the workforce of 4,500,000 were either on strike or locked out, in a struggle that finally demolished the prestige of the Swedish model of wage fixation. Not that everything was shaky in Sweden. Queen Silvia and King Carl XVI Gustaf provided the egalitarian Swedes with the relief of royalist euphoria when their first child, a daughter, was born. King Carl XVI Gustaf had his child baptised Victoria Ingrid Alice Desirée. The reference to Desirée, one of the founders of the Bernadotte dynasty, was not lost on the Swedes, nor on the rest of the Scandinavians.

Certainly the king's conspicuous egalitarianism was in tune with the democratic temper of most of his subjects. He and the queen made an attractive young couple, rearing their children in the peace of Drottningholm. They appeared often in public, at such formal occasions as the Nobel Prize ceremony, and such less formal ones as the world orienteering championship, presenting prizes for excellence. But in the ice age, prizes and excellence were hard to find.

If the King of Sweden looked back to the relative certainties of the nineteenth century, most of his fellow Scandinavians were looking forward anxiously to the twenty-first. The 1980s and the 1990s continued the trend of the 1970s. While instability and challenges were everywhere, there were three issues of prime concern: the leadership of the Scandinavian states, the problems of their relationship with the Soviet Union and the United States, and the environmental danger from the nuclear fuel cycle.

All of Scandinavia was affected by the Chernobyl disaster. Heavy radioactive fallout was deposited on the east coast of Sweden and in Swedish Lapland, and this precipitated a further reduction in the life expectancy of the Swedish nuclear power industry, with the Swedish prime minister suggesting that the country's nuclear power generation should stop before the end of the century. The Finns were incensed that their Soviet neighbours had not warned them to take precautions immediately the disaster unfolded, as the radio-active fallout drifted up from Chernobyl to Helsinki, Stockholm, Oslo and Denmark. The Norwegians lost huge areas of production in the Arctic Circle as the reindeer were affected by the radioactivity of their lichen diet, and the Danes were at one with their Scandinavian cousins in condemning the Soviet Union for its lack of consideration and responsibility.

Problems with the Soviet Union bedevilled Scandinavia, as did difficulties in accommodating the demands by NATO on the Nordic predisposition for neutrality. In 1984, Palme used the opportunity of a Stockholm peace conference to protest to Andrei Gromyko about Soviet violation of Swedish territorial waters and the overflight of a Russian military jet near Gotland in the Baltic Sea. Gromyko assured Palme that Swedish navy intelligence was mistaken but, in January 1985, a Russian missile went astray during firing exercises in the Barents Sea, crashing into Finland's Lake Inari after crossing Norwegian airspace. The Soviet Union apologised to both nations, the Finns accepting rather more readily than the Norwegians.

While Sweden, Finland and Norway were disturbed by the Soviet Union, Denmark began to display anxiety about the United States. Indeed, from the mid 1980s Denmark seriously reassessed its membership of NATO. At the party congress of the Danish Social Democrats, they passed a resolution calling for the banning of nuclear weapons from Denmark at times of peace or war.

One of the most dramatic events in Scandinavian–Russian relations in the decade was the unmasking of the Soviet spy Arne Treholt. Treholt, a Norwegian foreign ministry official and former junior minister, was arrested in January 1984 while attempting to leave Oslo with secret documents intended for the KGB. Described as the greatest quisling since Quisling, Treholt was convicted in June 1985 and sentenced to twenty years' imprisonment for spying. Treholt's conviction helped the United States in its attempts to stiffen morale in NATO by showing the determination of the Soviet Union to undermine the western democracies.

The new Scandinavian nation-states of the late twentieth century needed strong leadership in the difficult times as the new century was approaching. In Sweden and Finland especially, changes at the summit of the power pyramid were unsettling and disturbing.

Both Sweden and Finland lost through death their major father figures whose appeal, albeit fluctuating, was crucial to the development and maintenance of social harmony. Urho Kekkonen died on 31 August 1986 and his death was no less the end of an era in Finland than Palme's in Sweden. Kekkonen, who died at the age of eighty-six, had fought against the Bolsheviks in Finland's war of independence as a teenager. He had been president of Finland for twenty-five years – from 1956 to 1981 – and his diplomatic brinkmanship preserved Finland's independence and enhanced the nation's stature. In his youth, he had been the national high jump champion.

In his second year of office Mauno Koivisto, who became president of Finland in 1982 on Kekkonen's retirement, extended in unamended form the 1948 Treaty of Friendship,

Co-operation and Mutual Assistance with the Soviet Union, from 1990 to 2003. Koivisto was an ideal partner for his Russian equivalent, Mikhail Gorbachev, and the evolving Soviet aims of perestroika and glasnost neatly coincided with Finland's best interests. At the same time, President Reagan re-affirmed support for Finnish neutrality, thus enabling Koivisto to continue in the tradition of his predecessors by pursuing personally successful diplomatic initiatives to protect the nation. At the grass roots level, however, all was not so clear cut. Finnair pilots, for example, for a time boycotted flights to Moscow following the shooting down of a Korean Airlines Boeing 747 by the Soviet Air force, in a clear demonstration of hostility to Koivisto's strict neutrality policy. Nor were matters helped by the decision of Ahti Karjalainen to publish his memoirs. In these Karjalainen accused the Soviet Union of conspiring with the Finnish foreign minister Paavo Väyrynen in an unsuccessful attempt to defeat Mauno Koivisto in the 1982 presidential election. Väyrynen admitted he had talked to former ministerial counsellor Victor Vladimirov, who was described in the Finnish press as a general in the KGB. Koivisto believed Karjalainen, but argued that such behaviour was a thing of the past, a view endorsed by Gorbachev who said during a visit to Finland in October 1989 that the USSR had no right to interfere in the affairs of its neighbours.

On 9 May 1986 Norway also came under new management, when Gro Brundtland formed a minority Labour government, taking over from the Conservative-led, three-party coalition ministry of K.I. Willoch. Brundtland had previously made history in 1981 by being for a short while Norway's first female prime minister, but there were signs in 1986 that Brundtland would not be long at the helm. Her eighteen-person cabinet contained eight women – another record – and her first objectives were to cope with the collapse of world oil prices on which Norway's prosperity depended. With the economy dependent on falling oil prices, Gro Brundtland had little option but to continue with tight interest rates and tough budgets. Norwegians headed for the twenty-first century expecting austerity, reduced subsidies, higher direct and indirect taxation, and prepared for a period of comparative introspection, a symptom of which was the new crackdown on third world immigration. Among Scandinavians, Norway's immigration policy was the most liberal, but the burden of such groups as Tamil refugees from Sri Lanka led to a backlash from many Norwegians. Gro Brundtland resigned on 13 October 1989, after three and a half years in office. By then Norway's unemployment stood at 4.3 per cent of the labour force, and Norwegians turned to Conservatives to lead them in the 1990s, when Jan Peder Syse led the new government.

For Sweden in the 1980s the greatest problems were domestic, not international, and they focused on the mercurial personality of Olof Palme. In September 1985, Olof Palme's Social Democrats were re-elected for another three-year term. At that stage, the elections seemed to demonstrate the Swedish affection for their welfare state, but at the same time the Social Democrats lost sufficient seats to destroy their overall majority and make them reliant on the support of the nineteen Swedish Communist Party MPs. Palme's personal support was reduced, and he did little to help relations with the United States by making a stirring anti-American speech on US policy in Central America.

In a country attached to the democratic process, however, a fall in electoral popularity was unlikely to lead to political violence. Accordingly, when Palme was murdered on 28 February 1986 by an unknown assassin, Sweden suffered a collective nervous breakdown. Political murder had been unknown in Sweden since the late eighteenth century, and the spontaneous grief of the nation was eerie in its comprehensiveness. Olof Palme was shot dead outside one of the many entrances to the central underground station in

Stockholm. His blood froze on the ground where he fell. The spot was soon taken over by mourners who threw red roses on to the pavement, and while an extraordinary series of rumours swept non-Swedes in the capital, the Swedish nation rallied behind the new prime minister, Ingvar Carlsson. Palme was given a dramatic mid-winter funeral. He had been an atheist, and in deference to his wishes the Social Democrats and the men and women in the streets marched for hours round the old town until Palme was eventually buried in a central churchyard. With Palme was buried the cult of the individual in Sweden, as Ingvar Carlsson projected the more traditional self-effacing bureaucratic style that had served Sweden since the Middle Ages, and against which the Palme style was a contrast and an aberration. Whereas Palme had been from the Swedish upper class, Carlsson's parents were both workers. Indeed, Carlsson himself was an unknown figure outside Sweden, and in the normal course of events would have remained Palme's deputy, casting a small shadow compared with the prestigious stature of his leader.

The genuineness of the hunt for Palme's assassin was questioned as months passed without a clue to motive or murderer. In a witch-hunt setting, Swedish police raided the Kurdish exile community but, despite twenty arrests, no results were achieved. The police chief of Stockholm, Hans Holmer, resigned as scapegoat in March 1987. Finally, despite the misgivings of public opinion, Carl Pettersson was convicted in July 1989 and sentenced to life imprisonment for the assassination. Pettersson was found guilty mainly on the evidence of Lisbet Palme, the widow of the assassinated prime minister. In a face-to-face court confrontation, Lisbet Palme identi-fied Pettersson as her husband's killer. Pettersson was imprisoned for only a year before a police officer testified at appeal proceedings that Lisbet Palme was too distraught and hysterical to identify anyone. On 12 October 1989 a seven-member Swedish appeals court overturned the conviction. Pettersson, wearing an 'Alcatraz' sweater, immediately went on nationwide television and announced he would sue the state for record damages.

While the most efficient police force in Scandinavia, combined with one of the most effective bureaucracies in the western world, failed to find the murderer of its most famous twentieth-century prime minister, further cracks in the fabric of society were revealed by riots in Stockholm in August 1987, during which shops were looted, cars destroyed and Molotov cocktails thrown by bored Swedish school children at the end of their summer holidays. The nation's sagging reputation for rectitude and totalitarian social control received a further hammering when it was alleged that the premier Swedish arms manufacturer, Bofors, had illegally sold ground-to-air missiles to Dubai and Bahrain. Corruption, murder and moral collapse could now be found at home and abroad.

In the period 1968–93 there had been a burst of reformist energy followed by an important re-alignment of social forces. The bubble of optimism burst as the new trendsetters of Scandinavia came up against the massive decline in the power of the western world's economy that followed in the wake of the 1973 oil crisis. The new set of economic circumstances dashed to the ground the hopes of radicals and reformers, and led to the collapse of the attempt to construct an ideal society. For some Scandinavians, the period 1968–93 was a return to chaos. To a large extent, the crises faced by the nations of the north were outside their direct control. As had become usual in the past, all the nations responded differently. The gradual emergence of the European Economic Community as a world trading power forced Scandinavians to take stock of their room to manoeuvre. As the economic downturn intensified, Finland turned east, Denmark turned south, and Sweden and Norway turned in upon themselves. The only hope for the future of

Scandinavia collectively in the twenty-first century seemed to be a return to fierce, independent nationalism. National identity had to be re-defined and nurtured if the individual and his country were to survive and prosper. But it was with desperation rather than confidence that a self-conscious nationalism was advocated and promoted in the 1980s. Before then, the accepted rules of parliamentary democracy in a capitalist society had operated on a premise of progress no less enshrined in the north than were the values of Victorian Britain in the nineteenth century. After the retirement of Kekkonen, however, the murder of Palme, and the disaster of Chernobyl, the Scandinavians ceased to be sure of themselves and confident of their future.

The collective insecurity of Scandinavia was boosted at the turn of the decade by the extraordinary events in Eastern Europe: 1989 became the 1848 of the twentieth century. As the Berlin wall was demolished, foreign policy planners were forced to re-assess the direction of Nordic statecraft. The reforms of the Gorbachev era were as momentous as those changes made when Moscow and Ribbentrop signed their secret protocol, or Alexander I and Napoleon subdivided Europe. Scandinavians, with the rest of the world, watched in fascination the evolving policy of de-Russification. Finland and Norway, with land borders to the Soviet Union, were crucially important in the event of a breakdown in law and order in the Soviet Union if the Gorbachev reform movement pressures became too much. In the 1990s, Fazer's clientele in Helsinki debated the possibility of a thermidorian reaction against Gorbachev, knowing that once again the Finns were in the front line. The sight of a blue and white Finnish flag flying in Estonia during Gorbachev's historic visit of January 1990 was not only a diplomatic embarrassment to the Finnish government but also a sign that the Baltic States of Latvia, Lithuania and Estonia were determined to try to follow the Finnish example. They tried to persuade the Russians that it was better to have four friendly, neutral Finlands, than one friendly, neutral Finland and three recalcitrant Baltic states. An old age was dying, and a new century was about to begin, but from the Nordic point of view, illustrated best by the words of Baron Axel Carpelan, the Scandinavians were still not masters of their fate. Substitute tsar for president, and tsarist for communist, and Carpelan's observations in March 1904 have a haunting relevance: 'Tsarist Russia is like a great whirlpool, too large for the separate particles to grasp which way the suction is pulling. Desperate ukases are thrown out with increasing desperation around a confused, weak centre: the tsar. Strategy is being able to move the point of gravity quickly or divide it into several. The really important actors are waiting in the wings while Holy Russia tears itself into shreds, the chimneys smoke, the anarchists sharpen their weapons, the ice breaks up and hidden corpses are brought to light.'

By 1993 Carpelan's words were literally true as Scandinavia benefited from the breakdown in the structure of the Soviet Union, following the unsuccessful coup attempt against Gorbachev. Scandinavians were amongst the first to recognise the independence of the Baltic States, and to send ambassadors to Estonia, Latvia and Lithuania. The Nordic nations saw opportunities for trade in the newly emerging former constituent states of the Soviet Union, and were freed from the danger of having their Soviet neighbours overrun their borders in a disorderly flight from starvation. Finns heaved a sigh of relief that the Estonian mafia, who were setting up shop in Helsinki, could now be regulated on a bi-lateral basis. Norwegians were less confident, and expelled Russian spies in October 1991 from Oslo, but Sweden and Denmark were optimistic about the new market opportunities posed by the burgeoning infant states across the Baltic.

The breakup of the Soviet empire gave Scandinavian foreign policy makers their biggest challenge since world war two, but not their only one. The momentous decisions of the twelve member states of the European Community at their meeting at Maastricht in the Netherlands on 9 and 10 December 1991, forced the Scandinavian nations to re-assess their political and economic relationships with each other and the European community. The Maastricht view that it was essential to work towards closer relations between member states through common policies on foreign affairs, security and immigration, and the process of creating an economic and monetary union (EMU) plus a single currency (the ECU) and a European central bank, cut into the heart of Scandinavian national identity and under-mined twenty centuries of historical experience. If Scandinavia stayed aloof from the Maastricht deliberations, it risked economic isolation and collapse of the standard of living; if Scandinavia embraced the Maastricht philosophy, it risked watering down and eventually destroying the *raison d'être* of a unique collection of independent states. Denmark broke first. Although recognising its pivotal role as the link between Germany and Scandinavia by pressing ahead with the bridge building projects between Denmark and Germany and Denmark and Sweden, Danes declined to set in concrete their membership of the European community, and in a shock result voted for a time against the principles of the Maastricht Treaty.

In Sweden, however, Carlsson and the social democrats knew that they were in a no-win situation. If they took the bold step, and re-wrote party history by abandoning neutrality and seeking membership of the European Economic Community, they would be admitting their contemporary irrelevance. Bold they were. In June 1991, Carlsson and his party crossed the Rubicon, and Sweden applied to join the EEC. Since Finland, after a time, was inevitably bound to follow, the new economic game plans in the north appeared to involve a subjugation of Scandinavian national identity to the corporate collectivism of Brussels bureaucrats.

The fall of Scandinavian social democracy was less spectacular than the fall of the Soviet Union's ruling party, but both were part of the new ice age. Certainly Soviet watchers were caught on the hop by the abortive coup attempt on Gorbachev; not so observers of the Nordic scene. Before the 1991 election which swept the Swedish social democrats aside, the writing was on the wall.

In Scandinavia, as had been predicted by opinion polls, the economic problems caused by unemployment, inflation, failing productivity and an over-sized public sector took their toll when during the 1991 September elections Ingvar Carlsson's Social Democrats were swept away. By then social democracy, which had become sociologically inappropriate in Sweden, was so unpopular that a new prime minister, Carl Bildt, was elected to send the Swedish states in a new direction. The turning point – perhaps one should say the match point – was recognized at the time. It occurred when Germany's Boris Becker crushed Stefan Edberg in the men's tennis final of the Stockholm Open. In the autumn of 1990 Sweden's self-confidence was at its lowest point, and the Social Democrats under Ingvar Carlsson were blamed. While it would be an exaggeration to say that Sweden approached the state where sport was its most important touchstone of success (as in East Germany, or Rumania), the popular cultural heroes of Sweden were its world tennis champions and, as they were beaten, spectators ruefully acknow-ledged that so were the industrial giants which made Sweden's economic miracle the envy of the industrialised world. When Prime Minister Carlsson, and not the king, rose to present the prize to Becker, the audience booed. The match result was on the scoreboard, the Social Democrats were doomed. After Palme's murder, public opinion polls showed sixty per cent of Swedish voters had great confidence in Carlsson: by the spring of 1991, confidence had collapsed, and Carlsson's personal popularity stood at thirteen per cent.

Swedish industry epitomised the trend. Pehr Gyllenhammer, the celebrated chairman of Volvo, announced in 1991 that the new range of large family cars, the 800 series, was likely to be the last series to be developed alone by the Company. Future product generations would be developed with Renault of France, the Swedish group's industrial partner. General Motors acquired a fifty per cent stake in SAAB at the end of 1989: by the end of 1991 General Motors had invested $1.15 billion in SAAB-SCANIA. SAAB losses continued over the period and its car assembly plant in Malmö closed after only eighteen months operation as part of an effort to rationalise and reduce overcapacity.

Carl Bildt and a conservative coalition of Liberals, Christian Democrats and the Centre Party had a mandate to reduce the centralised power of the welfare state. Characteristically the Swedes rejected the extremist ultra-right new democracy which called for freedom of choice, except where alcohol was concerned, where they argued a neo-prohibitionist line. The new prime minister saw his role to be to bring Sweden into the EEC and protect the parties of free enterprise. This involved a difficult balancing act as Swedes – and the other Scandinavians whose political developments were running parallel at the time – were forced to subjugate essential elements of their national identity, while at the same time insisting defensively on their uniqueness. The daily lunch menus in the old town told the story: 'European community spaghetti' was becoming ever more popular and cheaper than the local speciality, but 'Jannson's Temptation' was fighting back.

The future for the Scandinavians was not, however, all black: as their societies were changed by entry into the European Community, so was the European Community bound to be altered by the presence of Scandinavians. Finns were not prepared to sacrifice their defence policy without the substitution of a European Community alternative. As one Finn put it, they were not prepared to give up their tried system of neutrality for a series of half-baked guarantees. Norway pressed for more active social policy. Gro Brundtland commented that the European Community would find Norway in a group wanting effectiveness on social concerns. Sweden asked for environmental standards to be improved. Acutely sensitive about their sovereignty and vulnerability as small states, the new Nordic members of the European Community promised to greatly strengthen the European community, by the changing axis of power in Europe from the big three – the UK, France and Germany – and working towards the ideals of a benevolent society that had always been hallmarks of their cultures.

CHAPTER 10

The Civilised Circle

During the last three centuries Scandinavia has often been seen by the rest of the world as an example: sometimes a good example, sometimes a bad example, sometimes as a black and sombre warning, sometimes as a bright, illuminating and encouraging portent. On the whole, however, the way in which Scandinavians, even in the most difficult and trying periods of their history, have devised institutions to stimulate co-operation in their region has been taken as an inspiration for others.

The Nordic Council was at the heart of a typically Scandinavian co-existence experiment. It paved the way for the breaking down of barriers, while still allowing members of the council the vital privilege of exercising sovereignty in areas where they chose to differ from a common norm. The Nordic Council agreement to formalise co-operation was signed on 23 March 1962. Although it was different from other superficially similar treaties, which had a clause on mandatory mutual assistance for defence, the attempt to draw closer together in non-military spheres and to keep recognised channels of communication open between career diplomats and cabinet ministers served as an emphatic deterrent to potential aggressors wishing to attack Scandinavia.

The Scandinavians clearly intended to signal to all their neighbours a respect for international law, while at the same time demonstrating to the citizens of their region that the rule of law would be observed in all the Scandinavian states. The members of the Nordic Council were also at pains to show that no clear disparities or any anomalies would exist in the interpretation and administration of Scandinavian civil and criminal law.

From a social legal foundation the governments of the Scandinavian states moved to develop and integrate as far as was practical appropriate economic and cultural links. In the economic field, the attempt was relatively successful. Obstacles to trade between the countries were reduced. Simplified customs arrangements made traffic easier and helped to stimulate commerce. Scandinavia was turned into a single passport-control area. Cross-border travel was simple and uniform – very different from the conditions earlier when the east and west were then divided by the Swedish-Finnish frontier at Haparanda, at the top of the Gulf of Bothnia, two hundred kilometres inside the Arctic Circle. At the Swedish end of the bridge, which then was the nearest and most convenient land crossing into and out of Russian Finland and hence into Russia itself, Swedish police watched their Russian equivalents, tsarist border guards. The Russians at the end of the nineteenth century were intent on stopping the smuggling of anti-government propaganda and weapons into Russia through its more liberal grand duchy, Finland.

By the 1990s, Russia was anxious to facilitate, not minimise, movement between west and east, if not east and west. The decision to re-name Leningrad St Petersburg was part of a deliberate strategy to stress the accessibility of Russia, and no doubt the mayor of St Petersburg hoped that the Venice of the north would have its own Orient Express running from Helsinki, chock-a-block with wealthy tourists who had hitherto been everywhere. Now that the decision to build a fourteen kilometre bridge between Sweden and Denmark across the sound is brought to fruition, cross-border travel between Scandinavia and Europe is as easy as travelling between Denmark and Germany. The bridge is, however, a rare apple of discord, facing opposition from the Finns, who fear their profitable and successful ship building industry will be destroyed as sea navigation is reduced by the height of the bridge, and opposition from the Nordic environmentalists, who fear everything.

The Scandinavians have always recognised the crucial role of education in creating a positive atmosphere in which friendly relationships could develop. While there was no gain-saying the differences between the Nordic states (often illustrated by the fierce, sometimes even bloody, sporting competitions between them) the Nordic Council set out to break down, as far as it could, existing cultural barriers through a bold educational experiment involving the allocation of scarce resources. The council agreed that each of the Nordic nation's teaching in the schools in the area should include language instruction and material explaining its culture and traditions. In this way they hoped to expunge from group consciousness the harmful stereotypes. In the space of a generation, the Nordic Council expected to wipe out through education, the view (incorrect, but nevertheless widely held) that Finns were quarrelsome and unintelligible knife-fighters, that Swedes were swaggering, boastful, introspective materialists, that Norwegians were a scattered group of puritan and bovine alcoholics and that Danes were bicycling pornography enthusiasts. To a large extent the council has been successful in Scandinavia, although outside the North stereotyping continues, reinforced by such decisions as the Danish parliament's agreement in 1989 for Denmark to become the first country to legalise civil marriage between homosexuals.

Besides trying to help local living standards and to blot out harmful stereotyping, the Scandinavians have aimed to be a force in the fight against Third World poverty. An important feature of the Nordic Council agreement was the insistence that the contracting parties should co-ordinate aid and work to help underdeveloped countries. The Scandinavians were well aware of the high level of their standard of living and the comparative good fortune Nordic citizens enjoyed. They had only to look in the glittering windows of such department stores as Stockmann in Helsinki, an emporium so famous that many Russians thought Stockmann was the capital of Finland.

Scandinavians have approached the problem of equity on two levels: the material and the political. Led by Sweden, and with the others following with greater or lesser degrees of enthusiasm and commitment, the Scandinavians have tried to promote economic growth in the most glaring cases of South American, African or Asian need. Most often the motive has been straight-out philanthropy, but in some cases Scandinavian companies have blended their commercial needs with those of the client nations. Often, but not always, under the aegis of the United Nations, Scandinavians have struggled to get projects underway that would lead to economic self-sufficiency in the most deserving areas. Cases of pump-priming have been matched by cases where high-technology, large-scale civil engineering programs have been carried out by Scandinavian experts, using their skills and talents in areas as diverse climatically as the burgeoning areas of Siberia, the Arab Emirates and even Australia, where Kockums-Celsius is in partnership with the Australian Submarine Corporation.

Although the Scandinavian contribution to European values and attitudes has been positive and outstanding, and although their forms of social organisation have correctly been described by Colin Simpson in the *Viking Circle* as civilisation with 'capital C', the equally vital influence of Scandinavian migration on receptor countries has been difficult to estimate in qualitative terms. Quantitatively, the numbers of Scandinavians migrating have been debilitating to their cultures. Sweden, Norway,/

Denmark and Finland lost much of their lifeblood through mass emigration in the nineteenth and twentieth centuries. The dramatic story of Scandinavian emigration is beyond the scope of this work, but the relatively poor Scandinavian countries of the emigration era were ill-fitted to lose so many of their finest, most adventurous and resourceful citizens in the prime of their lives. Sweden lost one-tenth of its population, over one million citizens, Norway lost almost as many, and Finland and Denmark about half a million each.

The emigrant Scandinavians' success at assimilating in the United States, and the ease with which the mother countries made good their population deficiencies, give a clue to the complex character of the region. In their mother countries, Scandinavians adapted their behaviour to the physical environment; in the United States they were equally successful in accommodating their values to the political climate. Scandinavians, on the whole, were not trouble-makers or recalcitrants at home or abroad. They tried to avoid exploitation and to tone down the level of local violence in their new homelands. A cathartic and necessary familiarity with hunting weapons was matched by a respect for nature and an understanding of the value of wilderness, this sensitivity readily translating to an urban setting as generally speaking most Scandinavians live cheek by jowl in exemplary city neighbourhoods.

It is common for those who do not share it to mock the Scandinavians' schizophrenic way of living, based on a complete change in routine from summer to winter. In the summer, celebrating by atavistic pagan bonfires, the typical city dweller escapes to his cottage by the sea or lake, there to live without central heating, double-glazing, or electric light. The simpler the life and the closer you come to nature, the happier the office or factory workers and their families. Braving sunburn, mosquitoes, boredom and the often fatal hazards of serious recreation, for two months or so the harried man of our times tries to identify with the peasant farmers of his ancestral stock. When the summer is over, the cottages and beaches are deserted for the year, and the apprehensive citizens drag themselves back reluctantly to lives of order, co-operation and direction, broken only by the mid-winter unseasonal migration of the increasing numbers of Scandinavians who take January holidays from the snow and darkness in Southern Europe, Northern Africa and South-East Asia.

The capacity of Scandinavians to assimilate and adapt to their surroundings has many positive aspects, not the least being the successful way in which individual Scandinavians, contemporary Denmmark notwithstanding, co-operate for the greater good of all in the largely social democratic Scandinavian welfare states. Several critics of the Scandinavian way of life have pointed out the negative aspects of modern Scandinavia, and pointed to the dangers of a too supine acceptance of norms set by governments and bureaucrats. But there is no doubting the good will and optimism that lies behind the Scandinavian experiment in communalism, and the determination to use pooled resources for noble purposes. Certainly, foreigners visiting the region are puzzled by the enthusiasm with which Scandinavians follow their leaders, and the superficial conformity of Nordic citizens is often disconcerting to those who do not share their values or understand the historical background of their origins.

To some Scandinavians, as to some outsiders, the balance sheet has not always been in the black. Denmark is now beyond the pale of the Civilised Circle. Some do not agree that Scandinavians have changed their trolls from giants to dwarfs and imps in two centuries. Those who are unwilling to share the taxation burden of running the welfare and social democratic state have voted with their feet and moved south, out of the clutches of the tax authorities. But those who have remained are left to share in the creation of a tolerant and good society, one that shows a welcome to foreigners and strangers, a respect for democratic institutions and a willingness to undertake difficult social engineering projects, based on a solid economic foundation of abundant natural resources, proven technological excellence and innovation, and a willingness from all to share the profits.

CHAPTER 11

The Sicilian Marriage

The year 1993 saw a nail in the coffin of pan-Scandinavianism when Norway, Sweden, Finland and Denmark began the process of European integration.

At the extreme north-west of the Scandinavian peninsula, the forces of geographic determinism, allied to undreamed-of national wealth in the form of north sea oil revenue, combined to make Norway the odd man out. Gro Harlem Brundtland was re-elected in 1993 for a four-year term as prime minister of a minority labour government. But far more significant was the acceleration of the anti-European Union Centre Party to the status of main opposition party. These Norwegian back-woodsmen concentrated on the damage which could be done to Norwegian farmers by membership of the European Union. Some Norwegian farmers received a 77 per cent subsidy from the Norwegian government. Norwegians rejected membership of the EU in a referendum on 28 November 1994. It was the second time in twenty-two years Norway had voted to stay aloof from European integration, the final result being 52 per cent against, and 48 per cent in favour of joining.

Political scientists attributed the narrow win of the anti-Europeans to the failure of Brundtland to convert the voters in northern Norway and the outlying regions. Local public opinion was that fishing and farming livelihoods would be destroyed by

Brussels bureaucrats. Women, on the whole, also opposed EU membership, giving as their reason that the social democratic gains of the Norwegian welfare state, and the high status of Norwegian women compared with their southern European counterparts, would be lost in the new enlarged Europe. And while it is true that the Norwegian parliament has always pursued an exemplary benevolent and tolerant attitude to racial differences, refugee migration and cultural differences between groups and nations, a popular slogan among conservative Norwegian voters in 1994, which eventually carried the day, was 'Would you like your daughter to marry a Sicilian?' Apart from this, the very word 'union' had negative historical associations from times when Norway was definitely the junior partner in a distinctly unpleasant union administered for centuries by Swedish and Danish monarchs.

Brundtland's ministry presided over a post-referendum boom in Norway. The decision to remain outside the European Union, far from damaging the nation, saw a dramatically improved economic performance for Norwegians compared with their Nordic EU neighbours, Denmark, Sweden and Finland. Whether this was due to staying out of the EU or was simply coincidence, in 1995 Norway's exports of oil, pulp and paper were so great, and economic growth reached such proportions, that net foreign debt and government budget deficits were expected to disappear. Unemployment was so low that it could not be expected to drop further. Norway neared the end of the millennium and the beginning of a new century in its best shape ever. Accordingly, to greet the first day of the new millennium, the government decided that the most appropriate symbol of the nation was an overall-clad worker, on a North Sea oil rig, beating on a metal barrel to the music of Grieg's 'Morning' while the sun rose over a bright and cloudless horizon.

By 1995 Norway was the world's second-largest crude oil exporter after Saudi Arabia. Norwegian politicians looked south and did not like what they saw, especially in the realm of oil politics. Learning from Dutch experience that revenue from Royal Dutch Shell oil could become a curse if squandered when windfall profits were distributed to a lucky generation, Norway sought to avoid cycles of boom, bust, high inflation and economic recession by establishing a petroleum fund, to be managed by the bank of Norway. Into this fund budget surpluses would flow, like North Sea oil, to be used for future foreign investment and to be used as a buffer for the oil-dependent economy in times of depressed world oil prices.

When Gro Harlem Brundtland unexpectecly resigned as Norwegian prime minister on 23 October 1996, she had been the most dominant political figure in the country for a decade. The smooth transition to the post-Brundtland era was a consequence not just of the Norwegian chacteristic of quietly getting on with things: in the period since Brundtland became prime minister Norway had grown to be the world's fifth largest oil producer. The rapidly rising standard of living had little effect on social values. Norwegians remained as parochial as ever, deeply suspicious of foreigners and threatened by the prospect of close ties to Europe, especially where inter-racial marriage was on the horizon. Despite years of effort by successive Norwegian governments, public opinion remained unconvinced that Swedish models of racial tolerance should be followed in Norway. The Norwegians nevertheless decided that although they did not want their daughters to marry Sicilians, they could at least help heat Italian pasta. A contract was signed in 1997 for 25 years to deliver six billion cubic metres of natural gas to Italy. Such was the growing importance of the gas fields that Norway accelerated its program of extraction and began building facilities to store liquefied natural gas, and pipelines to carry it to southern Europe.

While the women of Italy cooked pasta boiled with Norwegian gas, the women of Norway joined the labour force and worked as salaried employees at a level never possible before. By mid-summer 1998, 68.8 per cent of Norwegian women were in the work force. Paradoxically, as the prosperous Norwegian men and women alike entered the new millennium, their moods swung between optimism and pessimism. They were united, however, in deciding to ignore hostile world public opinion on whaling. Norwegians remained determined to continue to fish and to eat what most of the world saw as endangered species. Norwegians were more concerned to learn in September 1999 that the long boom, which had commenced in 1992, was over. The Norwegian reaction to this was to re-examine its relationship with Europe to see how far the nation could profit by a closer link on the Swiss model, not actually being part of the formal EU, but profiting from its proximity. Norway became a decaffeinated follower of EU guidelines. While not an espresso member of the EU, Norway adhered to watered-down EU economic and political policies and even, as a NATO member, sent troops into the former Yugoslavia during the Balkans crisis.

Norwegians were less concerned with world foreign policy than the question of who would marry Crown Prince Haakon, heir to the throne. This issue was resolved on 25 August 2001, when the Crown Prince married Mette-Marit Tjessem Høiby. Curiously, the new Crown Princess had an Australian connection; she had been an exchange student at Wangaratta. One might think this a perfect start in life for a Norwegian princess. Like many other fairytale princesses, she had experienced ups and downs before capturing her prince. Even in a country where everything is exaggerated – the depths of the fiords, the thickness of the glacier ice, the height of the mountains – she stood out: a single mother whose former boyfriend, and father of her child, had been imprisoned for assault and possession of cocaine. The Norwegians readily took to her as a model of how to be born again.

Denmark's relationship with the EU was initially not so ambiguous as Norway's. The Danish rejection of the Maastricht

Treaty in the summer of 1992 signalled a wish to be precise in its dealings with the European Union. Denmark's relationship with Europe, like the stability of its domestic political system, was perched on a knife's edge. In 1993 Poul Nyrup Rasmussen formed a new government led by social democrats which had a majority of only one seat in the 179-seat Folketing.

For almost three years, Danes had put the question of their precise relationship with Europe on the back burner, concentrating instead on getting to the bottom of the treatment of Tamil refugees in Denmark. Once a 6,000-page report was published, showing that Denmark had illegally restricted the entry of refugees, the serious business of contemplating a future as part of Europe began in earnest.

While the Danes in general were Euro-sceptics, Euroland itself welcomed Denmark, and placed no obstacles in the path of Denmark making a second effort to move closer to its eleven European partners. Europeans preferred dithering Danes to myopic Norwegians who, after all, many believed, had done nothing for the world except invent the paper clip and eat whales. Unpalatable aspects of the Maastricht Treaty were diluted for the Danes, who were to be permitted, if they chose, to opt out of plans for the European Monetary Union, joint defence, and EU citizenship. In May 1993 the second referendum votes showed 57 per cent of Danes were happy with the new arrangements. Some of those who opposed Maastricht then took part in what the newspapers called 'the worst riots in Danish history'. Fifty years after Denmark celebrated the anniversary of the humanitarian watershed involving the escape of Danish Jews from the Nazis, disenchantment with major political causes and alienation at a personal level led the Danes to elect an independent member to the Folketing for only the third time ever. Representing the western city of Aarhus, Jacob Haugaard secured a seat with 23,000 voters sharing his priorities: shorter lines at supermarkets, free kettles for old age pensioners, a tailwind for cyclists and the right of men to be impotent. His policies ridiculed the political system and the workings of parliamentary democracy, and called for a complete change of national perspective.

At the end of the twentieth century, Denmark became notorious not only for the innovative nature of its pornography, but also for the violence of its motorcycle gangs. In 1997, while the Bandidos and the Hell's Angels fought it out with anti-tank missiles and demolished clubhouses in gun, grenade and bomb attacks, Danes were treated to the worrying spectacle of the effects of a high standard of living and concomitant arms purchasing power on the criminal underworld in a social democratic welfare state. Prime Minister Rasmussen turned the clock back and enraged Danish civil libertarians by giving police powers to proscribe the free association of criminals and to enter their homes. Drug trading, arms trafficking and prostitution cartels controlled by bikie gangs were defended as stoutly as attacks on Danish fisheries by poaching Icelanders.

It was a dream of pan-Scandinavians, from the nineteenth century onwards, to have transport links strengthened to the extent that border crossing became unnoticeable. This helped not only the transport of goods and economic development, but also made easier clandestine and open crime, which although small in the obvious effects – only ten died in the Bandidos–Hell's Angels conflict – were psychologically disturbing to the Nordic enthusiasts for pastoral quietude. On 19 January 1997, Danish neo-Nazis were arrested for planning to send letter bombs to sports personalities in racially mixed marriages.

In May 1998 the Danish government faced its greatest *fin de siecle* problem when 500,000 private-sector workers went on strike for eleven days, protesting against the austerity package imposed by Rasmussen in response to global financial crisis. This industrial action cost the Danish economy a billion krone a day, slowing work in most Danish factories, disrupting transportation and halting progress on construction sites.

However, in a public relations coup, the Danes joined the Swedes in stressing the importance of the younger generation in building a new future for the Nordic peoples and their European neighbours in the new millennium. Crown Princess Viktoria of Sweden and Crown Prince Frederik of Denmark joined to inaugurate the road link between Denmark and Sweden. For the first time in 7000 years (when Denmark and Sweden were linked, and Nordic cave men could walk across Øresund) traffic could roll across the 16-kilometre Øresund road-rail bridge. It was obvious to all that the contemporaries of Crown Princess Viktoria and Crown Prince Frederik – the younger generation – would be the beneficiaries of this new burst of practical pan-Europeanism, if not pan-Scandinavianism.

Copenhagen was in the news for more bizarre reasons when the Little Mermaid statue, Denmark's iconic equivalent of the Statue of Liberty or the Sydney Opera House, was decapitated. The severed head of the mermaid was recovered in good condition, for the Danes, even their vandals, are proud of their civilised values. The criminal turned out to be a Danish TV camera-man – the second person in 35 years to cut off the head of the mermaid.

If the Danes supported Bill Clinton enthusiastically, they were even more in favour of George W. Bush and his foreign policy. The Danes alone among Scandinavians joined the 'coalition of the willing' in the 2003 Iraq War and were prepared to stick their neck out and go all the way with the US. The Norwegians sneered at this foreign policy decision, which was regarded as teaming up with the southern Europeans, the Spanish and the Italians.

While the Norwegians and the Danes exhibited varying degrees of hostility to incorporation in Euroland, the Swedes were less ambiguous in their determination to become part of, and indeed shape, the new Europe. On 13 November 1994 the Swedes voted to join the European Union after a referendum result that was a triumph for Prime Minister Ingvar Carlsson who, along with business leaders and the political establishment, advocated membership in the face of opposition from Swedes living in the sparsely populated northern region, and from environmentalists. Optimists hoped that a Swedish–Finnish–Danish bloc in the EU could counterbalance the southern shift which had occurred in the EU when Spain, Portugal and Greece joined a decade earlier. Since Sweden and Finland had warm ties with eastern Europe, it also cleared the way for the expansion of the EU to include Poland, Hungary and the Czech Republic. Nordic membership of the EU was especially important for the Baltic States – Estonia, Latvia and Lithuania – which were given the thumbs-up to join in October 2002. This decision was later regretted by the French who, like the Germans, were stung by US President Bush's description of the French and the Germans as 'old Europeans'. The Nordic foreign ministers were equally confused, and to some extent alarmed, by the ease with which the US State Department had manipulated the former members of the Soviet Union, turned them into client states of Uncle Sam, and used the Baltic bloc as weapons in the fight against 'rogue states'.

Despite high unemployment and the determination of Carlsson's social democrats to preserve welfare entitlements, Sweden was sufficiently economically powerful to be a net contributor to EU finances. In return Sweden expected to have a reasonable share in the decision-making process. This posed diplomatic challenges for the Swedes, who had to be tactful when Swedish values were at odds with the rather more traditional and conservative EU consensus – especially on social issues, the role of women, the environment and refugee immigration. Swedes continued to play a major role in the United Nations. Swedish technocrats led UN weapons inspectors following the 1991 Iraq–Kuwait crisis. By 2003 former Swedish foreign minister Hans Blix – the UN's chief weapons inspector –

was one of the best-known faces on world television as he wrestled with the dilemma of balancing the competing national interests of the United States and the members of the UN in the lead-up to the second war in the region in a generation.

The Finns, when given their chance, were more in favour of joining the EU than the Swedes, wanting to be at the table when important decisions were made in Brussels. Opposition to the EU in Finland was strongest amongst the Finnish farmers in the agrarian Centre Party, whose heavily subsidised production was quite outside the bounds of rational economics, even by Brussels standards. The farmers were supported by other smaller rag-tag groups, including communists and the curiously popular Christian Union Party. President Martti Ahtisaari and Prime Minister Esko Aho lined up with their long-term Swedish neighbour and hoped that record unemployment of 20 per cent would be alleviated by EU membership.

Initially both Finns and Swedes were disappointed. Investment did not flow north, food prices remained high, and the Swedish Social Democrats were forced to cut unemployment benefits to help reduce national debt. The Finns characteristically tried to run several EU policies. On some issues the president took one point of view, the parliament and the prime minister another, thereby satisfying everybody. President Ahtisaari warned the west against isolating Russia, signalled that Finland would not join NATO, and criticised Russia for having unsafe nuclear power stations and polluting industries. Finland was also able to claim cold-climate status – under which countries with severe winters were exempt from requirements of the EU farming regulations – and retained special farming subsidies. The Finnish government was allowed by Brussels to retain most of its state monopoly control over the sale of alcohol – ostensibly for health reasons, but in fact to preserve the golden fleece of a monopoly which added mightily to the government coffers from the purses of the bibulous Finns.

In October 1996 Prime Minister Paavo Lipponen summed up the Finnish dilemma as follows. Finland, said Lipponen, had to be among the first to join the EMU, so as to avoid becoming exposed and out on a limb, should Europe in the future divide again into eastern and western blocs. Finland's interests could not be pursued effectively with one foot inside the EU, and one foot outside. Nevertheless, old Finnish views, while dead, would not lie down. A former Finnish military commander, General Kari Hietanen, called for the will to right historic wrongs, and commented on the possibility that the disputed border region of Karelia could be restored to Finland. President Martti Ahtisaari responded that Finns could discuss anything they liked, but he as president would not raise this issue with Russia. At the same time, most Finns agreed that a never-played work of Dmitry Shostakovich, which the composer created to celebrate the victory of the Soviet Union in the Winter War, should remain unperformed on Finnish soil. Nor did Finnish membership of the EU change Finnish attitudes to foreigners, which, as in Japan, have resulted in a spectacularly low number of outsiders being accepted as residents. Finns were also in hot water for their attitude to gypsy applications for asylum: 1,000 Slovakian gypsies caused Finland a major embarrassment when Slovakia claimed that Finland did not have a minority policy in line with international human rights standards. In a corresponding and typical manifestation of Finnish xenophobia, a local council in Seinäjoki voted against accepting 30 Serb refugees for re-settlement.

Across the Baltic Sea in Sweden, Ingvar Carlsson's decision to cut welfare and increase taxes predicably led to consternation in the Trade Union Confederation, which correctly described Carlsson's government as attacking worker security. With double-digit unemployment in a country where public opinion demands full employment, worker security was a top priority. On 21 March 1999, Carlsson retired and former finance minister

Göran Persson was given responsibility for the new complexities of economic life in Sweden. Persson steered Sweden's financial institutions so well that within a year Sweden was one of a select group that qualified to be part of the new single European currency system. But skeletons continued to rattle in Swedish cupboards, even if the vampires of the previous century were long gone. Public opinion was very critical of government policy in the security and health areas. Sweden's security service breached a parliamentary edict by keeping dossiers on Swedish citizens because of their political views. The Health Ministry investigated claims that between 1935 and 1976, 60,000 Swedish women were forcibly sterilised as part of a government-sponsored eugenics program for some citizens of Sweden who came from non-Nordic backgrounds, or were mentally retarded. To make matters worse, Sweden approached the new millennium against a background of increasing neo-Nazi activities. Fascist activists shot two policemen during a bank robbery, murdered a labour unionist, and car-bombed a journalist's vehicle.

Violent and bloody confrontations at the EU Summit in Göteborg in June 2001 showed that another regional characteristic – Swedish tolerance for dissent – was gone forever. When anti-capitalist demonstrators against globalisation and the EU were shot by Swedish police using ball ammunition, Swedish television showed the victims unconscious and bleeding on Swedish soil. Appropriately enough, the excellent Swedish medical system patched them up, and none died. However, no longer were the political masters of the Nordic nations able to preach to the rest of the EU on questions of race, gender, the environment and immigration. French president Jacques Chirac – himself as moved and upset as were most members of the Swedish public – growled, 'You could have killed people'.

The anti-globalisation protests in the Nordic region were insignificant compared with the apocalyptic effect of September 11 on America, when the kamikaze terrorists attacked New York and the Pentagon. There was a sense, however, in which the high-rise buildings in Stockholm, Helsinki, Copenhagen and Oslo also shook. But by the time the dust in New York had settled, Nordic independent-mindedness (outside Denmark) re-asserted itself, and the people of Europe's northern peninsula thanked their lucky stars that they were far enough away and rich enough not to engage seriously in George W. Bush's war against terrorism. Most Scandinavians remained aloof from the sabre rattling as it developed into a mad vendetta against Iraq, couched in terms appropriate to a Tom Mix western of the 1940s. The Nordic nations still looked forward, with snug security, to fighting minor battles not with rogue states, but with trolls like the anti-Finnish Italian prime minister Silvio Berlusconi, who did not regard Scandinavian input into EU decision-making as worth taking seriously, especially where such sensitive matters as food standards were concerned.

Perhaps the best metaphor for the reality of Scandinavia's relationship with Europe was the crash of the Scandinavian Airlines System passenger jet which was destroyed on take off for Copenhagen on 8 October 2001, less than a month after September 11. In heavy fog the SAS jet collided with a small private aircraft on the runway at Linate airport. It was Italy's worst aviation disaster. All 114 persons aboard were killed, as well as four airport workers in the baggage shed, from where television crews filmed the foam-covered smoking remains. The crash and its aftermath showed the costs of European integration. What the crash meant to Italy was quite different to what the crash meant to the Nordic nations. But both blocs within the EU saw this major disaster as a opportunity to snuggle closer, rather than a time for recriminations and withdrawals.

What happened in Milan could not happen in Stockholm, Helsinki, Oslo or Copenhagen. In Milan ground radar had not worked for seven years. It stopped working in 1994. On 5 October 2001, shortly before the crash, the radar was removed altogether and was due to be replaced in December. The negligence and incompetence on the ground was unimaginable in the Nordic region: fifteen Italian unions were involved in long-running disputes with many levels of responsibility offering scope for inefficiencies and buck-passing. When the plane crashed the Italians thought it was the end of the world. Osama bin Laden had struck again. Fire rained from heaven. While Scandinavians faced technical problems and solved them, the Italian response was summed up by the airport director who spoke for all Italians when he said *'responsibilita non sono un problema mio'* ('this is not my problem') and left the aftermath to be dealt with by the Cardinal of Milan and a fuming Italian prime minister.

It was a core value of Scandinavian thought that responsibility had to be taken by the state and not the church. If a ferry sank in the Baltic, as did the *Estonia*, a requiem mass was insufficient. Responsibility, technical and administrative, had to be determined to avoid repeat disasters. Progress and bluster were not enough.

In the aftermath of S11 and the dangerous new world of the early twenty-first century, pan-Scandinavianism was impossible. The Nordic prime ministers kept in constant touch with each other by telephone as crisis after crisis unfolded, but they made little attempt to exactly coordinate their foreign policies as 'Scandinavians', preferring instead to act within the EU framework. This led to a perplexing loss of national identity for many.

Confusion, but not fear, was manifest in the post-S11 electoral results in the north. In Finland, public opinion stayed aloof from joining NATO. However, the Finnish president, Tarja Halonen, maintained her predecessor Kekkonen's track record by putting her foot in it over claims that she had opposed Estonia, Latvia and Lithuania joining NATO because it would leave Finland unprotected in the Baltic approaches to Leningrad.

Swedish prime minister Göran Persson was in the world eye in the first half of 2001 when Sweden had its term as EU president, but after S11 all the Swedes wanted to do was gloomily reflect on the bursting of the IT telecommunications boom which left Ericsson no longer 100 per cent Swedish but a partner of Sony. By far the greatest changes in the Nordic area after S11 were in Denmark, where Anders Fogh Rasmussen led the inaccurately named Liberal Party to national election victory on 20 November.

Rasmussen turned out the lights on Nordic cooperation in both domestic and foreign policy, made a right turn in the direction of tighter immigration laws, tough law and order provisions, cuts to overseas development aid and an inward-looking stress on what could almost be described as 'Fortress Denmark', albeit one made of Lego. In teaming up with the men of Sicily and Spain and joining the war against Iraq in defiance of international law, Denmark was right out of step with the characteristically caring Nordic character.

The Scandinavian nations have always been the least aggressive of the European countries, having devoted themselves to engineering social progress and enrichment. The Finns have been the most kind and gentle among the northerners, extending their taciturn courtesy even to trolls. Finns still believed in them. The most popular modern song played on Finnish radio was *Paivansade ja Menninkainen*, an exploration of troll habits. In 2000, the Finlandia Award for the best novel written in Finland went to Johanna Sinisalo's Troll, which described among other things how a photographer rescued a young troll from a group of drunken teenagers. For Sinisalo, trolls in the new millennium represented what could not be understood, had to be demonised, because 'trolls can always be found among us, releasing hurt, jealousy and new desires'.

Bibliography

Adelman, K.L., *Finlandization: A Model of Soviet Influence* (Washington, DC, 1978)

Allison, R., *Finland's Relations with Soviet Union*, 1944-84n (London, 1985)

Amundsen, R., *The Norwegian Expedition in the 'Fram'* 1910–1912 (London, 2000)

Andersen, H.C., *The Fairytale of My Life* (London, 1975)

Andersson, I.A., *History of Sweden* (London, 1968)

Andren, N.B.F., *Power-Balance and Non-Alignment – a Perspective on Swedish Foreign Policy* (Stockholm, 1967)

Arter, D., *The Nordic Parliaments* (London, 1984)

Austin, P., *On Being Swedish* (Coral Gables, Fla., 1969)

Bennett, J., *British Broadcasting and the Danish Resistance Movement, 1940–1945, a study of the Wartime Broadcasts of the BBC* (Cambridge, 1966)

Board, J., *The Government and Politics of Sweden* (Boston, 1970)

Carlgren, W.M., *Swedish Foreign Policy during the Second World War* (London, 1977)

Carpelan, B., *Axel* (Manchester, 1989)

Chew, A.F., *The White Death: The Epic of the Soviet-Finnish Winter War* (East Lansing, 1971)

Childs, M.W., *Sweden, the Middle Way, 3rd edition* (New Haven, 1947)

Childs, M.W., *Sweden, the Middle Way on Trial* (New Haven, 1980)

Dahlstrom, C.E.W.L., *Strindberg's Dramatic Expressionism, 2nd edition* (New York, 1965)

Davis, D.C.L., *Model for a Humanistic Education: The Danish Folk High School* (Columbus, 1971)

Deknatel, F.B., *Edvard Munch* (New York, 1950)

Derry, T.K., *A History of Modern Norway 1814–1972* (Oxford, 1973)

Derry, T.K., *A History of Scandinavia* (London, 1979)

Derry, T.K., *A Short History of Norway* (London, 1968)

Dunlop, I., *Edvard Munch* (London, 1977)

Eckstein, H., *Division and Cohesion in Democrats: A Study of Norway* (Princeton, NJ, 1966)

Eidheim, H., *Aspects of the Lappish Minority Situation* (Oslo, 1971)

Ekman, K., *Jean Sibelius: His Life and Personality* (New York, 1945)

Elder, N.C., *Government in Sweden: The Executive at Work* (Oxford, 1970)

Ell Mallakh, R., *Petroleum and Economic Development: The Cases of Mexico and Norway* (Lexington, 1984)

Engle, E. and Paananen, L., *The Winter War: The Russo-Finnish Conflict 1939–40* (New York, 1973)

Engle, E. and Paananen, L., *Essays in Finnish Foreign Policy* (Vammala, 1969)

Falnes, O.J., *National Romanticism in Norway* (New York, 1968)

Fitzmaurice, J., *Politics in Denmark* (New York, 1981)

Fox, A.B., *The Power of Small States: Diplomacy in World War II* (Chicago, 1959)

Friis, H.K., *Scandinavia between East and West* (New York, 1950)

Fry, J. (ed), *Limits of the Welfare State: Critical vies on post-war Sweden* (Farnborough, 1978)

Fullerton, B. and Williams, A.F., *Scandinavia*, 2nd edition (London, 1975)

Gad, F., *The History of Greenland* 2 vols (London, 1970, 1973)

Gerde, J., *From Peasants to Farmers: The Migration from Balestrand, Norway to the upper Middle West* (Cambridge, 1985)

Gjerset, K., *A History of the Norwegian Peoples* (New York, 1969)

Greve, T., *Haakon VII of Norway: Founder of a New Monarchy* (London, 1983)

Gripenberg, G.A., *Finland and the Great Powers: Memoirs of a Diplomat* (Lincoln, 1965)

Grundtvig, N.F.S., *Selected Writings of N.F.S. Grundtvig* (Philadelphia, 1976)

Hamalainen, P.K., *In Time of Storm: Revolution, Civil War and the Ethnolinguistic Issue in Finland* (Albany, 1979)

Hayes, P.M., *Quisling: The Career and Political Ideas of Vidkun Quisling* (Newton Abbott, 1971)

Heckscher, E.F., *An Economic History of Sweden* (Massachusetts, 1968)

Heltoft, K., *Hans Christian Andersen as an Artist* (Copenhagen, 1977)

Hoidal, O.K., *Quisling – a Study of Treason* (Oslo, 1989)

Horton, J., *Grieg* (London, 1974)

Hovde, B.J., *The Scandinavian Countries 1720–1865: The Rise of the Middle Classes* (Port Washington, NY, 1972)

Jacobs, T.B., *America and the Winter War 1939–40* (New York, 1981)

Jacobsen, M., *Finland Myth and Reality* (Helsinki, 1987)

Jagerskiold, S.A.F., *Mannerheim Marshal of Finland* (London, 1986)

Jakobson, M., *The Diplomacy of the Winter War: An Account of the Russo-Finnish War, 1939–1940* (Cambridge, Mass., 1961)

James, H.G., *Planning and Production in Sweden* (London, 1976)

Jansson, T., *Comet in Momminland* (London, 1968)

Jansson, T., *Finn Family Moomintroll* (London, 1970)

Jansson, T., *Moominvalley in November* (London, 1971)

Jenkins, D., *Sweden and the Price of Progress* (New York, 1968)

Johannesson, E.O., *The Novels of August Strindberg* (Berkeley, 1968)

Johansen, H.C., *The Danish Economy in the Twentieth Century* (New York, 1987)

Johansen, L., *Economic Planning in Norway: Methods and Models* (Oslo, 1970)

Jones, H.G., *Planning and Productivity in Sweden* (London, 1976)

Jutikkala, E. and Pirinen, K.A., *History of Finland* (London, 1962)

Kallas, H. (ed), *Finland: Creation and Construction* (London, 1968)

Karronen, L., *From White to Blue and Black: Finnish Fascism in the interwar era* (Helsinki, 1991)

Kekkonen, U., *Neutrality: The Finnish Position* (London, 1970)

Kirby, D.G. (ed.), *Finland and Russia 1808–1920 from Autonomy to Independence: A Selection of Documents* (London, 1975)

Kirby, D.G., *Finland in the Twentieth Century* (London, 1979)

Kjersgaard, E., *History of Denmark* (Copenhagen, 1974)

Klinge, M., *A Brief History of Finland* (Helsinki, 1991)

Klinge, M., *Let Us Be Finns: Essays on History* (Helsinki, 1991)

Koht, H., *Norway Neutral and Invaded* (London, 1941)

Koivisto, M., *Witness to History* (London, 1997)

Koivukangas, O., *Sea, Gold and Sugarcane: Finns in Australia 1851–1947* (Turku, 1986)

Koivukangas, O. and Martin, J.S., *The Scandinavians in Australia* (Melbourne, 1986)

Krosby, H.P., *Finland, Germany and the Soviet Union, 1940–1941: The Petsamo Dispute* (Madison, 1968)

Lamm, M., *August Strindberg* (New York, 1971)

Larsen, K., *A History of Norway* (Princeton, 1962)

Larsson, C., *A Farm* (New York, 1976)

Larsson, C., *Our Home* (London, 1976)

Larsson, C., *Our Family* (London, 1980)

Lauring, P., *History of the Kingdom of Denmark* 3rd edition (Copenhagen, 1960)

Layton, R., *Sibelius* (London, 1965)

Layton, R., *Sibelius and his World* (London, 1970)

Ibsen H., *Ibsen* (works) translated and edited by J.W. McFarlane (Oxford, 1977)

Leitenberg, M., *Soviet Submarine Operations in Swedish Waters, 1980–1986* (New York, 1987)

Lindbeck, A., *Swedish Economic Policy* (London, 1975)

Lindgren, H., *Corporate Growth: The Swedish Match Industry in its Global Setting* (Stockholm, 1979)

Lindgrund, R.E., *Norway-Sweden: Union, Disunion and Scandinavian Integration* (Westport, Conn., 1959)

Lowrie, W., *Kierkegaard* (New York, 1938)

Lundberg, E., *Business Cycles and Economic Policy* (Cambridge, Mass., 1957)

Magnusson, L. and Stråth, B. (eds), *From the Werner Plan to the EMU, In Search of Political Economy for Europe* (Brussels, 2001)

Magnusson, S.A., *Northern Sphinx: Iceland and the Icelander: from the Settlement to the Present* (London, 1977)

Mankell, H., *Firewall* (The New Press, New York), 2002

Mannerheim, C.G.E., *The Memoirs of Marshal Mannerheim* (London, 1953)

Mazour, A.G., *Finland between East and West* (Princeton, 1956)

Mead, W.R., *A Historical Geography of Scandinavia* (London, 1981)

Mead, W.R., *An Economic Geography of the Scandinavian States and Finland* (London, 1964

Mead, W.R., *Finland* (London, 1968)

Mead, W.R., *An Experience of Finland* (London, 1993)

Mead, W.R., and Hall, W., *Scandinavia* (London, 1972)

Messer, T.M., *Edvard Munch* (New York, 1973)

Meyer, M., *Henrik Ibsen* (London, 1967–71)

Miljan, T., *The Reluctant Europeans – The Attitudes of the Nordic Countries towards European Integration* (London, 1977)

Milward, A.S., *The European Rescue of the Nation State* (California, 1993)

Milward, A.S., *The Fascist Economy in Norway* (Oxford, 1072)

Misiunas, R.J. and Taagepera, R., *The Baltic States* (London, 1993)

Moberg, V., *A History of the Swedish People* (London, 1972–73)

Mortensen, B.M.E. and Downes, B.W., *Strindberg: An Introduction to his Life and Work* (Cambridge, 1965)

Nevakivi, J., *The appeal that was never made: The Allies, Scandinavia and the Finnish Winter War 1939–1940* (London, 1976)

Oakley, S., *The Story of Denmark* (London, 1972)

Paasivirta, J., *Finland and Europe: International Crisis and the period of Autonomy 1808–1914* (London, 1981)

Paasivirta, J., *The Victors in World War I and Finland: Finland's relation with the British, French and US Governments in 1918–1919* (Helsinki, 1965)

Palmblad, H.V.E., *Strindberg's Conception of History* (New York, 1966)

Palme, T., *The Finnish-Soviet Armistice Negotiations of 1944* (Stockholm, 1971)

Pauli, H.E., *Alfred Nobel – Dynamite King, Architect of Peace* (London, 1947)

Pentikainen, J., *Kalevala Mythology*, tr R. Poom (Bloomington, Indiana, 1989)

Polvinen, *Imperial Borderland* (London, 1995)

Popperwell, R.G., *Norway* (London, 1972)

Puntila, L.A., *The Political History of Finland 1809–1966* (London, 1975)

Richards, J.M., *800 Years of Finnish Architecture* (London, 1978)

Rintala, M., *Four Finns* (Berkeley, 1969)

Rintala, M., *Three Generations, The Extreme Right Wing in Finnish Politics* (Bloomington, 1962)

Rohde, P., *Søren Kierkegaard: An Introduction to his Life and Philosophy* (London, 1963)

Runblom, H. and Norman, H. (eds), *From Sweden to America* (Minneapolis, 1976)

Samuelson, K., *From Great Power to Welfare State: 300 Years of Swedish Social Development* (London, 1968)

Sandman, P.G. (ed.), *C.G. Mannerheim's Photographs from his Journey across Asia* (Helsinki, 1991)

Scase, R., *Social Democracy in Capitalist Society: Working Class Politics in Britain and Sweden* (London, 1977)

Schjelderup-Ebbe, D., *A Study of Grieg's Harmony with Special Reference to the Evolution of his Harmonic Style* (Oslo, 1974)

Schnitzer, M., *The Economy of Sweden: A Study of the Modern Welfare State* (New York, 1970)

Scobbie, I., *Sweden* (London, 1972)

Scott, F.D., *Scandinavia* rev. edition (Cambridge, 1975)

Scott, F.D., *Sweden: The Nation's History* (Minneapolis, 1977)

Screen, J.E.O., *Mannerheim: The Years of Preparation* (London, 1970)

Screen, J.E.O., *Mannerheim: The Finnish Years* (London, 2000)

Selznick, O., *Memo from David O. Selznick* (New York, 1972)

Simpson, C., *The Viking Circle* (Sydney, 1966)

Singleton, F.B., *A Short History of Finland* (Cambridge, 1989)

Smith, C.J., *Finland and the Russian Revolution 1917–1922* (Athens, Georgia, 1958)

Smith, J.B., *Munch* (Oxford, 1977)

Smith, L.F., *Modern Norwegian Historiography* (Oslo, 1972)

Stang, N., *Edvard Munch* (Oslo, 1072)

Stråth, B., *Organisation of Labour Markets. Governance, Culture and Modernity in Germany, Sweden, Britain and Japan* (London, 1996)

Stråth, B., *Europe and the Other, Europe as the Other* (Brussels, 2000)

Stråth, B., *Myth and Memory in the Construction of Community, Historical Patterns in Europe and Beyond* (Brussels, 2000)

Strindberg, A., *The Plays*, introduced and translated from the Swedish by Michael Meyer (London, 1964)

Tagil, S., *Regions in the History of Central Europe* (London, 1999)

Tanner, V., *The Winter War: Finland against Russia 1939–1940* (California, 1950)

Tarkka, J., *Neither Stalin Nor Hitler* (Helsinki, 1991)

Tawastjerna, E., *Sibelius, 1865–1905* tr. R. Layton (London, 1976)

Thaden, F.C., *Russification in the Baltic Provinces and Finland 1855–1945* (Princeton, 1981)

Timm, W., *The Graphic Art of Edvard Munch* (London, 1969)

Tomasson, R.F., *Sweden, Prototype of Modern Society* (New York, 1970)

Trulsson, S.G., *British and Swedish Policies and Strategies in the Baltic after the Peace of Tilsit in 1807* (Lund, 1976)

Upton, A.F., *Finland in Crisis, 1940–1941: A Study of Small Power Politics* (Ithaca, NY, 1965)

Verney, D.V., *Parliamentary Reform in Sweden 1866–1921* (Oxford, 1967)

Von Rauch, G., *The Baltic States* (London, 1995)

Walker, A., *Garbo: A Portrait* (London, 1980)

Wikander, U., *Kreuger's Match Monopolies, 1925–1930: Case Studies in market Control through Public Monopolies* (Stockholm, 1979)

Wilson, W.A., *Folklore and Nationalism in Modern Finland* (Bloomington, Indiana, 1976)

Wuorinen, J.H., *A History of Finland* (New York, 1966)

Wuorinen, J.H., *Finland and World War II, 1939–1944* (Westpoint Conn, 1083)

Wuorinen, J.H., *Scandinavia* (Englewood Cliffs, NJ, 1964)

Index

Index

Index

Hakkila, Väinö 152
Hallgrimsson, Geir 232
Halonen, Tarja 278
Hamar 169
Hambro, C.J. 166, 169–70
Hamina 19
Hammarskjöld, Dag 191–2
Hanko 147, 155, 221
Hanko Peninsula 152
Hansson, Per Albin 131, 176–7, 190
Hansteen, Viggo 171
Hardanger Fiord 47, 110
Hartling, Poul 227–8
Haugaard, Jacob 270
Hedin, Adolph 55–6
Hedtoft, Hans 197–8
Hegel, Georg Wilhelm 15
Heinrichs, General E. 156
Heligoland 10
Helsinki
  bombed 153, 157
  in Civil War 102–5, 107
  climate 5
  demonstrations and strikes in
    97, 99, 206
  Estonian mafia in 254
  harbour 59
  Olympic Games in 211
  prestige as international capital
    222
  proximity to St Petersburg 84, 153
  rail links 61, 106, 259
  reappearance of Russian imperial
    symbols 244–5
  rebuilt 28
  state of emergency 146
  visited by German navy 148
Helsinki Orchestra 95
Helsinki School of Arts and Design 94
Helsinki University
  Sibelius involved with 86–8
  student unrest 218
  Viipuri Student Corporation 87
Hietanen, General Kari 275
Himmler, Heinrich 168
Hird, the 171
Hitler, Adolf
  Christian X birthday greetings 163
  and Norway 135, 170–1
  and Mannerheim 151, 157
  and Sweden 173–6
Holmer, Hans 251
Holsti, R. 148
Hospitals, Swedish 186, 235
Homosexual marriages, Danish 261
Huntford, Ronald 186–7
Hunting licences, Norwegian 110
Husqvarna 133

Ibsen, Henrik
  general 86, 91, 135
  life and career 40–2, 44–6, 113
  nationalism 43, 46, 64, 73
  supports Denmark 40
  supports Finland 82
  and women's rights 43–4, 51, 73
  and the working class 44, works 32,
    41–3, 71–3, 86
Ibsen, Sigurd 73–4
Iceland
  becomes independent 166, 230
  Danish possession 10, 140, 229
  joins NATO 184, 231
  Vikings discover 7
  in World War II 230–1
Icelandic Marine Research Institute 232
Ignatius, Major-General Hannes 122
IKEA stores 240–1
Immigration policies 2, 250, 255
Imperial Chemical Industries (ICI) 58
Industrial relations
  Finland 146
  Sweden 125, 130–1, 223, 246
Industries
  Danish 197
  Finnish 28, 261
  Norwegian 233
  Swedish 133–4, 242, 256–7
Inflation
  general 256
  Danish 198–9, 228
  Icelandic 231
  Norwegian 202
  Swedish 121, 223, 236
Ireland
  comparisons with Finland 6, 26, 81, 84,
    103, 106
  Iceland 140
  Norway 6, 24, 51
  Russia 136
  Sweden 71, 236
Iron ore, Swedish 5, 147, 167, 174–5, 223
Isted, Battle of 34
Italy: Scandinavians visit 13, 45, 64, 101

Jaabak, Søren P. 49
Jaegers
  Danish 162
  Finnish 96, 101, 105–7, 143, 156
Jakobson, Max 160
Jan Mayan Islands 140
Jansson, Tove 207–8
Japan
  relations with Finland 98
  with Sweden 128
Jarlsberg, Wedel 22
Jarring, Gunnar 192